Exploring Childhood in a Comparative Context

Exploring Childhood in a Comparative Context meets an increasing need for students focusing on early childhood to be familiar with alternative practices in other countries. Providing a ready-made source of information about a wide range of countries including Finland, the Netherlands, the United States, New Zealand, Japan, South Africa and many more, the book clearly describes the way each country understands and conceptualises childhood.

Each chapter includes contextual information about the country, an introduction to the theory that has shaped practice and describes the curriculum for pre-school and primary education. Including vignettes from practitioners working in each country to illustrate practice, the chapters explore key themes such as:

- Child development
- Parental involvement
- Teaching and learning
- Professionalism
- Assessment
- Pupil experience.

Accessibly written and including opportunities for reflection, this timely new book will give students a valuable insight into alternative education systems that is essential if they are to become practitioners with a current and global approach.

Mabel Ann Brown is Senior Lecturer on the Foundation Degree in Children's and Young People's Services and the BA Child and Youth Studies at the University of Derby, UK.

Jon White is Senior Lecturer in BA Early Childhood/Education Studies and MA Education at the University of Derby, UK.

Exploring Childhood in a Comparative Context

An introductory guide for students

Edited by Mabel Ann Brown
and Jon White

Routledge
Taylor & Francis Group

LONDON AND NEW YORK

First published 2014
by Routledge
2 Park Square, Milton Park, Abingdon, Oxon OX14 4RN

and by Routledge
711 Third Avenue, New York, NY 10017

Routledge is an imprint of the Taylor & Francis Group, an informa business

© 2014 Mabel Ann Brown and Jon White

The right of the editors to be identified as the authors of the editorial material, and of the authors for their individual chapters, has been asserted in accordance with sections 77 and 78 of the Copyright, Designs and Patents Act 1988.

British Library Cataloguing in Publication Data
A catalogue record for this book is available from the British Library

Library of Congress Cataloging in Publication Data
Library of Congress Cataloging-in-Publication Data
Exploring childhood in a comparative context : an introductory guide for students / edited by Mabel-Ann Brown and Jon White.
pages cm
Includes index.
1. Early childhood education--Cross-cultural studies. 2. Early childhood education--Handbooks manuals etc. I. Brown, Mabel-Ann.
LB1139.23.E94 2013
372.21--dc23
2013004277

ISBN: 978-0-415-69651-7 (hbk)
ISBN: 978-0-415-69652-4 (pbk)
ISBN: 978-0-203-14304-9 (ebk)

Typeset in Adobe Garamond Pro
by Saxon Graphics Ltd, Derby

MIX
Paper from
responsible sources
FSC
www.fsc.org   FSC® C013056

Printed and bound in Great Britain by
TJ International Ltd, Padstow, Cornwall

To those we have lost.

Contents

Contents

List of figures

List of tables

List of contributors

Mabel Ann Brown has a Master's degree in Education and has worked in schools for 28 years prior to commencing working in Higher Education at the University of Derby. She has researched early year's education in Finland and participated in a 'Skype for learning' project linking a German school with an English school. She is particularly interested in providing children with a relevant and wide curriculum that will support them through life.

Jon White qualified as a teacher in 1978 and first taught in a boy's secondary modern social-priority school. Following six years with the Department of Defence, he took up a post as Head of Biology in a large 11–18 comprehensive school in the West Midlands. As a Senior Lecturer at the University of Derby, he has a particular interest in transition practice and the development of resilience, as well as the promotion of European links.

The contributors

Michelle Appleby (United States)
Michelle Appleby was educated in the United States and trained as an elementary school teacher in the state of Michigan where she taught for eight years. She is currently the Education subject leader and Senior Lecturer at the University of Derby in the United Kingdom. She leads modules on Education Placement Experience and Reflection, Alternative Schooling, Cognitive and Language Development and Social and Emotional Development. Her postgraduate research is related to literacy assessment and support for literacy attainment. She is particularly interested in developing learners' sense of self by supporting emotional and social needs in learning environments.

Simon Brownhill (Australia and New Zealand)
Dr Simon Brownhill FHEA was previously a Senior Lecturer in the School of Education at the University of Derby and is now a Senior Teaching Associate at the University of Cambridge in the United Kingdom. His teaching experiences span the 3–13 age phase with

a particular emphasis in the early years (3–7) where he was formally an Assistant Head Teacher of the Early Years at a large multicultural primary school. His infinite fascination with children's behaviour and its effective management has been the focus of both his undergraduate and postgraduate research, and of four collaborative/single-authored books.

Chris Bryan (South Africa)

With a background as a teacher, a teacher trainer and a tutor on a Master's Education programme, Chris Bryan is committed to *quality* teaching and learning provision in schools. Her longitudinal research in South Africa has allowed her to develop an international perspective, focusing on both teacher professional development and the learning of the child, within a disadvantaged socio-economic community. She believes that a fundamental principle of quality teaching and learning is an understanding of the complex contextual interaction of the child, school and society.

Jan Dekker (Netherlands)

Dr Jan Dekker is a Senior Lecturer at Hogeschool Edith Stein, a mono-sectorial and interreligious teacher training college for pre-primary and primary education in Hengelo, the Netherlands. He studied Psychology and Andragogy and after his graduation he specialised in the field of pedagogy and education. In his work at Edith Stein the focus is on competence-based learning, reform education and the international perspectives of education. While teaching classes in pedagogy, he has been the cornerstone of the Erasmus exchange programme, connecting Dutch students with a range of institutions across Europe and beyond.

Mara Dirba (Latvia)

Dr Mara Dirba has been teaching in different teacher education courses for 12 years at the University of Latvia. She actively participates in educational projects both on European and Latvian level, and conducts workshops and seminars on European Diversity Education. She is interested in diversity and inclusive education and her research themes are inclusive and intercultural education. She manages the 'University Educational Circle' organising seminars and workshops for teachers from different European countries.

Anita Gulczyńska (Poland)

Anita Gulczyńska PhD, is a Lecturer at the Department of Social Pedagogy at the Faculty of Educational Sciences of the Łódź University, Poland. Her areas of interest in both research and teaching are socio-pedagogical aspects of social life in impoverished local communities, critical and radical social work and qualitative methods of research in general with a special attention to socially engaged research. She was a conducting participant of a three-year study of youth socialization in the context of one of the Łódź impoverished neighbourhoods.

Bart Hempen (Belgium)

Bart Hempen, MSc, obtained his Master's degree in Medical Biology (1995) at the Rijksuniversiteit Groningen (Netherlands) and at the Université Libre de Bruxelles (Belgium). He studied biology for teacher training at the Vrije Universiteit Amsterdam (1998). He is currently working as a university college biology teacher educator at Hogeschool-Universiteit Brussel and as the Co-ordinator of European educational programmes. He has undertaken various publications.

Yukari Iguchi (Japan)

Yukari Iguchi is a Lecturer in Hospitality and Culinary Arts at the University of Derby and has previously worked in various sectors within the hospitality industry in Japan, Switzerland and the United Kingdom. Yukari is interested in cultural diversity and researches in the area of international students' experiences at universities in the United Kingdom, presenting at several conferences and workshops on this theme. Also, she researches in the area of managing cultural diversity within hospitality small- and medium-sized enterprises.

Jana Kantorová (Czech Republic)

Jana Kantorová lives in Olomouc, a city in the Czech Republic. Her main field of study was the teaching of education, science and music for secondary schools. In 2003 she had the opportunity to work at the Faculty of Education of Palacký University in Olomouc as an Assistant Professor at the Institute of Education and Social Studies. In her profession as a university pedagogue she focuses on general educational science, school climate, alternative schools and didactics of educational science.

Penelope Louka (Greece)

Dr Penelope Louka holds a BSc (Hons) in Psychology and an MSc in Health Psychology from the University of Luton, United Kingdom, and a Doctoral degree (Ph.D.) in Social and Health Psychology from the University of Westminster, United Kingdom. She has worked for several years as a Professor at the University of Westminster at both undergraduate and postgraduate levels. She is also a Chartered Member (CPsychol) of the British Psychological Society (BPS). At present, Dr Louka is the Co-ordinator of the School of Social Sciences and the Head of the Psychology Department at Mediterranean College, Athens, Greece.

Angeliki Papangeli (Greece)

Dr Angeliki Papangeli studied Greek Philology and Linguistics at the University of Athens and then followed an MSc in Human Communication at UCL, United Kingdom. She did her Ph.D. at the University of Reading (School of Psychology and Clinical Language Sciences). She has worked for several years as a Greek teacher in the United Kingdom (teaching bilingual children and adults). Her interests focus on typical, atypical and bilingual language development, multi-cultural education, research methods and statistics. Currently, she leads HND and BSc Early Childhood Studies programmes at Mediterranean College, Athens, Greece.

Michèle Vanleke (Belgium)

Michèle Vanleke, MA, obtained her Master's degree in Romanic Languages (1996) at the Katholieke Universiteit Leuven, Belgium (her thesis was in the field of Sociolinguistics: 'Subject positions in oral discourse'). Michele studied French and Spanish for teacher training (1996) and is currently working as a university college French linguistics and methodology teacher educator at Hogeschool-Universiteit, Brussels. She is the Co-ordinator of a European and Educational Intensive programme.

Pavla Vyhnálková (Czech Republic)

Pavla Vyhnálková lives in the Czech Republic. Her main field of study was social education science. During her studies she gathered a lot of practical experience as a pedagogue in extracurricular organisations for children and young people. In 2007 she had the opportunity to work at the Faculty of Education of Palacký University in Olomouc as an Assistant Professor. In her profession she focuses especially on leisure education, communication and gerontology.

Monika Wiśniewska-Kin (Poland)

Monika Wiśniewska-Kin is a Doctor of pedagogical sciences and works at the Institute of Theoretical Foundations of Early Education at the Department of Preschool and Early School Education at the Faculty of Educational Sciences, University of Łódź, 91–408, Łódź 46/48 Pomorska Street. For many years, she has been dealing with research concerning the cognitive competences of children in the early school age. She is also a member of the Elementary Education Team at the Pedagogical Committee of the Polish Academy of Sciences and a member of the Self-Education Doctoral Team at the Pedagogical Committee of the Polish Academy of Sciences.

Acknowledgements

The editors acknowledge the contributions of all the authors, who completed the chapters for this book whilst continuing with their other work commitments. Second, we would also like to acknowledge the support of their respective institutions and colleagues. Third, we would like to thank Annamarie Kino and the publishers David Fulton/Routledge for their guidance in editing this book.

All aspects of this book have been collated in good faith but should corrections or updates be necessary we would welcome suggestions that could be incorporated in revised editions.

Mabel Ann Brown and Jon White

Abbreviations/terminology

(Further country specific terminology can be located in some of the chapters.)

DfE (Department for Education) England
ECM (Every Child Matters)
EPPE (Effective Provision for Pre School Education)
EYEC (Early Years Education and Care)
EYFS (Early Years Foundation Stage)
EYPS (Early Years Professional Status)
HCAM (Helping Children Achieve More)
PISA (Programme for International Student Assessment)
OECD (Organisation for Economic Cooperation and Development)
ZPD (Zone of Proximal Development)

USA abbreviations

ACT (American College Testing)
AYP (Adequate Yearly Progress)
ELL (English language learners)
ESL (English as a Second Language)
ESOL (English speakers of other languages)
FAPE (Free and appropriate public education)
FCAT (Florida Comprehensive Assessment Test)
IDEA (Individual and Disabilities Education Act)
IEP (Individualized Education Program)
LRE (Least restrictive environment)
MEAP (Michigan Educational Assessment Program)
NCLBA (No Child Left Behind Act)
SAT (Scholastic Aptitude Test)

Introduction

Mabel Ann Brown and Jon White

In the last few years (2006–2009) the Organisation for Economic Cooperation and Development (OECD) Programme for International Student Assessment (PISA) results have indicated a decline in the United Kingdom education system whilst other international countries (e.g. Finland) have continued to excel; thus international perspectives have been considered as a way forward as exemplified in the Department for Education Review of the National Curriculum (DfE 2012). This book considers education from other perspectives and invites the reader to consider alternatives and contest ideas of education and childhood.

Change and progress are always with us, thus education in England is changing to meet the demands of a changing economy (post-2008) and an ever changing world. A range of writers from within different countries have agreed to share their educational perspectives in order to create this publication. This book also includes the voice of the child in an international context in order to contextualise the comparisons in educational provision, policy and practice.

The rationale for choosing these countries is that they offer the reader a broad perspective and an insight into different global educational practices, some of which appear to be more successful.

The information in this book is current. It will only date as practice changes in each of the participating countries and this tends to take a number of years to move from idea into practice.

This book is relevant to any reader wishing to explore and implement the best practice for children today.

The aim of this book

The purpose of this book is to provide an accessible introduction into alternative education systems. The book is intended to provide a ready source of information about each country and present a picture of the way in which each country treats children and conceptualises childhood. This understanding is essential if students and teachers are to become practitioners with a current and global approach.

Another feature of this book is to provide an initial insight into alternative systems for the purpose of widening ideas and creating global vision when considering educational practice. This book is recommended for all students undertaking Educational, and Early Years and Childhood courses in higher education.

This global perspective deepens understanding of any similarities and differences, as well as raising international awareness and encouraging aspects of citizenship, all of which are necessary in a world that needs to see the wider picture. The ideal citizen, as Rousseau (1991:5) describes, is one who 'understands his good to be identical with the common good'. Yet if we are to follow Rousseau's thinking, 'by nature' we only care for self preservation. Thus our childhood nature can become compromised in a system that educates children for the common good. Each of the following chapters therefore tries to share with the reader how their country tackles this issue of educating children for the common good whilst encouraging children's natural nature.

Content

The content is provided by a group of academics from a range of countries and backgrounds, each contributing to a chapter that considers the education system in their country. The chapters refer to the country's philosophy regarding education and incorporates vignettes based on current observations of practice and current pupil/student reflections about their experiences. The writer (or writers) for each country also refers to curriculums, theorists and the OECD PISA, if this is applicable. The indicative age range for each chapter is from pre-school through to the end of primary education, 0–11 years approximately, depending on each country's system.

The vignettes and case study examples consider the following aspects of education: early years experience, child development, primary education, parental involvement, teaching and learning in different subject areas, inclusion, school meals, professionalism, testing and assessment, travel to school, holidays and standards. The contributors have gained current reflections for the vignettes from a range of different age groups, for instance early years views, primary children's views or even secondary. In the case of secondary students they have reflected back on their own childhood experiences. The authors of the chapters have also referred to personal observations of practice and include case study examples.

Each chapter has a brief introduction to the country and their system with an introduction to the historical, social and cultural influences that have shaped the education system. The chapters also consider how childhood is perceived in that country. General information on education is provided as are the phases of the education system, for instance pre-school, primary and secondary. There is information about the curriculum, the teaching and learning at the various stages and an indication as to what a typical day might look like.

There is a consideration of what childhood is and how it might be perceived. Chapter 1 is concluded by an adapted chart illustrating the OECD PISA 2009 positions of the countries considered in this book. Depending on the each country's position within this league table, they might either applaud these statistics or refrain from referring to them. This is clearly demonstrated by the chapter from Japan (Chapter 7). However, statistics only demonstrate a small part of a child's development and skills, and values are distinctly considered by many of the chapters as being of perhaps even greater importance than statistics and league tables.

The focus of Chapter 2 is on the education in Flanders, Belgium. This chapter considers the provision that can be provided within such a diverse country. Flanders has seen a significant movement of people and this has created or exacerbated some of their problems.

The population in Flanders in 2004 was 6,016,024 (4.8 per cent of the population were foreign). (Information adapted from www.oecd.org/belgium/38529279.pdf.)

The population in Flanders in 2010 was 6,251,983 (http://en.wikipedia.org/wiki/Demographics_of_Belgium#Population).

At the beginning of 2012 '25% of the people of Belgium were of foreign background' (http://en.wikipedia.org/wiki/Demographics_of_Belgium#Population).

Migration in the 1990s was 25,000.

Migration in 2003 was 35,000 (information adapted from www.oecd.org/belgium/38529279.pdf).

Belgium has to offer an education system in more than one language depending on the region and overall make-up of the communities. This in itself is a problem for the organisers of the education system. Many readers of the Belgium chapter (Chapter 2) will find the range of topics in primary education of interest.

Chapter 3 introduces the reader to the Czech Republic and the education system that has developed since World War Two and post-1993 when the Czech Republic was internationally recognised. The Czech educational system is searching for ways to face the challenges of today's world such as globalization, immigration and information technology. This chapter also raises the idea of balancing inequalities.

The next chapter (Chapter 4) focuses on the education system in England. This is currently facing many changes and challenges in order to provide children with an appropriate and relevant system. In England, politics and finances frequently determine some of the practice changes. This can mean that the education children receive is more politically motivated than ideal for children, although many changes are influenced by academic research or reviews such as the *Independent Review of the Primary Curriculum* (DCSF 2009) or the *Cambridge Primary Review* (Alexander 2010).

Chapter 5 takes the reader to Finland to consider their successful system and familiarises the reader with a philosophy that appears to work. In Finland the children start school at a later age and yet still succeed. The children are encouraged to be independent learners from a very early age.

This is followed by Chapter 6 which considers pre-school and primary education in the current economic climate in Greece. Greece is a country that has been shaped by history. Its origins are based in an intellectual society of great strength that has been changed and shaped by war, occupation and immigration. Greece was producing philosophers, such as Aristotle, and great thinkers long before many other nations.

Chapter 7 takes the reader over to the east for an insight into the Japanese system. This system places a real emphasis on social and moral development and is a fascinating insight into a precise and determined philosophy.

The book then takes the reader back to Europe for an insight into Latvia in Chapter 8. Latvia, due to its geographical position, has been influenced by both the east and the west. It is culturally diverse and struggles to teach children who come from such diverse backgrounds.

Chapter 9 then discusses the Netherlands' perspectives. The Netherlands is also influenced by its diversity and many children are potentially hindered in reaching their full potential by the location they are born into.

Chapter 10 takes the reader down under to explore the Australia and New Zealand education systems. This also introduces the reader to the New Zealand document *Te Whāriki* and as Papatheodorou and Moyles (2012:142) remark, '*Te Whāriki* has attracted world wide interest respect and admiration'. It fosters positive identities and dispositions in children with Learning stories assessment, not just describing what children can do but rather indicating what needs to happen next. *Te Whāriki* has an emphasis on holistic development, the family and children's well being.

Chapter 11 moves back to Europe to consider what is happening in Poland. This chapter concentrates on the effects of neighbourhoods. Chapter 12 then takes the reader to South Africa and tries to summarise what is happening within this large geographical area.

The final chapter is across the ocean to the United States. In this chapter the author considers the structure and organisation of American education although this is difficult in such a large and diverse country.

Each chapter has much to offer the reader. The reader can consider the structural organisation, the flexibility of the systems, the professionalism, the curriculums, the creativity and statistics plus consider the challenges that face education internationally. This book is a must for any person with an interest in children's futures.

Welcome to this book exploring childhood in a comparative context!

References

Alexander, R. (2010) *Children, Their World, Their Education: Final Report and Recommendations of the Cambridge Primary Review.* Abingdon: Routledge.

DCSF (2009) *Independent Review of the Primary Curriculum: Final Report.* Nottingham: DCSF.

DfE (2012) *Review of the National Curriculum in England: What Can We Learn From the English, Mathematics and Science Curricula of High Performing Jurisdictions?* Research Report DFE-RR178.

Papatheodorou T. and Moyles J. (2012) *Cross-Cultural Perspectives on Early Childhood.* London: Sage.

Rousseau, J.J. (1991) *Emile or On Education.* (Introduction, translation and notes by Allan Bloom) London: Penguin.

1

What is childhood?

Mabel Ann Brown

Acknowledgements

I would like to acknowledge the support and opportunities provided by colleagues at the University of Derby.

Introduction

In Fisher (2002:87), Bertram and Pascal claimed, 'laying the foundations on which a child's edifice is to be built is a complex, skilful and very responsible task', so is childhood a time to lay these foundations or is it a time for something more?

Personally I believe it is something more as it is a time when a child finds out who they are and how they can relate to other children. Childhood is a time when children can feel acknowledged and loved or they can feel inadequate and become self doubting. The responsibility for fostering confidence lies with the adult; they are indeed laying the foundations for the future. What these foundations are or need to be is debatable and frequently based on adult's perspectives at that time. Is it the skills, knowledge or even a sense of identity that we need to impart? It is unclear. Whichever it is, the adult plays a significant part.

The role of the adults

'It is the quality of interaction between adult and child that defines the quality of the whole educational experience', Trudell says in Fisher (2002:69). Children will build upon their early experiences. Piaget defines this as assimilation and accommodation as the children first absorb experiences and then change and adjust, as explained in Bruce (2005:41). Thus we need to consider if positive experiences with adults are the key to a successful adulthood.

Woodhead (1999:19) refers to the 'social child' and in this image the child has status within society and has their own abilities and interests. In this instance the practitioners, adults and parents become the facilitators enabling children to grow in competence. The adult has a responsibility to respect the child and their competences and structure the environment to support this.

However, in some societies childhood is not viewed as a time to assimilate or empower; it is viewed more as a preparation for adulthood. In this context childhood becomes a time to acquire the skills necessary to be an adult. This could, according to Woodhead (1999:18), be the 'developing child' paradigm with children in a state of 'not yet being' or 'projects in the making'.

Perspectives on education and its purpose

Education is a part of modern day childhood but what is it? Aristotle in Ross (2008:15) identified three variations on the purpose and nature of education that are still valid today. The first variation was designed to produce 'citizens that are useful to a society'; the second variation was a system that produces individuals who can relate to other human beings; and the third variation a system that supports 'exceptional accomplishments' (Ross 2008:16). Thus in terms of Aristotle, childhood is a time to develop personally but also a time to develop social skills and values whilst also meeting the needs of the greater picture of being useful to society. Alexander (2010:197) identified 12 aims for education: to promote well being, engagement, empowerment, autonomy, respect and reciprocity, interdependence and sustainability, awareness of citizenship, culture and community, knowing and making sense of the world, skill development, opportunities to excite the imagination and an ability to contribute to dialogue. Each of these is highly important but is it taught or is it acquired? Healthy children are considered as willing to engage in learning as they often want to know and often say 'why?' or 'what is that?' Knowledgeable adults will empower children by giving them the answers or opportunities to find out for themselves. Some of Alexander's (2010:197) aims will be achieved as part of a hidden curriculum but other aspects may need to be taught.

Social engineering

Education can be transformative and encourage mobility from one social group to another but it is often underpinned by the politics at that time and could be just a response to a capitalist system (Ross 2008:19). 'Schools re create the social and economic hierarchies of the society in which they are embedded' (Ross 2008:20), thus some children can be discriminated against particularly if they begin life in a deprived locality or situation. These early limitations can reduce the opportunities to receive higher education. This in turn will affect the child's future earning potential. The OECD (2009a:71) recognises a clear link 'between education and the average earnings of individuals'. Graduates generally earn more than those who leave school with basic qualifications. Politicians and school organisers can try to address this by enabling some children to receive an education outside their normal locality. This is frequently described as social engineering.

Another view is socialization and an attempt to foster certain social groups for political or economic reasons. John Dewey (1907) cited in Ross (2008:17) 'proposed an alternative and transformative model of education' that 'enabled an opportunity to escape from the limitations of the social group in which he was born'. Thus childhood could also be considered a time for social engineering by the prevailing powers of authority. Alexander (2010:174) defines the aims of education as 'ethical and political'. Ethical in that we may be trying to improve the lot of some groups of people but political because we are trying to maintain certain agreed social groups. Education is to some extent agreed by consensus or by the way people vote particularly in the United Kingdom.

An obedient prepared workforce

Rousseau (1991:7) considers that man is naturally inclined to be independent, self sufficient and upon whom 'inclinations are imposed'. Thus preparing children for a workforce is completely contrary to man's natural instinct. 'Capitalist society needs a docile obedient motivated workforce, school prepares us for this in three ways by expecting, subservient conformity, hierarchical acceptance and motivation by external rewards', (Ross 2008:115). However, as Trevarthen (2011:173) points out 'educational reformers since ancient times ... have reacted to the imposition of the formal practice of schooling to urge that children should be respected for their intuitive abilities and not just trained in skills'. Alexander (2010:191) refers to the need for 'balance' between the intention of preparation for work and the needs of the child's individual development; it confirms the notion that 'one size does not fit all' and that children have individual needs too.

Responsible citizens

The life skills to survive are innate within each child or as Rousseau (1991:7) points out 'his sole concern is his preservation and comfort', but this does not necessarily agree with countering individual desires and inclinations for the common good.

Children need to become responsible citizens one day but how do we achieve this and when should it be achieved by? The time when children move from childhood into adulthood has long been debated; in fact the school leaving age in Britain has been raised several times. In 1972 the school leaving age was raised to 16. Yet in Britain 'people cannot vote until they are 18' (Goldson et al. 2002:10). Does this mean that a 16 year old is still a child or does it mean that adulthood only begins when we are 18? Inherent in this is the notion of personal responsibility and the movement from adults as a controlling influence to personal choice and freedom to act in a way that they wish. If the supervising adults have empowered the children, this transition will be less fraught with problems. Positive role models, as Bandura's Social Learning Theory (Macleod Brudenell and Kay 2008:118) observed, can make a significant difference particularly as children 'observe and imitate' the behaviour of important adults in their lives.

Meeting children's needs

In the 'pre modern era', children were thought to have distinct needs and requirements; it was assumed they went through 'identifiable periods of development', (Goldson et al. 2002:18). Vygotsky moved this argument or debate forward in the 1930s with his Zone of Proximal Development (ZPD). This is supported and reflected upon by Alexander (2010:94) when he says, 'Plowden building on Jean Piaget's development theory, made plain the view that until a child is ready to take a step forward it is a waste of time to try to teach him to take it'.

As the skills that were required for work changed, so too did the childhood for children. 'The new childhood discovered by Aries', follows 'the notion that the child is engaged in the process of becoming an adult', (Goldson et al. 2002:19). This particularly applied to more affluent families but working class children had 'modern childhood' imposed upon them (Goldson et al. 2002:20). A distinct 'decline in child labour' (Goldson et al. 2002:22) and the 'expansion of education' plus the concept of rights of the child have led to the system children experience currently. For some, this is an imposed cultural experience whilst for others it is an expectation of their class in society. This means that for some children there is a clash between the home culture and the educational culture, which can have serious psychological consequences particularly if the child feels inadequate.

Child development

Maslow, a humanist psychologist, believed that there is a hierarchy of needs and that until these needs are met learning cannot successfully take place, thus it is important that children 'feel valued, accepted and included', (Petty 2004:53–54). They also need all their psychological needs met such as food and water. 'Maslow observed that if we feel deficient in any of these needs then problematic behaviour' will be apparent (Petty 2004:53).

Cooper in Fisher (2002:2) advocates that 'the best learning opportunities are those that give children the space, time and support to be independent and effective learners'. Petty (2004:56) expresses this as 'active learners' – where the learner is doing something to themselves; and not 'passive learners' – to whom something is done. The Fins would appear to advocate this approach and their children are achieving according to the OECD (2009b). Brunner (in Ross 2008:130) also advocated three 'ways of knowing' through action, imagery and the medium of symbols. In his view all three were needed to be most effective in terms of teaching and learning. However, if children are in a nursery or school do they have opportunities for action and imagery? To a great extent this depends on the ethos of the staff, the setting and the national education system.

Alexander (2010:169) considers whether children should start school or a provision early as they do in the United Kingdom or should we observe the Steiner view that children are more ready academically after the age of six? Interestingly, the OECD (2008 cited in OECD 2009a: 10) claimed that 69.4 per cent of all 3–4 year olds are enrolled in education with the highest levels of subsidised provision in Denmark and Sweden. This level of engagement and interest in the early years is emphasised by research. 'Research from diverse countries suggests a common conclusion that the investment in young children brings significant benefits not only for children and families but also for society at large' OECD (2009a:69). However, the quality of that early years experience is important. In 2004 the Effective Provision for Pre-School Education (EPPE) clearly demonstrated what was needed for effective provision.

Childcare provision has freed up many women for the labour market, however, with growing unemployment this may not be ideal. Lack of employment opportunities may lead to a return to one parent caring for their own children at home to reduce childcare costs.

Hearing the voice of the child

Lavalette and Cunningham, cited in Goldson et al. (2002:24), claim 'children are best placed to describe and analyse this world'. If this is the case it is important to hear their voices.

One way to give children confidence is to listen to their perspectives on the world. Williams (2009) also prioritises the benefits of listening to children's views: 'Children who feel empowered are more likely to be better and happier learners'. He further goes on to say that it shows that it is not the age of early years interventions but their nature which lead to developmental benefits when 'the biological, social, emotional and intellectual aspects of learning are inextricably interwoven' (Williams 2009). Thus there is a need to meet children's basic needs as Maslow indicates but also to hear what they are saying. Children will need to be 'adaptive, responsive and self believing' if they are to succeed in an unknown world (Petty 2004:56); in fact they need to be active learners rather than passive.

The empty vessel perspective

Williams (2009) reflects on the Cambridge Primary Review and claims 'Much schooling worldwide relies on models of teaching seeing the student as an empty vessel into which knowledge is poured'. The National Curriculum (1988) in the United Kingdom in many respects supported this perspective as does the testing and assessment regime prevalent in the United Kingdom systems. Yet Woodhead (1999:19) reminds the reader of Piaget's goal which was to 'encourage respect for young children's ways of thinking and behaving' with 'developmentally appropriate' learning opportunities. Assessments do take into account stages of development as suggested by Piaget (1886–1980) but they fail to allow for children developing at their own individual speed. Piaget reasoned that 2–4 years was the pre conceptual age; from 4–7 years was the intuitive phase; and 7–11 years was the concrete operational stage but there are always children who fall outside these ranges. This greatly influenced the idea in England of certain educational phases.

TABLE 1.1 Educational phases in England

Educational phases in England	
Nursery	0–4 year olds approx.
Foundation Stage	4–5 year olds
Key Stage 1	5–7 year old
Key Stage 2	7–11 year olds

Williams (2009) argues that these developmental stages are not sufficient:

> Scientific studies using new technologies are challenging long held assumptions: forget developmental stages, right brain/left brain functions and learning styles. It shows that it is not the age of early years interventions but their nature which lead to developmental benefits when the biological, social, emotional and intellectual aspects of learning are inextricably interwoven.

He argues that background and social and emotional development are all highly influential in a child's development. This is highlighted in some of the international systems such as Finland or Japan. Vygotsky (1978) also made the point that learning is usually in a social context thus the child's peers, family and community all play a significant part in the learning process. Kay (2005:39) explains that 'adults can closely observe the child's activity and offer relevant support to help the child function at the next stage of his development (the ZPD)'. This approach is born out in Finland in their pre-school system.

Dewey (in Ross 2008:109) refers to 'having an experience' and 'knowing an experience', thus children need to move from knowing to actually understanding and acting upon the learning. Kolb and Fry (1985), in Ross 2008:111, interpret this in terms of experiential learning, the process of a concrete experience, the reflection, leading to the formulation of an abstract concept and the testing out of this within a new context.

Emotional, social, physical and academic development

Childhood is a time to encourage emotional, social, physical and academic development, possibly for political and economic reasons or simply because we want to offer children every opportunity and possibility for egalitarian and philanthropic reasons. In many respects it is in our interests to do this as their future abilities are our future too.

How we achieve this is approached differently by different nations. Finland has adopted a more initial socializing process whereas the United Kingdom has for decades focused on intervention and education with a focused curriculum and defined learning outcomes. More recently the OECD (2009b) statistics have indicated that this was not working and that the United Kingdom children were losing out whilst the Fins were achieving consistently. The government in the United Kingdom has sought to address this and the Cambridge Primary Review (Alexander 2009) supported the growing need for a change as did many teachers.

The question is what kind of a change? Trevarthen (2011:187) claims that 'the big decisions that administrators of education make have to be concerned not with nature vs nurture but with nature vs institutional structure and nurture vs instruction'. Lavalette and Cunningham, cited in Goldson et al. (2002:9), remind the reader that children are 'vulnerable', 'incomplete' and not yet 'fully rational', therefore administrators and all adults do have a huge responsibility to ensure that the provision is appropriate whatever that may be.

One of the views of what childhood should be is that 'it is free from adult worries and responsibilities a time of learning and play a period of happiness and relative freedom', as described in Goldson et al. (2002:9). However, in the current world this can be far from true as Palmer (2007) infers in her book *Toxic Childhood*. Families are frequently broken or re-established and children often have to deal with turbulent home lives. In the words of Goldson et al. (2002:11), 'in Western societies many children's lives do not match the ideal but are scarred by sexual abuse, violence, poverty and discrimination'. For these children worry and mental disturbance are the daily features of their lives. Their life chances are significantly reduced and their childhood is something that has passed them by.

Settings frequently have to deal with children who need to work out these problems and one way this can be achieved is through opportunities to play or dramatise ideas. In Finland this kind of activity is frequently offered to young children. Play has long been debated in terms of child development and 'Froebel made the distinction between play and work, play is what children are involved in when they initiate the task and work is what they do when they fulfil a task required by an adult' (Bruce 2005:19).

International perspectives

The OECD PISA results are merely one tool that could be considered or ignored particularly as learning is so much more than a few tested subjects. However, the OECD PISA results do encourage readers to ask whether they are indicative of a more successful childhood academically particularly as children at 15 in some countries do seem to consistently do well.

TABLE 1.2 Adapted comparisons from *PISA 2009 Database*

	Reading	*Science scale*	*Maths*
Belgium (Flanders)	11th	507	515
Czech	34th	500	493
United Kingdom	25th	492	514
Finland	3rd	554	541
Greece	32nd	470	466
Japan	8th	539	529
Latvia	30th	494	482
Netherlands	10th	522	526
Australia	9th	514 (10th)	527 (15th)
New Zealand	7th	519 (7th)	532 (13th)
Poland	15th	508	495
Spain	33rd	488	483
USA	17th	502	487

Source: Adapted from OECD (2009b)

Finally to demonstrate how important childhood is, Table 1.3 shows the births and deaths based on statistics that are available. Each birth in the United Kingdom is potentially an employee for the future. Childhood should be a part preparation for this but it is an unknown future, therefore there must be flexibility to allow children to develop in line with the world. Essentially all children need the skills to adapt.

Each birth is a potential member of the workforce and any significant increases or declines in the birth rate can impact on the workforce in the future. Table 1.3 makes no attempt to consider the movement of people which also significantly changes a workforce potential within a particular region. Therefore some children may become part of the workforce in another country and others may migrate here and become part of the United Kingdom workforce. Thus in educational terms, an international perspective on education is vital to prepare this potential workforce for work in whichever region of the world they eventually work in.

The employment rates within the European countries covered by this book are shown in Table 1.4.

Whether the employment rate is indicative of a successful education system or of a locality that is succeeding or struggling is debateable but perhaps worthy of consideration when reflecting on different education systems.

TABLE 1.3 Adapted information from the Office for National Statistics (England and Wales 1988–1998)

	1960	1970	1980	1990	1998	2001	2009	2010	2011	2012
UK births info@statistics.gov.uk +OPCS Digest of statistics 2010 England and Wales only	914,000	848,000	707,000	706,000	635,000		706,248	723,165	723,913	
UK deaths info@statistics.gov.uk	624,000	658,000	661,000	564,000	555,000		491,348	493,242	484,367	
In employment aged 16+										**29.59 million (June–Aug 2012)**
Total number of residents in England and Wales					**52.2 million (1997)**	**52.4 million**			**56,170,900**	
			1987	1997			2009		2011	
Migration inflow			212,000	285,000			411,000		252,000	
Migration outflow			210,000	225,000			226,000			

Source: Adapted from Office for National Statistics (1998, 2011, 2012a, 2012b)

TABLE 1.4 Employment rates in Europe

Country	2010 Employment rate %	2011 Unemployment rate %
Netherlands	74.7	4.4
Czech Republic	65.0	6.7
United Kingdom	69.5	8.0
Finland	68.1	7.8
Greece	59.6	17.7
Latvia	59.3	15.4
Poland	59.3	9.7
Japan	70.1	4.6
USA	66.7	8.9

Source: Adapted from Eurostat (2012a, 2012b)

Reflective questions

What do you think childhood should be?

In what ways is childhood different in other countries?

How do we prepare children for an unknown future world?

Current challenges

Moss (cited in Waller 2006:142) argues that 'there are two possible constructions of early childhood institutions: as a place for pre determined outcomes or as children's spaces which provide opportunities for children and adults, the consequences of which are unknown'. The former is perhaps more reliable but the latter enables greater future potential as there is room for creativity and ingenuity however some would fear this. One challenge is therefore to provide a space for children that will both inform them and allow them to develop for an unknown future.

Lavalette and Cunningham, cited in Goldson et al. (2002:23), claim that 'childhood is not a static merely biological phenomenon' but rather that it is 'affected and shaped by wider social and cultural elements'. Thus a current challenge is to provide children with a positive childhood experience at a time when the economic climate nationally and internationally is somewhat unstable.

Conclusion

Depending on what society believes childhood is for, will determine what is offered to children. The adults will decide children's futures but what they choose will impact everyone's futures. The economy and state of the world will also influence what is provided.

The children could be merely participants of a service or we could empower them with positive experiences so that they will surprise us by their ingenuity in the future.

References

Alexander, R. (2010) *Children, Their World, Their Education: Final Report and Recommendations of the Cambridge Primary Review*. Abingdon: Routledge.

Bruce, T. (2005) *Early Childhood Education*. 3rd edn. London: Hodder Arnold.

Eurostat (2012a) Employment Rate, Age Group 15–64, 2000–2010 [Online]. Available at: http://epp.eurostat.ec.europa.eu/statistics_explained/index.php?title=File:Employment_rate,_age_group_15-64,_2000-2010_(%25).png&filetimestamp=20111117142634 (Accessed on 31 October 2012).

Eurostat (2012b) Unemployment Rate, 2000–2011 (%).png [Online]. Available at: http://epp.eurostat.ec.europa.eu/statistics_explained/index.php?title=File:Unemployment_rate,_2000-2011_(%25).png&filetimestamp=20120502100338 (Accessed on 31 October 2012).

Fisher, J. (ed.) (2002) *The Foundations of Learning*. Buckingham: Open University Press.

Goldson, B., Lavalette, M. and Mckechnie, J. (2002) *Children, Welfare and the State*. London: Sage.

Kay, J. (2005) *Teaching Assistant's Handbook Primary Edition*. London: Continuum.

Macleod Brudenell, I. and Kay, J. (eds) (2008) *Advanced Early Years for Foundation Degrees and Levels 4/5*. 2nd edn. Essex: Heinemann.

OECD (2009a) *Education Today: The OECD Perspective*. OECD Publishing.

OECD (2009b) *PISA 2009 Database* [Online]. Available at: http://www.oecd.org/dataoecd/54/12/46643496.pdf (Accessed on 18 March 2013).

Office for National Statistics (1998) Birth statistics, England and Wales (Series FM1), No. 27, 1998 [Online]. Available at: www.ons.gov.uk/ons/rel/vsob1/birth-statistics--england-and-wales--series-fm1-/no--27--1998/index.html (Accessed on 31 October 2012).

Office for National Statistics (2011) Births and Deaths in England and Wales. [Online]. Available at: www.ons.gov.uk/ons/rel/vsob1/birth-summary-tables--england-and-wales/2011--final-/sb-births-and-deaths-in-england-and-wales--2011--final-.html (Accessed on 31 October 2012).

Office for National Statistics (2012a) Labour Market Statistics October [Online]. Available at: www.ons.gov.uk/ons/rel/vsob1/birth-summary-tables--england-and-wales/2011--final-/sb-births-and-deaths-in-england-and-wales--2011--final-.html (Accessed on 18 March 2013).

Office for National Statistics (2012b) Population Estimates for England and Wales, Mid-2011 (2011 Census-based) [Online]. Available at: www.ons.gov.uk/ons/rel/pop-estimate/population-estimates-for-england-and-wales/mid-2011--2011-census-based-/index.html (Accessed on 31 October 2012).

Palmer, S. (2007) *Toxic Childhood: How the Modern World is Damaging Our Children and What We Can Do About It*. London: Orion.

Petty, G. (2004) *Teaching Today*. 3rd edn. Cheltenham: Nelson Thornes.

Ross, A. (2008) *A European Education: Citizenship, Identities and Young People*. Stoke-on-Trent: Trentham Books.

Rousseau, J.J. (1991) *Emile or On Education*. (Introduction, translation and notes by Allan Bloom) London: Penguin.

Trevarthen, C. (2011) *What Young Children Give To Their Learning Making Education Work to Sustain a Community and Its Culture*. European Early Childhood Education Research Journal, Vol. 19, No. 2, June 2011, pages 173–193.

Vygotsky, L. (1978) *Mind in Society*. Cambridge, MA: Harvard University Press.

Waller, T. (2006) *An Introduction to Early Childhood: A Multidisciplinary Approach*. London: Paul Chapman.

Williams, J.R.A. (2009) *International Perspectives on "Children, Their World, Their Education: Final Report and Recommendations of the Cambridge Primary Review"* October 2009 [Online]. Available at: www.eenet.org.uk/resources/docs/Cambs_Primary_Review.doc (Accessed on 27 July 2012).

Woodhead, M. (1999) *Towards a Global Paradigm for Research into Early Childhood Education.* European Early Childhood Education Research Journal, Vol. 7, No. 1, 1999, pages 5–22.

2

Education in Flanders

Bart Hempen and Michèle Vanleke

Introduction: education in Belgium – one state, three systems

The kingdom of Belgium is a small but densely populated country in Western Europe that was established in 1830, after gaining independence from the Netherlands. In the course of its history this part of Europe was ruled by Celts, Romans, Franks, Carolingians, Spanish, Austrians, French and Dutch. Borders between Latin and Germanic cultures are still crossing the country. Most of the Dutch-speaking Belgians live in the north, French-speaking Belgians mainly live in the south and a small group of German-speaking Belgians inhabit the east of the country. This linguistic diversity resulted into still-active political conflicts forming the bases of a complex system of government, resulting in far-reaching reforms of the formerly unitary Belgian state into a federal state.

Depending on where a Belgian lives (s)he belongs to a certain region, depending on which language (s)he speaks a Belgian belongs to a certain community. Belgium comprises three regions (Flanders, Wallonia and Brussels) as well as three communities (Dutch, French and German). Personal affairs such as education are community matters; more geographical issues such as road infrastructure are dealt with at a regional level. As the federal state of Belgium recognises three different communities (as well as three official languages) this also means Belgium has three educational structures and education policies, respectively coming from a Dutch-speaking Ministry of Education or from the French-speaking or the German-speaking counterpart. Though the organisation of education displays a lot of diversity, the quality of education in Belgium is excellent. According to the OECD's PISA study results, Belgium is one of the top-performing countries in reading literacy, mathematics and science (OECD 2010).

Since 1989, Belgium's Dutch, French and German-speaking communities have acquired almost full authority for education. Only the age limits of compulsory education, the age of retirement and teachers' degree diploma requirements are dealt with by the federal government. In principle, all schools are mixed as a school is not allowed to refuse pupils on the grounds of gender.

How childhood is perceived in Flanders

According to the Belgian constitution, each child has a right to education. Compulsory education was introduced in order to guarantee this right to education. Compulsory education is supposed to be free of charge, i.e. primary and secondary schools financed by the government are not allowed to charge an enrolment fee. Furthermore, in nursery and primary education, parents do not pay for school materials and activities which are necessary to meet the objectives of education. In secondary schools, parents do pay for school materials and activities.

Case study

Dirk, 32 years old, father of Lieven, 10 years old, who attends a primary state school in Brussels:

The school my son Lieven attends is situated in the middle of Brussels. It is a Dutch speaking school, in the middle of a city where 85 percent of the population speaks French. At home we speak Dutch, for this reason we chose this school. All lessons are in Dutch, the teachers also want the children to speak Dutch in the playground.

We are not charged any entrance fees. Also I am very pleased that all school materials needed to meet the attainment targets are free of charge. We only need to pay for school materials in case of loss and for certain school activities like excursions.

The most stressful moments for me are the mornings when I bring Lieven to school. Lessons start at 8h30. The teachers ask us to immediately leave the playground after bringing our children. Nevertheless, there always is an enormous traffic jam around the school between 8h and 8h30. My wife picks-up Lieven after school (3h30 pm). Children can be picked up until 6h pm. We are asked to inform the teacher in advance if Lieven is being picked up by someone else.

At least three times a year, the school organises a parents' evening when we are invited to speak with Lieven's teacher. She writes a school report, five times per school year. The report summarizes the results: all subjects are graded on a scale from 1 to 10. Furthermore all reports are provided with additional information and tips on guidance and remediation. We are asked to sign the report and give it back to the teacher. Our son does well, next year he'll hopefully be in his final year of primary school.

Compulsory education starts on 1 September of the year a child turns six, lasting up to 12 full years of schooling. In Belgium, compulsory education does not imply school attendance. Children do not necessarily have to go to school to learn. Home education is an option, but in reality it is rarely done.

Another fundamental right for every Belgian is written in the constitution: freedom of education. Every natural person or legal body has the right to organise education and establish institutions for this purpose. They are entirely free in choosing teaching methods and are allowed to base their education on a certain educational view, determining their own curriculum and timetables as well as appointing their own staff. However, as schools only receive governmental funding and recognition if they make sure the pupils will at the end of their school career meet the attainment targets elaborated by the Ministry of Education, the amount of different kinds of schools in Belgium is limited. Many of them belong to a certain educational network.

TABLE 2.1 Education phases in Flanders

Education phases in Flanders	
Under six years old	Pre-school
6–12 years old	Child starts school
12–18 years old	Secondary education

Education in Flanders

In Flanders there are three educational networks:

(1) Publicly run education organised by the public body acting under the authority of the Flemish Community. This educational network is required to be neutral.
(2) Publicly funded, publicly run education comprises both provincial education (organised by provincial authorities) as well as municipal education (organised by local authorities).
(3) The publicly funded, privately run schools (mainly catholic schools) deliver education organised by a private person or private organisation.

About 70 per cent of all Flemish pupils attend a catholic school; two times 15 per cent of pupils attend schools organised by one of the other two networks. Pupils at catholic schools are considered to be more disciplined. In Brussels, non-Flemish-speaking families tend to send their children to Dutch-speaking schools for this reason.

Comparing schools

Veerle: 11 years old, attends a privately run Catholic Primary School, Saint Pieter's College, Flanders:

> At school we have to wear our uniform. I don't really like the blue, grey and white colours. However, I find it really easy not having to choose my kind of clothing in the morning! Then again, we always have to wear our uniform, even in summer we are not allowed to wear short skirts, not even when it is hot.
>
> Our teachers are friendly, but our director is very strict, we always have to stand up when he enters the classroom. This year we have three different teachers: one for maths, Dutch and French, one for world orientation and sports and one teacher for music who is really cool.
>
> I like going to school, especially on Tuesday when they serve chips at the cafeteria. In the afternoon we play volleyball during our weekly sports lesson, this is my favourite sport. Too bad we only play sport once a week. After school, we study in the library doing our homework. This always happens in silence.
>
> Last Wednesday afternoon my mom and I were selling waffles we baked at school. The money goes to our Zambia project. We also sell pencils from Oxfam.
>
> Friday we get a free desert at lunch time when we had good grades on our weekly tests. I always look forward to this! In general I really like going to school!

Medi: 11 years old, attends a primary state school in Brussels:

> I have a lot of fun at school. My favourite subject is sports. Sometimes we even go to the swimming pool for swimming. During sports we have to wear a special T-shirt with the school logo, during swimming lessons we must wear a swimming cap. I don't like that. At normal lessons I can wear whatever I want. My favourite clothes are my nike sweater and shoes, my grandpa gave me for my birthday.
>
> With grandpa I speak Turkish, with my parents and friends I speak French and at school we have to speak Dutch. Sometimes I make a mistake and say something in Turkish to my teacher. Sometimes he is angry about this. Last week I was punished for chatting in Turkish with my neighbour during the lesson. The teacher made me stay over for an extra hour. This was during the so called "thick sweater day", a day when the heating system is turned lower for one day and we have to wear extra warm clothes. Our world orientation teacher explained this is done as a sustainable development measure.
>
> During playtime, I see my Turkish friends from other classes. Most of the pupils at my school come from non-Belgian families. We often talk about what we are going to do after school when we go to the city centre.

Each network translated the educational goals in their own way, resulting in three different kinds of educational curricula. This situation also exists in the French- and the German-speaking parts of Belgium. If all educational networks within the three educational systems (i.e. the Dutch, the French and the German speaking) were to be dealt with, this chapter would be three times as voluminous. Therefore we restrict ourselves to education in Flanders (attended by 60 per cent of Belgian pupils).

In nursery, primary and secondary schools, the school year starts on 1 September and ends on 30 June (officially it ends on 31 August). Besides mainstream nursery (2.5–6 years old) and primary education (6–12 years old), special nursery and primary school also does exist for children with special needs, i.e. eight different types of special education.

The content of the curricula offered in nursery and primary education is based on the developmental objectives (as they are called in nursery education and special needs schools of primary and secondary education) or the attainment targets (as they are known in mainstream primary and secondary education) elaborated by the Ministry of Education.

Reflection: the Flemish attainment targets for primary education

Visit http://ond.vlaanderen.be/dvo/english/corecurriculum/primary/indexprimary.htm and choose your subject of preference. Compare the Flemish goals indicated with the curriculum of your country. Which goals are similar, which differ? Could you include them in your own practice to enhance and enrich the learning experiences of your pupils?

The nursery education curriculum

The developmental objectives form the common core curriculum. These were formulated for five *areas of learning*:

- *Art education*: visual arts, music, drama, dance, media and attitudes;
- *Dutch*: listening, speaking, reading, writing and linguistics;
- *Mathematical initiation*: numbers, measuring and space (geometric initiation);
- *Physical education*: motor skills, healthy and safe lifestyle, self-awareness and social integration;
- *World studies*: nature, technique, humankind, society, time and space.

All schools must offer their pupils activities in all these areas of learning. In the course of its full inspections, the inspectorate checks whether the developmental objectives have been met. The school boards draw up a curriculum containing the developmental objectives, which are approved by the government upon the advice of the inspectorate who subsequently checks that the curriculum is also followed.

The primary education curriculum

In primary education two kinds of attainment targets are distinguished: subject-specific ones and cross-curricular ones. The subject-specific attainment targets regard the pupils' knowledge, skills and attitudes towards arts, Dutch, French, mathematics, physical education and world studies. Cross-curricular attainment targets are minimum objectives which do not specifically belong to one area of learning but can be aimed at by several areas of learning or educational projects. The cross-curricular attainment targets concern 'learning to learn', 'social skills' and 'use of computers'. Subject-specific attainment targets concern the following topics:

- *Art education*: visual arts, music, drama, dance, media and attitudes;
- *Dutch*: listening, speaking, reading, writing, strategies, linguistics and (inter)cultural focus;
- *French*: listening, reading, speaking, oral interaction and writing;
- *Mathematics*: numbers, measuring, geometry, strategies, problem-solving skills and attitudes;
- *Physical education*: motor skills, healthy and safe lifestyle, self-awareness and social integration;
- *World studies*: nature, technique, humankind, society, time and space, and use of resources.

Reflective task

You may wish to compare these curriculum areas with your own system.

TABLE 2.2 Year 1 (age six) Flanders' timetable

	Mon	*Tue*	*Wed*	*Thu*	*Fri*
8:00–8:40	Arrive at school				
8:40–9:30	Maths	Maths	Dutch	Maths	Maths
9:30–10:20	Maths	Maths	French	Maths	Maths
10:20–10:35	Morning break				
10:35–11:25	World studies	Dutch	Religion	Dutch	World studies
12:15–13:20	Lunch break				
13:20–14:10	Religion	Arts	—	World studies	Arts
14:10–14:25	Afternoon break				
14:25–15:15	Sports	World-orientation	—	Sports	Arts

Note: On Wednesdays schools end at 12:15

These six specific school subjects in primary education are not meant to give a certain structure to the education the school provides. Schools decide individually how they offer certain contents of learning. School boards draw up a curriculum making sure that it meets the attainment targets at the end. This curriculum is then approved by the government upon the advice of the inspectorate who subsequently checks that the curriculum is adhered to.

The same division into areas of learning is operated throughout nursery and primary education. This underlines the developmental line throughout elementary education. The same cross-curricular themes can be found in secondary education.

Creative world studies

Some teachers in Flanders approach the primary school subject of 'world studies' through the Edward de Bono approach: de Bono's Six Thinking Hats. The Maltese psychologist, Edward de Bono, developed a thinking tool using 'Six Thinking Hats' which provides means for groups to think together more effectively and to plan thinking processes in a more detailed way. Each of us tends to think about matters in a specific way. Some people approach situations in their life more scientifically, where others deal with them more emotionally. By using de Bono's thinking tool, students begin to realise that one can look at a particular topic from various perspectives. When dealing with controversial issues, de Bono's Six Thinking Hats are very effective in making students sensitive to other points of view. The scientific base behind this method is that the human brain thinks in a number of distinct ways which can be accessed using the de Bono technique, allowing someone to develop strategies for thinking about particular issues in life.

De Bono identifies six distinct states of mind. In each of these states the brain will bring aspects of the issue into our consciousness (e.g. a positive approach or a more pessimistic way of judging, or...). Each hat represents one of these six different ways of thinking. The six hats encourage the wearer to view an issue from different perspectives, thus encouraging a more creative way of thinking.

TABLE 2.3 De Bono's Six Thinking Hats and their representing approach towards phenomena

De Bono hat colour	Way of thinking/approaching a phenomenon
Black	The serious colour encouraging the thinker to be cautious about a phenomenon. Probably the most important hat preventing the student's emotions from dominating the situation. Wearing this hat makes you the devil's advocate, asking questions which are exposing weaknesses in a situation.
Blue	The colour of the sky, thus suggesting having an overview of the student's way of thinking. The blue hat is a meta-cognitive hat. It challenges the thinker to be self-analytical, evaluative and to think holistically.
Red	The colour of blood. This is a hot colour encouraging the student to show their emotions, intuition and general feelings without any need for justification. This hat is the emotional hat; here emotions are more important than thinking.
Green	The fresh colour of newly growing plants, welcoming new beginnings and creative ideas. It is the hat that invites creative solutions and innovative suggestions.
Yellow	The bright and positive colour. It requires the student to look at the good points of a phenomenon, an issue or a situation.
White	The sterile colour of a hospital. This is a clinical or neutral colour, demanding the student to discover facts concerning the phenomenon in an objective manner. The white hat represents facts. It is the hat for data, detail, figures, information and the asking of useful questions.

Source: Adapted from De Bono 2000

De Bono's thinking tool gives students a more balanced view when debating controversial issues. These issues have always been at the heart of science and in the future will be of even greater importance when scientific discoveries contribute even more towards daily life issues. This might require that the future science teacher moves up to a 'next level' that is not exclusively scientifically approaching certain phenomena but also approaches them in a more social way. The future science teacher will more often be asked to put on the de Bono blue hat and look at complex issues in a holistic way.

Reflective questions

Download a copy of the Six Thinking Heads brochure (available from www.debonogroup.com/six_thinking_hats.php) and critically reflect on its content. Consider your responses to the following questions:

■ Do you stimulate creative thinking with the pupils you work with?

■ What do you consider to be the benefits or limitations?

Language education in Flanders

In Dutch-speaking Flanders, French is a compulsory subject for pupils in 5th and 6th grade. In Brussels and some other bilingual peripheral municipalities, pupils start learning French from the 3rd grade onwards. Nevertheless, introductory French lessons (enhancing language awareness) can be offered from the start of nursery education. Such language awareness lessons may also be offered in another language, in schools that already offer French-language awareness lessons).

Communication is the basis for learning a foreign language. Children start communicating easier by being asked to talk about their hobbies, personal characteristics ... and letting children look in the classroom and describing persons with whom they share things, differences (interpersonal intelligence). Or by letting them talk about a topic (verbal intelligence) illustrating it with pictures (visual/spatial intelligence) of what they like or don't like (intrapersonal intelligence), or depicting which movie star they like to resemble physically (body intelligence). With a little preparation and imagination, each lesson can be a multiple intelligence lesson (see p 26).

Teaching methods and materials

Due to the constitutionally guaranteed principle of 'freedom of education', decisions regarding teaching methods and teaching aids belong to the freedom of the school board. There are no official guidelines. In nursery and primary education many school activities are often centred around a specific topic. These topics are linked to seasonal festivities, but may also concern topics the child brings in.

As an organisational structure, the 'working in corners' method can be found in many nursery and primary schools in Flanders during some hours per week. In these corners children simulate, experiment, discover and discuss about everyday situations or about finding a solution to a problem, either with the help of other children (and the teacher) or independently. This approach is an important tool helping children to acquire some independency when preparing for primary education.

Another often used approach in nursery and primary education is named 'contract work'. This formula is about dealing with individually chosen activities within a certain period of time (written down in a contract). To complete the tasks chosen, children are given a certain amount of class time in which they can decide relatively independently about the duration and sequence of their activities.

Many nursery (as of four years old) and primary schools in Flanders have introduced personal computers or tablet as a learning process support tool. What children should be able to do with a computer, also called 'Information and Communication Technology competences', is mentioned in the cross-curricular developmental objectives/attainment targets. Every school can freely decide from what age they will start to work on this.

Finally, it needs to be mentioned that the Flemish Ministry of Education does not oblige the purchase of certain teaching aids, school books or audio visual study material. Schools can freely choose from the teaching materials that are available on the educational market.

Secondary education in Flanders

Secondary education starts when the child turns 12 and lasts up to the age of 18. Full-time compulsory secondary education lasts until the child turns 16 (or in some cases when the child is still 15, i.e. when the first two years in secondary education are completed). Part-time compulsory secondary education equals a system of working and learning (at least one day per week).

All levels of secondary education in Flanders last for at least six years. The first two years in mainstream secondary education are supposed to be the same for all Flemish pupils. Then the differentiation phase begins: a child and its parents have to decide if the child will attend a more general form of secondary education (Algemeen Secundair Onderwijs, ASO), a more technical way of secondary education (Technisch Secundair Onderwijs, TSO), a more artistic way of secondary education (Kunst Secundair Onderwijs, KSO) or a more vocational secondary education (Beroepssecundair Onderwijs, BSO).

Further specialisation within the type of secondary education chosen also exists, e.g. within ASO a child can opt for a choice of subjects preparing him/her for studying fundamental sciences, or for a choice of subjects preparing him/her for social studies. The curriculum of secondary education comprises both subject-related attainment targets as well as cross-curricular attainment targets (e.g. on sustainable development). Any diploma of secondary education obtained in Flanders gives unlimited access to higher education.

Higher education includes higher vocational education, professional bachelor study programmes organised by university colleges (in Dutch: hogescholen) and academic study programmes mainly organised by universities (be it in some cases by university colleges).

Challenges for education in Flanders

The current teaching staff is ageing, resulting in an increasing shortage of teachers. This should be avoided by making the profession more attractive and giving it a better image. Lifelong learning should become the solution for enhancing the attractiveness of the profession: learn on the job by offering in-service training opportunities to teaching staff. Teachers must learn how to constantly fascinate and stimulate their pupils sufficiently in order to make them responsible for their own development and future. The Ministry of Education wants schools to transform their pupils from young adults into active citizens with strong personalities, open minds and a sense of sustainable development.

The ideal teacher not only refreshes their learning materials constantly but also acts with enthusiasm and inspiration to challenge and stimulate their pupils. They are the inspiration for their further development. They believe in the pupils and have a passion for the job, are prepared for all possible developments and trends, and know the daily world of the pupils. Didactically they have an eye for individual learning possibilities and are alerted to the social and cultural background of each child. They also guide pupils in their search for information and are no longer the only source of knowledge. The Ministerial Paper makes it clear that young people do not only learn at school, but also learn outside the school context, acquiring an open view on the world.

Creating teachers that can deal with these 'new' demands also requires a lot of teacher training institutes when preparing future teachers adequately. The Ministerial Paper suggests that during their teacher training, students should not only develop an analytical way of thinking but also be stimulated in developing creativity and multiple intelligences.

Independent research

What are your country's challenges for education in general and for teacher training specifically? Search on the Internet and read some government documentation mentioning future plans for education by your local authorities.

Teacher training

The content of all teacher education programmes in Flanders – be it nursery, primary, lower or upper secondary teacher education – is chosen by the school of education which the student attends. The school's freedom, however, should always reflect both the Flemish Ministry of Education's subject-specific attainment targets in secondary schools and the basic teacher competencies. There are ten basic teacher competencies which describe the roles of the teacher as: (1) facilitator of learning and developmental processes, (2) educator, (3) content expert, (4) organiser, (5) innovator and researcher, (6) partner of parents/guardians, (7) member of the school, (8) partner of external organisations, (9) member of the education community and (10) cultural participant.

Case study

Teacher Stefanie, 27 years old, has been teaching at a publically run municipality school for five years:

Every Wednesday afternoon when there are no lessons, I give aerobics lessons in the sports centre of our village. In this way I get to know our village children in a different way!

When I'm at the bakery on Sunday, I usually run into the parents of my pupils. That may not always be pleasant because they immediately start talking about their children and the school. An unofficial parent pupil review meeting at my bakery! Just when I want to get home to enjoy my breakfast!

Sunday afternoons I start my preparations for the week. I try to offer lots of different working methods in my lessons. Children aged 8 are not able to concentrate for a very long time. Fortunately I know a lot of games thanks to my previous scout's club membership!

I also find humour very important when teaching. The subject I really do not like to teach is music. This is really not my strongest characteristic, that's why I use a lot of CDs.

The multiple intelligence classrooms

Pupils love variety and like to taste different things. What they like, they keep; what cannot fascinate them has irrevocably served its turn. As a teacher it is important that you excite them, stimulate them, take their point of view on the world into consideration and incorporate this into your lessons. It is equally important to know what goes on in their minds, to know their interests and to encourage them in maintaining their best characteristics and to challenge them in improving their weaker skills.

What is true for pupils is even more important for students in higher education. Having an eye for what students like to do and watching their strengths are the two fundamental pillars of a successful lesson. Bringing variation into your lessons and approaching students according to their own learning style as well, can be achieved with the help of the multiple intelligences theory developed by Howard Gardner (1983/1993). In teacher training we distinguish three main approaches in the theory of multiple intelligences: matching, stretching and celebrating.

When a teacher trainer focuses their lessons on the main students' intelligences present, we speak of matching. Students, who are best at physical intelligence, can be stimulated even more by permitting them to move when they need to. Students with a strong rhythmical intelligence can be stimulated even more by allowing them to write songs or compose music. The theory of multiple intelligences is not just about focussing on the main intelligences present (matching), but also focussing on the development of weaker intelligences (stretching).

A third approach is known as celebrating. By acquainting students with the theory of multiple intelligences, they learn to understand that there are different ways of being intelligent and that everyone has a unique intelligence pattern. Being aware of this ensures that students and teachers become more skillful in associating with each other. Know-how of their own intelligences make them feel prouder and have more faith in themselves. Besides, they become more involved in the learning of their development of other intelligences. By learning to see and appreciate the talents of others, they feel more accepted and become more self-confident. They also learn to accept mutual differences and become more successful in forming social relationships.

Activity

Download a copy of the free multiple intelligences test for young people (available from www.businessballs.com/freepdfmaterials/free_multiple_intelligences_test_young_people.pdf) and do the test. Evaluate your score: are your results in accordance with your expectations?

Conclusion

According to OECD's PISA study results, Flanders, as well as the other educational systems of Belgium, belong to the top-performing countries in reading literacy, mathematics and science. The ways of instruction in primary schools in Flanders is diverse, but still very often teacher-centred and strictly curriculum-focused. One of the main challenges for education is leaving this strict path and evolving in the direction of a school of openness, tolerance and solidarity.

References

De Bono, E. (2000) *Six Thinking Hats*. London, UK: Penguin Books. [Online]. Available at: http://www.edwdebono.com (Accessed on 1 May 2012).

Gardner, Howard (1983/1993) *Frames of Mind: The Theory of Multiple Intelligences*, New York: Basic Books.

OECD (2010) PISA 2009 Results: What Students Know and Can Do – Student Performance in Reading, Mathematics and Science (Volume I). [Online]. Available at: http://dx.doi.org/10.1787/9789264091450-en (Accessed on 1 May 2012).

3

Education in the Czech Republic

Pavla Vyhnálková and Jana Kantorová

Terminology

FEP (The Framework Education Programme) is a document that defines the compulsory content, scope and conditions of education in the Czech Republic.

FEP PE is *The Framework Education Programme for Pre-school Education* (pre-primary).

FEP EE is *The Framework Education Programme for Elementary Education* (primary).

Introduction

The following chapter deals with the educational system and the educational perspectives in the Czech Republic. First, we mention the historical and cultural context of the Czech Republic, then we introduce the main principles of education in this country and finally we are dedicating ourselves to the pre-primary and primary education in detail. The chapter is closed by the short thinking about the problems and challenges of the education in the Czech Republic.

The Czech educational system is searching for ways to face the challenges of today's world (post-modern relativity of values, massive development of information and communication technologies, globalisation and immigration, etc.) and also how to deepen cooperation with inherent social structures, particularly with family and community.

Historical, social and cultural influences

The Czech Republic is a continental state lying in the middle of Europe. It lies on the area of three historical countries – Bohemia, Moravia and a part of Silesia – and has an area of 78,867 km². The Czech Republic has altogether 10,535,811 dwellers (calculated on 31 March 2011). It is divided administratively into 14 autonomous regions and the capital city is Prague.

The important watershed of modern history of the Czech Republic was the Velvet Revolution, which started on 17 November 1989. It overthrew the communist regime and allowed the renewal of democracy and the development of market economy. From 1990 federalisation started to be belatedly brought into practice, although disagreements between the two parts of the federation, the Czech Republic and Slovakia, grew quickly. Finally it led to the disintegration of the common state. As a subject of the international law, the Czech Republic started to exist on 1 January 1993.

The Czech Republic is a democratic state with a liberal constitution and a political system based on the free competition of the political parties and movements. The President is the head of the republic; the top legislative organ is a bicameral parliament of the Czech Republic. The Czech Republic has gradually become involved in west-European political structures. On 12 March 1999 it was accepted to NATO and on 1 May 2004 it entered the European Union. It is a member of OSN, Council of Europe, OECD and other international groups.

Social and cultural values of the Czech Republic

Within the last 20 years, the Czech society has undergone an intensive and uneasy transformation process. After the stormy evolution in the 1990s, the economy gradually stabilised, mainly because of the non-state sector and private business. The Czech society considerably changed socioeconomically. The impact of a worldwide crisis and the necessary saving measures realised on the state level were very perceptible for a lot of people. Simultaneously, people, who lived out the overwhelming part of their life in communism, often still have the paternalistic conception of the state. The political situation is corresponding to this. The governance changes alternately between conservative and social democracy.

The Czech people are a nation rich in culture and they still have live traditions, which may captivate Europe and even the world. The Czech nation has given birth to plenty of important scientists, artists and statesmen. Even though the western crisis of values concerns Czechs as well, they are (mainly in hard times) capable of deep solidarity and selfless help.

Independent education has also always been well valued in the Czech lands and it has a long and rich tradition. It has a great pedagogue of worldwide importance, whose bequest is still being followed by modern Czech teachers such as Jan Amos Comenius who was born and lived for part of his life in the Czech Republic.

Childhood in the Czech Republic

A *child* in the Czech Republic, in conformity with the Convention on the Rights of the Child, is considered to be every person *younger than 18 years*. The Convention on the Rights of the Child was ratified by the Czech Republic in 1991 and there is also a well-developed system of *child protection*.

The surroundings have a great impact on children as they go through their childhood and this is evident on every level from micro-environment (family, school, group of contemporaries), through local and regional surroundings to macro-environment (state and media). In particular, the individualistic family ambiance creates different starting conditions for education and life in society, just by the structure of the family relationship itself (a lot of children grow up with one parent), and also by its economic, cultural and especially its emotional characteristics. Society and the school provide support and help for any disadvantaged children.

Case study 1

Peter is six years old. He lives in a flat in town. His parents are both employed; he has no brothers or sisters. Peter gets up at 6:30 a.m. Mum takes him to school by car. After the lessons Peter goes to the youth centre. He trains at ice hockey three times a week, and he is taken there by car by his dad. Apart from this, Peter also attends a school of music; he has started to play the piano. When it is 17:00 p.m., his parents take him from the youth centre or from the training and he still has to write his homework. Peter watches television or he plays on the computer in the evening. He goes to bed at 20:00 p.m. During the weekend, when his parents have no work, the family goes on a trip and Peter is really glad that he can spend time with his parents. His desire is to have more free time and would like to play more according to his own ideas. He wishes to have a sibling too, or at least a little pet.

Case study 2

John is six years old. He lives in a village in a family house. His dad goes to work; his mum stays at home with his younger brother, who is three years old. John gets up at 6:30 a.m. His mum accompanies him on his walk to school and after lunch she picks him up again. Once a week in the afternoon John has an art club at school and he has also started to attend the volunteer fire department for young people in the village. There are no more possibilities in the place where he lives and his parents lack the financial funds to drive him to the city. At home John writes his homework and then he plays inside the house or outside with the dog. Sometimes he has to look after his little brother, which he does not enjoy very much. During the weekend, his parents work in the house or in the garden and John helps them. Occasionally he visits his grandma and grandpa who live not far away. His wish is to have a radio-controlled car and he would like to go on a trip with his parents sometime.

Introduction to education in the Czech Republic

Current changes and tendencies in the education in the Czech Republic

The transformation of education and of the educational system in the Czech Republic has taken place during the last 20 years (and more intensively in the last ten years). This process is connected mainly with the gradual democratisation and humanisation of the Czech society.

After 1989, the perennial grammar schools, independent schools and church schools were renewed and there became a possibility to establish schools inspired by alternative pedagogical directions. Still bigger attention in binding documents and in practice is paid to the groups of pupils with individual characteristics – foreigners and members of national minorities, talented pupils and students, pupils and students with a health handicap or with a sociocultural disadvantage. Integrated education of pupils with special educational needs is preferred (*The Framework Education Programme for Elementary Education (FEP EE),* pp.

111–116; *ACT No. 561/2004 Coll.*, Section 14, 16–20; *Organisation of the Educational System in the Czech Republic 2009/2010*, p. 85).

The most conspicuous contribution of the school reform is the establishment of a *new two-stage curricular system*.

Further reading

The Framework Educational Programme. (*Organisation of the Education System in the Czech Republic 2009/2010*, p. 85).

National Programme for the Development of Education in the Czech Republic : White Paper.

The Framework Educational Programmes among others 'shall define the compulsory content, scope and conditions of education. These shall be binding for the development of School Educational Programmes, the evaluation of children and pupils' results in education, the development and assessment of textbooks and teaching texts' (*ACT No. 561/2004 Coll.*, Section 3).

Education in a particular school and in an educational institution shall be pursued according to the School Educational Programme, issued by the director of the school and of the school facility and shall be publically accessible (*ACT No. 561/2004 Coll.*, Section 5).

Considering the content, the education in the Czech Republic has opened to the new topics since 1989. Targets and content of education are not determined and formulated ideologically any more. The current Czech school aspires to educate and bring up a new generation prepared for life in a democratic and pluralistic society.

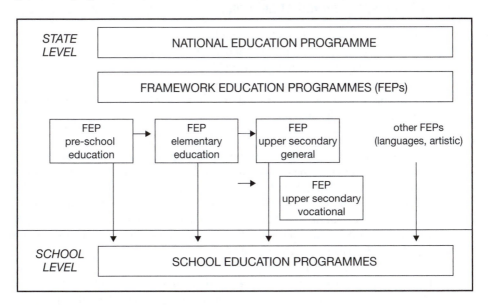

FIGURE 3.1 The Czech system of curricular documents
Source: FEP EE, p. 5

Targets and principles of education in the Czech Republic

According to the education law, the education in the Czech Republic is based on the principle of equal approach of every person in the country, and of other member states of the European Union as well, towards the education. The right to get the education cannot be refused for the discriminatory reasons of race, colour of the skin, gender, language, faith or religion, nationality, ethnic or social origin, material possession, family life or health condition. Esteem, respect, tolerance, solidarity and dignity should predominate among all participants of education and the individual needs of every person should be taken into account.

Education in the Czech Republic is also based on the principle of free propagation of knowledge corresponding to the contemporary knowledge of the world. There is an aim to keep the process of education and evaluation of results improving (*ACT No. 561/2004 Coll.*, Section 2).

The general aim of education in the Czech Republic is to develop the character of a human being equipped with the 'knowledge and social competencies, ethnical and spiritual values for their personal and civil life, for the execution of a profession or working activities, and for acquiring information and learning in the course of life' (*ACT No. 561/2004 Coll.*, Section 2).

Among the values that should be acquired by the educated person belong the principles of democracy, fundamental human rights along with responsibility and a sense of social coherence, equality of men and women in society, national and state citizenship awareness, respect for the individual identity of every person, knowledge of global and European cultural values and traditions, protection of the environment, etc. (*ACT No. 561/2004 Coll.*, Section 2).

What I have studied at school...

… plenty of important things helpful for life.
… respect for others and expression of opinions.
… responsibility (for myself in the first place).
… cooperation with friends and the development of interpersonal relationships.
… reading, writing and calculating above all; that is what I use, and many other things which I have already forgotten.

Pupils and students in the Czech Republic have a right to be educated and to use the school services provided in the intentions of the law. Adult pupils and students may be elected into the school council, all pupils and students can establish self-governing bodies in the school and they can be elected there. Then, pupils and students have the right to express their opinions on every decision which concerns their education, they have the right to be informed about the results and about the course of their studies and they are supposed to be helped with this business in the case of need.

Above other responsibilities, pupils and students have firstly a duty to attend the school duly, to educate themselves, to adhere to school and internal Rules of Order and other school rules. They should also respect the instructions given by the pedagogical staff of the school (*ACT No. 561/2004 Coll.*, Sections 21–22).

The educational system and the organisation of education in school

The educational system in the Czech Republic is composed of *schools* and *school facilities*. The types of schools are 'nursery schools, basic schools, secondary schools [...], conservatories, tertiary professional schools, basic artistic schools and language schools authorised to organise state language examinations' (*ACT No.561/2004 Coll.*, Section 7) and then also universities, whose functioning is defined by a special legal rule. Education in school is then supplemented and supported by the education and services of school facilities.

Schools and school facilities in the Czech Republic are created by the municipalities or a union of municipalities (nursery and basic school), by a region (secondary schools), registered churches and religious societies, and in the case of some specific schools or school facilities directly by the state and its individual ministries (*ACT No. 561/2004 Coll.*, Section 8).

Direct educational, specially pedagogical or pedagogical-psychological activities in schools and school facilities are practiced by *pedagogical staff*, where apart from the teachers and tutors, there are also special pedagogues, psychologists, pedagogues of free time, assistants of pedagogues, trainers and the head pedagogical worker. Qualification for the performance of their function, particularly concerning the professional qualifications and compulsory further education, are determined by special legal rule (*ACT No. 563/2004 Coll.*).

Pre-primary education

Pre-school (pre-primary) education in the Czech Republic is intended for children from three to six years. It is realised in *nursery schools*, nevertheless the preparatory classes correspond to the *pre-school degree* as well, and they are established for children with some social disadvantage in order to balance the possible sociocultural differences.

The participation of children in pre-school education is not compulsory, however, it is strongly recommended, particularly a year before the beginning of the compulsory school attendance, where a child has this right given by a law and where it is provided free of charge in state and public institutions (*Organisation of the Education System in the Czech Republic 2009/2010*, p. 73).

Nursery schools in the Czech Republic work with a considerable liberty of organisation. We may find here, for example, nursery schools of a Waldorf type, Montessori school, schools of Christian orientation and other schools working according to some specific programmes (for example, Step by Step – Start Together, Health Promoting schools, etc.) (*Organisation of the Education System in the Czech Republic 2009/2010*, p. 79).

The role of pre-school education is the support of the versatile development of personality on intellectual, emotional and physical level. Pre-school education contributes to the acquiring of basic rules of behaviour, values and relationships which prepares a child for further education. It also has an important role for balancing inequalities in the development of children (*ACT No. 561/2004 Coll.*, Sections 33–34). Institution of pre-school education should closely cooperate with children's families and it should enrich the family education with other initiatives. Pre-school education also carries out a diagnostic function, mainly in a relationship with children who have special educational needs.

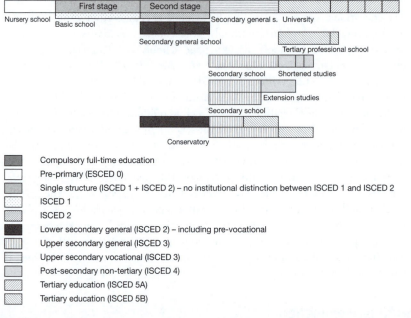

FIGURE 3.2 Organisation of the educational system in the Czech Republic
Source: Organisation of the Education System in the Czech Republic 2009/2010, p. 83

Further reading

The Framework Education Programme for Pre-school Education (*Rámcový vzdělávací program pro předškolní vzdělávání* 2004) (further written as *FEP PE* or *RVP PV*).

This document determines the following three targets of pre-school education:
1. development of a child, its education and cognition, and
2. acquiring the basis of values, which determine our society,
3. obtaining personal self-reliance and the ability to express as an independent personality influencing its surroundings (*RVP PV*, p. 8).

There are five *key competencies* which should keep developing during the pre-school education:

1. Learning competencies,
2. Problem-solving competencies,
3. Communication competencies,
4. Social and personal competencies,
5. Civic and activity competencies.

Education is realised in a biological field (*child and its body*), psychological (*child and its psychology*), interpersonal (*child and the other one*), socially cultural (*child and the society*) and environmental (*child and the world*). One of the most important principles in the formation of a school educational programme should be *the integrated approach* – educational content should be provided to children in natural coherence (*RVP PV*, pp. 7–8).

The daily order in the nursery school should be regular, although also flexible, in order to provide sufficient space for taking the individual possibilities of children into account and for fulfilling their actual or currently changed needs. The daily programme has to respect the need for activity and rest of individual children; the physical activities and activities realised outside which contribute to the strengthening of health should be included as well (*RVP PV*, pp. 31–34).

> Suitable methods and forms of work are learning by experience and in cooperation through play. These activities that are based on direct experience support children's curiosity and their need to discover, they stimulate children's joy in learning; their interest in learning new things, gaining new experiences and mastering other skills. [...] Learning should take the form of play, where the children are engaged according to their interests and personal choices. [...] Spontaneous and directed activities should be interlinked and balanced. [...] The teacher should guide children on their path to knowledge, stimulate their active interest and their desire to look around themselves, to listen and to discover.
>
> (*Organisation of the Education System in the Czech Republic 2009/2010*, p. 76)

The voice of the child

In the nursery school I liked...

... that we played, and that we studied in an entertaining way and we had good snacks.
... that I was in a group of children from the early childhood.

The most important thing I have learned in the nursery school is...

... being self-reliant.
... the cooperation with others in the team.
... an art of sharing and lending.

In the nursery school, I found a little bit problematic...

... that I bore badly being without parents in the beginning.
... that I did not want to eat and sleep after the lunch.

The long lasting and relentless monitoring and evaluation of the child's progress is really important in pre-school education. Primarily, it should enable the teacher to lead the child individually and sensitively in correspondence to its natural development in the direction of a support of his further studies and universal progress. But, continuous evaluation also has a significant diagnostic dimension and it can be a clue for prompt and suitable intervention causing the benefit of a child (*RVP PV*, p. 41).

TABLE 3.1 Number of children, classes, nursery schools and teachers in the Czech Republic

	2005/06	2006/07	2007/08	2008/09	2009/10
Children	282,183	285,419	291,194	301,620	314,008
Schools	4,834	4,815	4,808	4,809	4,826
Classes	12,409	12,494	12,698	13,035	13,452
Teachers	22,109	22,367	22,744	23,567	24,584
Children/class	22.7/1	22.8/1	22.9/1	23.1/1	23.3/1
Children/school	58.4/1	59.3/1	60.6/1	62.7/1	65.1/1
Children/teacher	12.6/1	12.8/1	12.8/1	12.8/1	12.8/1

Source: Organisation of the Education System in the Czech Republic 2009/2010, pp. 80–81

Primary education

Compulsory school attendance

'School attendance shall be compulsory for a period of nine years, however no longer than until the end of the school year when a pupil reaches seventeen years of age' (*ACT No. 561/2004 Coll.*, Section 36).

> Compulsory school attendance shall start at the beginning of the school year following the date when a child reaches six years of age. [...] A child who reaches six years of age at the period between the beginning of a relevant school year and at the end of the calendar school year may be admitted to compulsory school attendance. [...] If such a child is physically as well as mentally adequately mature and if his/her statutory representative so requests.
>
> (*ACT No. 561/2004 Coll.*, Section 36)

Based on the written request of the child's statutory representative and a recommending assessment from the relevant specialists, the head teacher may put off the beginning of compulsory school attendance by one year if the child is not suitably mentally or physically mature after having reached six years of age (*ACT No. 561/2004 Coll.*, Section 37).

TABLE 3.2 Pupils entering the compulsory education later than at six years of age in the Czech Republic

	2005/06	2006/07	2007/08	2008/09	2009/10
Number	23,172	21,735	21,155	21,152	21,368
In % of new entrance	25.2	23.7	23.1	22.8	22.8

Source: Organisation of the Education System in the Czech Republic 2009/2010, p. 107

Structure and organisation of elementary education

Elementary education in the Czech Republic comprises of the primary and lower secondary education. The *primary education* is realised from the 1st–5th year of elementary school (the first stage); the *lower secondary education* from the 6th–9th year of the elementary school (the second stage); or on the lower stage of six-year or eight-year secondary general school, or on the corresponding part of an eight-year educational programme of a conservatory.

Pupils fulfil the compulsory school attendance by the presence in the elementary education. Municipality has a duty to provide the conditions for complying with the compulsory school attendance for children having the place of residence in their region. In order to ensure the geographical school accessibility, for small children particularly, it is possible to divide the two stages of elementary school organisationally and to establish a school made just by the first stage. In the first stage, there is also an alternative to put pupils from different grades into just one class (small schools with composite classes). Elementary education is free of charge, apart from public and church schools which can demand fees (*Organisation of the Education System in the Czech Republic 2009/2010*, pp. 83, 89–90).

Concerning the alternative structures, elementary schools in the Czech Republic can follow the principles of Waldorf and Montessori's pedagogy and of the Jena or Dalton Plan, in the intentions of current law. At the first stage of a basic school, under some conditions it is possible to comply with the compulsory school attendance in the form of *individual (home) education* (*Organisation of the Education System in the Czech Republic 2009/2010*, p. 103).

During the elementary education, pupils are placed in classes according to their age; the maximum for one class is 30 pupils. For the teaching of some subjects it is possible to divide classes into groups, create groups of pupils from the same year or from different years or to join classes. It is usual that *just one pedagogue* teaches pupils at the first stage (often the same person for several years), however, the teaching of selected subjects can be authorised by other teachers as well (*Organisation of the Education System in the Czech Republic 2009/2010*, p. 92).

The teaching of elementary education is time divided into the *teaching lessons*. Each one lasts 45 minutes and they can be divided and connected in reasoned cases. In the first and second years of an elementary school, the number of compulsory teaching lessons is determined from 18–22 hours a week; from the first to the fifth year it should be from 22–26 hours a week. The earliest time when the teaching may start is 7 a.m. and it has to finish by 5 p.m. at the latest. Lunch break needs to be at least 50 minutes; other breaks have to be ten minutes as a minimum (*ACT No. 561/2004 Coll.*, Sections 23–26; *Organisation of the Education System in the Czech Republic 2009/2010*, pp. 93–94).

Targets and content of elementary education

Through basic education pupils shall acquire necessary learning strategies on the basis of which they should be motivated for lifelong learning, learn how to think creatively and solve problems, effectively communicate and cooperate, protect their physical and mental health, creative values and the environment, learn how to be considerate and tolerant towards other people, different cultures and spiritual values, to recognise their abilities and real possibilities and to apply these together with knowledge and skills acquired in deciding on their life path and professional career.

(*ACT No. 561/2004 Coll.*, Section 44)

TABLE 3.3 Number of pupils, classes, elementary schools and teachers in the Czech Republic

	2005/06	2006/07	2007/08	2008/09	2009/10
Pupils	916,575	876,513	844,863	816,015	794,459
Schools	4,474	4,197	4,155	4,133	4,125
Classes	45,769	44,527	43,433	42,498	41,941
Teachers	63,157	62,657	60,973	59,492	58,417
Pupils/class	20/1	19.7/1	19.5/1	19.2/1	18.9/1
Pupils/school	204.9/1	208.8/1	203.3/1	197.4/1	192.6/1
Pupils/teacher	14.5/1	14.0/1	13.9/1	13.7/1	13.6/1

Source: Organisation of the Education System in the Czech Republic 2009/2010, pp. 108–109

It is evident that the educational targets are defined not only at the *cognitive level*, but also at the *level of skills* and mainly at the *level of attitudes and values* (*Organisation of the Education System in the Czech Republic 2009/2010*, p. 88).

From 1 September 2007, the binding document called *The Framework Education Programme for Elementary Education* (further written as *FEP EE*) determines the targets and content of elementary education and the individual school educational programmes of different elementary schools are worked on its basis. Similarly, like in the case of pre-primary education, the *key competencies*, which should accompany the schooled individual, are defined in this document:

1.   Learning competencies,
2.   Problem-solving competencies,
3.   Communication competencies,
4.   Social and personal competencies,
5.   Civic competencies,
6.   Professional competencies.

Each of these competencies is closely related to each other; they are interdisciplinary. 'The entire educational content and all of the activities taking place at school must therefore be aimed at and contribute to forming and developing these competencies' (*FEP EE*, p. 11).

Education in elementary school comes true together in nine educational fields: *Language and Language Communication, Mathematics and Its Application, Information and Communication Technologies, Man and His World, Man and Society, Man and Nature, Arts and Culture, Man and Health, Man and the World of Work*. Some of these fields are then divided further into constituent branches (*FEP EE*, p. 15). The fields of actual problems of modern world are represented in the *FEP EE* as so-called *Cross-Curricular Subjects*, which

> represent an important formative element of elementary education, create the opportunities for individual engagement of the pupil as well as mutual cooperation and contribute to the development of the pupil's character, primarily in the area of attitudes and values [...] The thematic areas of the cross-curricular subjects traverse various educational areas and allow for the interconnection of the educational content of more educational fields, hence contributing to the comprehensiveness of the pupil's education.

[…] The pupil is thus given the opportunity to form an integrated view on a given issue and to apply a broad spectrum of skills.

These cross-curricular subjects are defined in elementary education: *Moral, Character and Social Education, Civic Education for Democracy, Education Towards Thinking in European and Global Contexts, Multicultural Education, Environmental Education, Media Education* (*FEP EE*, p. 91).

TABLE 3.4 The framework timetable for basic education in the Czech Republic

Educational areas	Educational fields	Stage 1	Stage 2
		1st–5th forms	6th–9th forms
		Minimum time allotment	
Language and Language Communication	Czech Language and Literature	35	15
	Foreign Language	9	12
Mathematics and Its Applications		20	15
Information and Communication Technologies		1	1
Man and His World		12	–
Man and Society	History Civics	–	11
Man and Nature	Physics Chemistry Nature Geography	– – – –	21
Arts and Culture	Music Fine Arts	12	10
Man and Health	Health Education Physical Education	– 10	10
Man and the World of Work		5	3
Cross-curricular subjects		C	C
Available time cllotment		14	24
Total compulsory time allotment		*118*	*122*

Source: FEP EE, p.106
Note C = must be included and implemented with all pupils in the course of education at the relevant stage; the time allotment may be drawn from the unallocated time allotment.

The conception of *FEP EE* allows the taking of needs and possibilities of individual pupils into account thanks to the fact that the teaching might be organisationally variable, individualised and internally differentiated.

The voice of the child

What I liked about the first stage …

… the stamps for praise.
… breaks spent outside on the playground.
… new children and a kind Ms. Teacher.
… the fact that I had good marks.

The most important what I have studied on the first stage of elementary school is…

… mainly reading and passion for books.
… accepting older people and teachers as an authority.
… cooperation and communication with classmates.
… bases of almost everything.

What I found the most difficult on the first stage of the elementary school was…

… getting used to commuting.
… finding a friend.
… getting used to a new regime and developing independent learning skills.
… standing silent the whole lesson, sitting on a place and keeping concentrated added to this.

Assessment

The evaluation of results of the education on the basic school is expressed in the form of classification levels, orally or in the combination of both ways (*1 = excellent, 2 = very good, 3 = good, 4 = satisfactory, 5 = unsatisfactory*). Pupils are evaluated in individual subjects continuously and then also at the end of every half year when they are given a school report also including information about the pupil's behaviour and overall results. If a pupil fails at the end of second semester or the evaluation is not possible, he usually repeats the year; if he fails from two compulsory subjects at most, he makes a corrective commission exam (*ACT No. 561/2004 Coll.*, Sections 51–53; *Organisation of the Education System in the Czech Republic 2009/2010*, pp. 99–100).

The voice of the child

For me, marks represent…

… the evaluation of my efforts and my knowledge, although I am not convinced that they are especially important.
… marks represent nothing to me – they may not express the true character of a person.

Educational and social function of school

As it has already been mentioned above, school has not only got a function to educate in the sense of passing on knowledge, but it also educates in the formative, emotional, attitudinal and voluntary way. Educational moves used in the Czech Republic are, for example, approbations or other appreciation; on the other hand, there are also disciplinary measures – school reports, reprimands or other punishments. Behaviour is evaluated at the end of every semester on a three-point scale (*1 = very good*, *2 = satisfactory*, *3 = unsatisfactory*) (*ACT No. 561/2004 Coll.*, Section 31; *Organisation of the Education System in the Czech Republic 2009/2010*, p. 99).

Further reading

Special educational needs

Organisation of the Education System in the Czech Republic 2009/2010, p. 102.

Apart from education, schools also often provide the whole day upbringing in school facilities for leisure education, which are parts of their organisations.

TABLE 3.5 Typical day in the nursery school and in the 1st stage of the elementary school in the Czech Republic

1st stage of the elementary school	
08:00–08:45	Czech Language
08:45–08:55	Break
08:55–09:40	Mathematics
09:40–10:00	Main break
10:00–10:45	English Language
10:45–10:55	Break
10:55–11:40	Man and His World
11:40–11:50	Break
11:50–12:35	Physical Education
12:35–13:15	Lunch break
13:15–16:30	Optional leisure education in the youth centre (if parents register the child)

Problems and challenges of education in the Czech Republic

Although the transformation process mentioned above started a lot of positive changes in the Czech education system, there are also problematic points where a Czech school meets with difficulties. Some are a bequest of a 40–year communist dictatorship, others are connected with the state of post-modern society and are specific for the Czech conditions. In the following part, we try to outline briefly some of these problems and challenges.

Concerning the content of education and mainly the fulfilment of its targets, schools have already overcome the initial difficulties connected with the start of the Framework Education Programme (FEP) and with the establishment of the School Education Programme (SEP). However, some schools do not cope as easily with certain methodological freedoms of the FEP. According to the report of the Czech School Inspection, 'deficiencies in descriptions of SEPs, syllabi, curricula and self-evaluation of schools […] have persisted' according to the principles mentioned in FEP. In the range and quality of SEP, there are considerable differences between individual schools and only one third of evaluated SEP is worked on fully in accord with FEP (*Annual Report for the 2009–2010 School Year*, p. 38).

The common problem of the Czech schools is the low level of skills teachers have with information and communication technologies, and the insufficient technological facilities schools provide, which represents a barrier to the effective usage in lessons (*Annual Report for the 2009–2010 School Year*, p. 40).

The next problematic field is the quality of the foreign language lessons, mainly from the point of view of the teacher's qualification.

International comparisons

A weaker result of Czech pupils in the international field of literacy and numeracy (PISA) is a serious issue. The name of literacy in schools is interpreted

> in different ways. Current findings on reading literacy and on options for its development often escape schools' attention. The FEP (2007) offers only very limited guidance on what goals school should achieve in the field of reading literacy. […] The results indicate a moderate improvement of pupils' skills to retrieve information from texts and to assess the form of texts. A weakness prevails in the abilities to assess the content of texts and to interpret them.
>
> (*Annual Report for the 2009–2010 School Year*, pp. 31, 33)

As for numeracy at the first stage of an elementary school, for example, the numerical computation and the correct usage of mathematical terminology and symbolism can be evaluated positively. 'There were discrepancies in developing independence when solving examples, justifying pupils' answers and developing the competences necessary for problem solving' (*Annual Report for the 2009–2010 School Year*, p. 33). The measure in this field should chiefly lead to further education of pedagogical staff, to the development of subject didactics and to the methodological support.

Finally, the single defining of values, to which a young generation should be educated, is not easy nowadays. As Petr Piťha correctly points out, generally there is an accordance that school should prepare children for life and it should contribute to the inclusion into society of a successful individual. However, the problem is how we evaluate the current society. On the one hand, we criticise it a lot; on the other hand, its condition fascinates us. In the sharpened form we might express the dilemma in the following way: leading children to courtesy and moral patterns will make them vulnerable and it will harm them. And if you do not lead them in this way, the society will collapse; it will fall into still bigger brutal chaos (Piťha, 1999).

The teacher is perceived by the society as …

… the one who has spare time during the holidays, who hangs around all the time and in fact find that being a teacher is just an enjoyment, it is not work at all.
… the one who has a poorly paid job full of stress and is frequently undervalued by the society.
… a respected profession, only the salary does not correspond to the work done.

Further education for teachers is …

… Important – time has changed as have the demands on teachers.
… Essential – when a teacher educates himself it is a contribution for pupils too.

According to Spilková (2003) the centre of professionalisation is the concept of a teacher as a facilitator of pupil's development and education; as someone who tries to get every pupil to his personal maximum; guides on the way of knowledge; shows things; helps to orientate; excites; inspires; furnishes with the feeling of competence and self-confidence.

Current situation in the pre-primary sector

From the outer difficulties of the Czech education system let us mention for instance the problems of financing, which appear mainly in the fields of pre-primary education by the insufficient capacity of the nursery schools (in the 1990s, in the time of demographic decline, a lot of nursery schools were cancelled).

TABLE 3.6 The number of rejected requests for admission to nursery schools in the Czech Republic

	2001	2002	2003	2004	2005	2006	2007	2008	2009
Rejected	2,770	3,813	4,673	6,128	6,810	9,570	13,409	19,996	29,632

Source: Organisation of the Education System in the Czech Republic 2009/2010, p. 81

From the studies of pedagogical publications and articles it is evident that the problems outlined above do not appear only in the Czech Republic, but also in other states. We do not want to judge the Czech situation in a disproportionally negative way. We perceive the troubles and imperfections, which should be removed, but at the same time we become aware of the fact that the realisation of the process of change is not easy and it requires time. The knowledge of what should be done and how it should be done is not sufficient. We also need enough determination and will and often the power to change ourselves.

Reflective questions

Can you compare the Czech education system with the education system in your country and in other countries?

Where do you see the main differences?

What are the main changes in the Czech education system over the last 20 years?

Is the development of the Czech education system similar to the development of the education in other post-communist countries?

How can the cross-curricular subjects in the various educational fields (see Table 3.4) be implemented?

Further reading

ACT No. 561/2004 Collection, on Pre-school, Basic, Secondary, Tertiary Professional and Other Education (the Education Act), as amended.

The Framework Education Programme for Elementary Education (FEP EE).

National Programme for the Development of Education in the Czech Republic: White Paper.

Organisation of the Education System in the Czech Republic 2009/2010.

European Commission (Education, Audiovisual & Culture Executive Agency), 2010. Dostupné z WWW: http://eacea.ec.europa.eu/education/eurydice/.

List of terms

Compulsory school attendance
Cross-curricular Subjects
Educational area
Educational consultant
Elementary school
Framework Education Programme
Framework timetable
Key competencies
Nursery school
Preparatory class of elementary school
School Education Programme
School prevention coordinator

Bibliography

ACT No. 561/2004 Collection of Law, on Pre-school, Basic, Secondary, Tertiary Professional and Other Education (the Education Act), as amended. Dostupné z WWW: www.msmt.cz/dokumenty/act-no-561-of-24th-september-2004.

Annual Report for the 2009–2010 School Year. [online] Praha, 2010. Dostupné z WWW: www.csicr. cz/en/85477-annual-report-for-the-2009-2010-school-year.

Česko. In *Wikipedie – otevřená encyklopedie.* [cit. 2011-07-30] Dostupné z WWW: http://cs. wikipedia.org/wiki/Česko.

The Framework Education Programme for Elementary Education (FEP EE). Praha: Výzkumný ústav pedagogický, 2007. Dostupné z WWW: www.vuppraha.cz/ramcove-vzdelavaci-programy/ zakladni-vzdelavani.

Kantorová, Jana. *Meritum : Řízení školy 2009. Část 2 – Klima školy.* Praha: ASPI Wolters Kluwer, 2009, s. 41-118. ISBN 978-80-7357-413-0.

National Programme for the Development of Education in the Czech Republic: White Paper. Praha: Ministerstvo školství, mládeže a tělovýchovy, 2001. Dostupné z WWW: http://aplikace.msmt.cz/ pdf/whitepaper.pdf.

Organisation of the Education System in the Czech Republic 2009/2010. [online] European Commission (Education, Audiovisual & Culture Executive Agency), 2010. Dostupné z WWW: https:// webgate.ec.europa.eu/fpfis/mwikis/eurydice/index.php/Czech-Republic:Overview.

Piťha, Petr. *K problémům vzdělávání v ČR.* Případová studie sdružení Lípa. Příspěvek přednesený ve dnech 26. – 28. 11. 1999 ve Špindlerově mlýně. [online] Dostupné z WWW: http://lipa.cz/ temata.htm.

Rámcový vzdělávací program pro předškolní vzdělávání (RVP PV). [*The Framework Education Programme for Pre-school Education (FEP PE).*] [online] Praha: Výzkumný ústav pedagogický, 2004. Dostupné z WWW: http://www.vuppraha.cz/ramcove-vzdelavaci-programy/predskolni-vzdelavani.

Spilková, Vladimíra. Priority v praktické přípravě studentů učitelství – současný stav a perspektivy. [Priorities in the teaching practice in the framework of pre-service teacher education – current state and perspective.] In *Pedagogická praxe.* 1. vyd. Praha : PedF UK, 2003, s. 28-32. ISBN 80-7290-105-2.

Tuček, Milan aj *Prestiž povolání.* Praha: Centrum pro výzkum veřejného mínění, Sociologický ústav Akademie věd České republiky, 2011. Dostupné z WWW: http://www.cvvm.cas.cz/upl/ zpravy/101176s_eu110725.pdf.

4

Education in England

Jon White

Acknowledgements

I would like to thank friends, family and colleagues for their contributions to this chapter. Their support and discussion has enabled this consideration of childhood through the eyes and voice of a child.

Introduction

Over the last 50 years or so, it is fair to suggest that Early Years Education and Care (EYEC) has undergone a revolution in England. Policy and political imperatives have been influenced and interwoven with both the radical idealism of the far Right and Left, together with the competing psychological and sociological dogma of academia. There is little wonder that, when considering the journey made by EYEC providers, there is much to reflect on.

It is taken that when discussing the 'Early Years', the age group being referred to in England is from birth to about eight years old (DfES, 2008). Some authorities will discuss the time pre-birth and, while this is a valid perspective, it is not one which will be introduced in this chapter. Nevertheless, there is increasing concern over the pre-natal environment in which some children develop and it is therefore unreasonable to underestimate the potential impact of adult behaviour on unborn children.

The main focus becomes the activities of adults. It is of concern because what we as adults do is what the child experiences. We impact on the social construction of the world in which children operate, be it in the home or in the many and varied institutions in which children operate. We also control how children move between these places – their transitions – whether these movements are planned and organised, or whether they are unexpected and chaotic (Brooker, 2002). Anyone who has ever taken a child to hospital in the middle of the night will understand how traumatic it can be for all concerned. We are in a position to make a real difference in the lives of the children in our world: so how are we doing?

It is recognised that the education of children and their achievements in their early years will be the principal determinants of their happiness and the prosperity of their, and subsequent, generations. As such, it is critical to establish with some clarity what we want for children and what we expect of those who are entrusted with their education and care.

On agreement of a direction for EYEC practice, there can be an exploration of how that is achieved. What kind of physical environment is needed? What is the institution for? How is it organised in relation to the connections made to society outside of the nursery door? What are the expectations of the adults who work with children and how their efforts and activities are to be valued? What qualifications may we reasonably expect them to have? Finally, what is the experience of being a child today and how might it compare to children from earlier generations?

Consider

These are all questions which are debated in the popular and professional press:

To what extent does this debate involve adults and children? Where do they find a voice in these discussions?

In the era of digital technology and mass communication, how effective are Wikis and Blogs in helping find voices for those people who are often not heard?

Setting the context

In England, we find ourselves located on an island on the north-west edge of the European continent. England is part of four 'countries' making up the United Kingdom: Scotland, Wales and Northern Ireland comprise the other three. The phrase 'Great Britain' refers to the four partners and is generally regarded as a geographical name, rather than a political statement. There are ties between these four countries which go back many years, with the main Government being in London. Each partner has its own seat of Government, providing some independence and self-determination, while matters such as tax and defence are controlled centrally from London. The organisation and management of the relationship between the partners of the United Kingdom is in the process of continual evolution. It is worth noting that the four partners have their individual distinctiveness in their approaches to education and care. This chapter retains a focus on England.

As with many Western economies, England is far from a homogenous country. There are large cities with pockets of wealth alongside acute social and economic deprivation. There are many cultures rubbing alongside each other, often making for vibrant communities. Suburban sprawl can house a mixture of prosperity or desperation, while rural life presents the same inequality that may be hidden underneath a veneer of apparent tranquillity. The theme that emerges from this picture of Englishness is one of inequality of opportunity and outcome. It is argued that the story of educational policy and practice in England is the story of how repeated Governments have battled to remedy this injustice.

England is relatively close to France, our nearest neighbour, and has incredible air and rail connections between the major cities and the hub cities of the European Union and beyond. However, while we look back at military collaboration against Fascism, we are at times reluctant to adopt the social and political stance of our European neighbours. A key belief, enshrined in the European psyche, is that public services need to be supported by social wealth in order to mitigate against inequality and that the state has a central role in integrating services and private enterprise. This may be known as the 'infrastructure of justice' (Rawls, 1973) or the 'social contract' between the citizens and the state.

So while we are geographically close to Europe, it may be that we are politically and culturally closer to an American ideology, one in which the practice of conservative capitalism is the leading dynamic. One in which the State level of intervention is seen as potentially interfering with the rights of the individual to exercise their own power. Not just with language (broadly similar), but with academia and research the United States and its pro-market individualism has shaped British EYEC custom and practice for a generation.

It is the impact of this drive to which we now turn.

The historical, social and cultural influences and the drive for quality

The 1970s had witnessed the loud rumblings of discontent over the state of the education system. The Prime Minister had given a speech at Ruskin College, Oxford, in which he expressed the commitment of the Government to drive up the standards of delivery through more effective partnership between taxpayers and teachers (Callaghan, 1976). Education was no longer going to be left in the hands of the professionals: accountability had arrived. There was a need to ensure that teachers were offering value for money and that the provision, funded by the taxpayer, was of the highest quality. The way forward was partnership between parents, business and teachers. What sounds quite regular now was bold thinking in 1976.

Consider

How do you adapt to change?

Are you someone who groans and says 'Oh no – not more new ideas'... or are you someone who thinks 'I can ignore this – it will go away soon and everything will go back to normal'... or are you someone who leaps up and says 'Great – let's do it!'?

The reflective practitioner takes on change thoughtfully – so what do you think the feeling was when the Prime Minister openly criticised the education establishment?

So the 'Ruskin Speech' (Callaghan, 1976) raised the question of quality, putting the activities of professionals under the spotlight of publicity. It was suddenly seen as acceptable to question the autonomy of teachers, their methods and the structure and delivery of the curriculum. Many reasoned, with rising unemployment and the perception that standards were not what they once were, that someone was to blame. These concerns were dismissed at the time by the Liberal Left, but the seeds of change had been sown and the New Right was on the way at the start of the new decade.

There was a sea-change in Britain in the 1980s as the Conservative Government set about the task of changing the social and economic landscape for a generation (Cashdan and Harris, 1993). There were some strategic changes at the start of this period, including an increase in parental choice of school, but the landmark legislation came in 1988 with the Education Reform Act. This introduced several new policies: the National Curriculum, local financial management of schools and league tables.

For the first time in many years, Head Teachers and School Governors were holding real power.

This legislation mirrored the changes seen in other areas of society, driven by the New Right. The belief was that people would be motivated to improve themselves through competition and the drive for success. In the context of schools, this vision put the pressure on Head Teachers and School Governors to perform well in the Local Authority league tables so as to ensure good reputations were made and parents saw their school as the natural choice for children who would be guided to success. Good schools would grow, while less successful schools would become driven to improve: the inexorable drive for 'quality' had begun, but with little in the way of discussion of how 'quality' can be a contested concept and the subject of multiple understandings (Moss and Petri, 2002).

As a consequence, successful teaching was an imperative and an inspection regime, spearheaded by the Office for Standards in Education (OFSTED), reported publically on the performance of all schools under Local Education Authority control, with the newly acquired authority to manage their own finances and a degree of flexibility in staffing; the outcome was intended to be a rise in quality of experience through competition. This again reflected the American dream of marketplace economics being the driver of quality and value for money, in which British education would produce a generation of children better equipped to meet the demands of employment in a global economy.

This was the connection that had been made in the public consciousness. Teachers were not entitled to just teach, to work with children and to exercise their professional autonomy. There had to be a measurable outcome for the nation-state and the nation-state could and should have a say in what teachers were doing. Education had become a commodity which could be bought and delivered, irrespective of the social context and economic climate.

Following the landslide victory of the Labour Government in 1997, there was an expectation that some of the legislation of the previous decade would be repealed. However, in an attempt to impress on the public the commitment it had to education, there was a series of legislation and policy initiatives introduced in the early years of the administration (Cole, 1998). They maintained the principles of the New Right but tempered them with a social democratic flavour by a commitment to combat the social exclusion caused by the policies they inherited. It appeared that the new administration was keeping 'standards, choice and accountability', but moving away from an American model towards something distinctively more European. This combination of New Right policies and New Labour ideology (or neo-liberalism and state-socialism), led to this approach being labelled the 'the third way' (Giddens, 1998).

Some of these changes can be observed in the following statistics:

TABLE 4.1 The number of teachers and teaching assistants in England

Full time equivalent in Local Authority maintained schools and academies in England	2000	2010	2011
Teachers	405,800	448,000	438,000
Teaching assistants	79,000	194,200	219,800

Source: Adapted from www.education.gov.uk/researchandstatistics/statistics/a00205723/

The number of teachers has remained static since the year 2000 but the number of teaching assistants has increased significantly. The ratio of teachers to pupils in the maintained primary sector is one to 21 pupils currently. Approximately 94 per cent of teachers are qualified to a degree level whilst teaching assistants are in the process of raising their academic level to a level three or above.

Consider

You will recall the issue raised earlier of *good intentions* resulting in *disappointing outcomes*.

Many millions of pounds have been spent on early years education – invested with good intentions.

Are there measureable outcomes that could have been used to assess the effectiveness of this huge expenditure?

What might they be?

The number of pre-school children attending a setting has increased but the number of primary age children has remained about the same since 2005.

The implications of these shifts will now be considered in relation to some specific provision.

TABLE 4.2 The number of pupils in England

	Number of pupils				
	2005	*2010*	*2011*	*2012*	*2013 projected figures*
All schools in England, under five year olds	753,000	811,000	828,000	865,000	897,000
All schools in England, primary age 5–11 year olds	3,670,000	3,501,000	3,521,000	3,567,000	3,647,000

Source: Adapted from www.education.gov.uk/researchandstatistics/statistics/statistics-by-topic/schoolpupil characteristics/ pupilnumbers/a00201305/dfe-national-pupil-projections-future-trends-in-pupil-numbers-december- 2011%20%2016.8.2012

Early years provision

With over 50 per cent of mothers in employment there was a general consensus and need for quality early years provision. In addition, there was a desire by the Government to increase children's potential achievement and avoid the gap of disadvantage. Provision was provided both by the private (Private Day Nurseries) and the public sector (Sure Start and Children's Centres).

Initially Early Childhood and Care was provided for three and four year olds and then extended for two year olds during the Labour Government post 1997 and prior to 2010. Currently in 2012 there is some funding for two year olds and above to attend a nursery or similar provision. Nursery schools provide education primarily for children below the age of five. Local Authorities also provide Sure Start Children's Centres to meet local needs and support particularly vulnerable children and their families following the Childcare Act 2006.

Sure Start Children's Centres in England

[Information adapted from www.education.gov.uk/inthenews/inthenews/a00200125/number-of-children-centres:

June 2010: 3,631 Children's Centres

8 September 2011: 3,507 Children's Centres

There is some consolidation of provision but the early years is still an area of public spending, as the Nutbrown Review (2012) reported: 'Quality early years provision has a lasting positive impact on child outcomes.' The difficulty is achieving quality provision and understanding what is required to achieve it, particularly as the term quality 'is too variable,' Alexander (2010:491).

TABLE 4.3 Staff qualifications in the early years in England

Workforce qualifications in the early years	% of staff at this level
Below level 3	30
Level 3	50
Higher than level 3	20

Source: Adapted from Nutbrown (2012)

The Labour Government intention pre 2010 was ideal to lay firm early years foundations, but there were issues surrounding quality and the need for qualified staff with reasonable remuneration (Alexander, 2010:491). Frequently the staff working in the Early Years or pre-school were poorly qualified although this was addressed post-2006 with the drive to professionalise the workforce (Papatheodorou and Moyles, 2012:195).

Consider

To what extent should practitioners be qualified to work with children and how might this impact on the children?

The Effective Provision of Pre-School Education (EPPE) Project (2004) had demonstrated the need for a qualified workforce within the early years and the push to address this came post-2006. The skills, knowledge and aptitudes the staff needed to deliver quality education and care raised awareness of the importance of good training and nationally recognised qualifications for all staff working with even the youngest children (Boddy et al., 2007).

In June 2012 the Nutbrown Review was published recommending a quality workforce 'who engage with children, supporting learning and interaction with their environment through play', and 'affecting their well being, development and achievements' (Nutbrown, 2012:15–16).

The pre-school curriculum

Changes in the early years were based on a significant research (EPPE, 2004) which confirmed that children benefitted from greater continuity between the ages of birth to seven (Anning and Edwards, 2006). Play was the central driver for learning and development: this approach, implemented nationally for all children, provided parents with the knowledge that their child would receive high-quality education and care in whatever context they were looked after.

The strategy developed during this period was a single framework of guidance from birth to five, known as the Early Years Foundation Stage (EYFS) incorporating national standards for both childminding and day-care. The DfES (2007) covered six areas of learning:

- personal, social and emotional development
- communication, language and literacy

- problem solving, reasoning and numeracy
- knowledge and understanding of the world
- physical development
- creative development

The DfES (2007) for children aged 0–5 was welcomed for its intentions but the assessment pressure to reach certain levels by the age of seven meant that the children's curriculum by the age of seven was not sufficiently balanced (Alexander, 2010:491). As part of the monitoring of children's progress the EYFS Profiles were introduced. All pre five year olds were subject to an assessment profile. The difficulties with this, as Alexander (2010:163) points out, is that children may feel that they cannot achieve and therefore become disinterested and demonstrate less effort to learn.

There were also issues around the transition from a statutory play-based EYFS to a more subject-based curriculum after the age of five.

However, while the EYFS has certainly been welcomed by many practitioners, concerns remain. One concern is that the outcomes are driving the provision of activities. In September 2012 the new EYFS was introduced. The Childcare Act (2006) requires local Government to work towards reducing disadvantage through targeted early years services. As the effectiveness of this policy is judged through the EYFS profiles, it appears a reasonable assumption that the activities of a setting will be focussed on delivering targets which are measured, rather than activities which may be more developmentally appropriate. The pressures of inspection and externally applied standards are in danger of over-riding the judgement of practitioners. Some of the OECD PISA statistics in 2006 and again in 2009 implied that this change in early years practice may not be achieving the anticipated desired results.

Further reading

www.oecd.org/pisa/

Primary

Primary schools consist of infant schools for children aged 5–7, frequently referred to as Key Stage 1 (KS1) and junior schools for those aged 7–11, or Key Stage 2 (KS2). Many primary schools also provide a nursery class for the under five year olds.

When they reach the end of the EYFS, the children move into KS1 of the national curriculum. This is at the end of the school year in which they have their 5th birthday. This transition is a major milestone, as they move from a play-based curriculum (with six areas of learning) to a far more formal curriculum (originally with ten subjects).

This transition experience was giving cause for concern, so a Government review (led by Sir Jim Rose) was commissioned in 2008 in order to assess the experience of children. The recommendations made, including a reduction in the number of areas of learning at KS1, were aimed at improving both the continuity and effectiveness of this provision.

In 2012 the transition from reception (4–5 year olds) into Year 1 (5–6 year olds) attempts to extend the play-based curriculum whilst introducing children to the national curriculum and extending the children's learning and development. Teacher autonomy and the use of professional judgement is becoming more acceptable (DFE, 2010).

There is, not unreasonably, a need for the reception and feeder settings to communicate with Year 1 in the school and this is achieved formally through the EYFS Profile. Again, the child's experience and achievement is reduced to a document, conveniently delivered so that the appropriate continuity of provision can be maintained.

The voice of the professional

A Head Teacher of a city primary school was asked about the impact of the EYFS:

> Interesting question! On one side, it has been a chance for us to work together with people in a whole new way – making the pathway children follow a bit more of a steady journey. But on the other hand, and we try not to do this but there is pressure on the nurseries and our feeder settings to prepare children for when they arrive with us. So they are often (and I think that this often comes from parents) expected to do the serious stuff and this worries me a bit.
>
> From this answer, can you decide whether this Head Teacher is satisfied with the statutory guidance?

Further review of the EYFS is planned as the early years provision continues to evolve.

The primary curriculum

The curriculum followed in settings has been a source of tension between drivers for 'care' and 'education'.

Documents have come and gone: *The National Curriculum Handbook for Primary Teachers in England* (QCA/DfEE, 1999), *Birth to Three Matters* (David et al., 2002) and the *Curriculum Guidance For the Foundation Stage* (QCA/DfES, 2000) are no longer with us, although for some years they were seen as the Keystones of provision. They reflected a set of beliefs regarding what should occupy children, but also a hidden agenda regarding the pace and style of provision that was firmly removed from the hands of those responsible for delivery.

The Government implemented these changes as part of its far-reaching strategy to improve the quality of provision for young children. This ten-year plan was spearheaded by a multi-agency approach titled *Every Child Matters* (DfES, 2004a), supported by *Choice For Parents, the Best Start For Children* (DfES, 2004b). These initiatives came one after the other, leaving many practitioners, teachers and parents in something of a blur.

Many argued that between 1988 and 2010

an over specified National Curriculum and punitive inspection regime coupled in later years with National Strategies specifying the timetabling and teaching methods for core

subjects of literacy and numeracy have reduced the idea of a teacher to someone who …
maintains order teaches to the test and follows standardised curriculum scripts…

(Hargreaves 2003 cited in Thomas 2012:4)

It was clear that there was Governmental concern regarding what was happening with young children, but the interventions were, according to some, quite overwhelming.

Debbie: an experienced Year 1 teacher in a city school.

When you asked me about the changes in the last few years, it filled me with a sense of amazement that we have coped with everything. We have had changes in the inspection system, changes in the curriculum, changes in our contracts and pensions, changes in the school day and…. Need I say more? The workload has been relentless and it is a wonder that I'm still sane.

What stays the same is that some children don't do as well as we want them to for reasons that are often out of our hands.

Consider how Debbie can resolve the conflict between her own ideas of professionalism and the external pressures for performance.

Play and creativity have often been treated as poor relations to the basics of education (Tizard et al., 1988). The targets and profiles devised to measure the progress of children are mainly quantitative tools that provide information in chunks that can be managed. There have been calls for this to be reconsidered. One of the earlier calls came from the National Association of Child Contact Centres (NACCC) in May 1999, in which there was recognition of the benefits of creative partnerships between schools and organisations in wider society. Artists and storytellers, builders and painters could make the learning environments more expressive and involving. While there were numerous local initiatives, there were pressures to limit this type of learning to specific times and places, without seeing the need to integrate creative play to the wider curriculum and a daily experience.

Tom, aged eight.

What do I like best at school … well, what I really like is when we can do a project and all the kids get to do a bit of it and then we work at it for ages and then get to see what everyone else has done and they get to see our bit as well, but not everyone can do everything so we all have to work together to make it good and the teacher helps us when we get stuck. We did one last term on fish that was good and I got to be the bottlenose dolphin in the school play.

My mum and gran came to watch, and we talked about it for ages after.

What is the impact of this approach on Tom's confidence?

This project-based approach is becoming increasingly popular in schools and may be seen to reflect the way in which most adults have to operate in their family and working lives.

Learning the skills of flexibility and resilience, as children may, encourage the growth of these characteristics into adulthood. Reports and research continue to demonstrate the value of learning appropriate skills.

In March 2012, Thomas (2012:8) quoted a teacher who said 'Our ideal curriculum would be one that is constantly evolving and is pertinent to our context. Learning which reflects our stakeholders and diversity.'

Two useful reports

Field, F. (2010) *The Foundation Years: Preventing Poor Children From Becoming Poor Adults* London: HMSO.

Allen, G. and Duncan-Smith I. (2008) *Early Intervention: Good Parents, Great Kids, Better Citizens* London: Centre for Social Justice.

Have a look at the executive summaries in these reports and consider whether our national priority is really investing in the early years to benefit the children or as a strategy to reduce the dependency on benefits.

For some years now, following one of the recommendations of the Green Paper (Note: Green paper: the Government is investigating something) Excellence for All (DfEE, 1997), there has been an acknowledgement that staff training is a priority. This leads to the question of what we see as the appropriate qualifications and rewards for those who work with children.

It is clear that there are a wide range of skills, knowledge and experience required to be effective in this field of work (David et al., 2002).

In England, these are defined by two levels of achievement. The first level will be at school and the requirement to have achieved pass grades in five subjects (including English and Maths) at GCSE, the examination taken at 16 years old. If a pupil wants to go on to study beyond 16, they have either academic or vocational routes available. Many who are interested in working with children will follow a high-quality, practical vocational route with a small range of nationally recognised two-year foundation degrees available. However, increasing numbers are taking academic subjects and continuing at University with undergraduate programmes, e.g. B.A. (Hons) Early Childhood Studies. There is a generation of students who have followed this route and are able to apply their knowledge and understanding within the early years setting in which they are employed. Many will go on to postgraduate training in education, health and social care, as well as management posts in early years settings.

Alternatively, many students will pursue their interest in children to train as teachers. There are intense demands for places and the entry qualifications are higher now than they have ever been (DfE, 2012). The four-year training has been supported by the Government, but there is currently uncertainty regarding the support that future generations of trainees will receive. There is a shift towards work-based learning and thus future generations of teachers may experience greater practice prior to qualifying as a teacher.

However, one of the factors which may distinguish these two career pathways is the salary structure for graduate employees. Broadly speaking, the status of those who 'teach' and have 'qualified teacher status' is reflected in the far higher salaries of those who are 'caring for children'. While there has been a huge investment in provision in both the education and care sectors, with ambitious building programmes and a commitment to 'quality', there remains an entrenched view of the early years sector as being no more than a preparation for school and not of value in its own right. To recognise and reward the contribution of the early years workforce in the same way as 'qualified teachers' are recognised and rewarded will enhance the status of the workforce and play its part in the integration of childcare and education services. Surely this is one of the key steps to be taken in order to respond to the EPPE (2004) findings, which demonstrate the beneficial effects of high-quality provision on children's intellectual and social development (Sylva et al., 2008).

Consider

If you consider many European countries' regulations regarding the qualifications and conditions of service, you will find that they appear to value their early years workers. They also expect them to be highly qualified.

What do you consider to be the advantages and disadvantages of this strategy?

How might the success of this policy be measured?

Conclusion

This takes us to a concluding thought: what is it like growing up in England today?

Sam, aged nine. So, how are you doing?

There is always so much to do, with telly to watch and games to play. My brother just got a Playstation and he lets me borrow it sometimes. I quite like school, but I wish there was more time to really get things done – they're always rushing you on to the next thing. Maybe it will be worse when I go on to the next school.

Does Sam have a point? The message in this little conversation was clear – lots to do to fill the time of childhood, but no spare time: no time to think. Is this typical of children in England?

Current challenges

Have we been making progress in recent years? Of course we have; in England the majority of children enjoy good health and are free from disease and the worse effects of poverty (Dahlberg et al., 2007). Children can go to high-quality early years settings when they are young and then move into school as they become older. There are health and social care services in place to promote and protect their welfare. Their world, it seems, is constructed around them and they can be confident that the adults who surround them have their best interests at heart.

But in spite of this, there is a growing movement towards seeing the experience of children from the child's perspective and to question the dominant paradigm of developmental psychology and economic necessity. As Foucault (1980 cited in Dahlberg et al. 2007:165) argued 'the Western culture and Western rationality cannot claim to have universal validity.' In England there is a slow change in the understanding of learning, with the stirrings of a willingness to explore alternatives. Pence and Moss (1994) describe this as an 'open architecture' approach, and it is a useful way of stimulating debate over practice. Not content with 'truth' or 'correctness' but an evolving curiosity over how to best engage with, and listen to, children.

The ripples of this engagement with children are just beginning. Will we hear what they say and have the confidence to trust their competence?

Children need the space to grow and staff need the confidence to demonstrate their professionalism. The challenge is to achieve quality and hear what children have to say. A further challenge is to provide a viable, quality service and facility for children that can be upheld in a difficult economic climate.

References

Alexander, R.A. (2010) *Children, their World, their Education: Final Report and Recommendations of the Cambridge Primary Review.* Abingdon: Routledge.

Anning, A. and Edwards, A. (2006) *Promoting Children's Learning from Birth to Five.* Buckingham: Open University Press.

Boddy, J., Cameron, C., Moss, P., Mooney, P., Petri, P. and Statham, J. (2007) *Introducing Pedagogy into the Children's Workforce.* London: Thomas Coram Research Institute.

Brooker, L. (2002) *Starting School – Young Children's Learning Cultures.* Buckingham: Open University Press.

Callaghan, J. (1976) *Towards a National Debate.* Education 22 October, p. 332.

Cashdan, A. and Harris, J. (1993) *Education in the 1990s.* Sheffield: Sheffield Hallam University Press.

Cole, M. (1998) *Globalisation, Modernisation, Modernisation and Competitiveness: A Critique of the New Labour Project in Education.* International Studies in the Sociology of Education 8 (5) 315–322.

Dahlberg, G., Moss, P. and Pence, A. (2007) *Beyond Quality in Early Childhood Education and Care: Languages of Evaluation,* 2nd edn. London: Routledge.

David, T., Gooch, K., Powell, S. and Abbott, L. (2002) *Birth to Three Matters: A Review of the Literature Surrounding the Framework to Support Children in their Earliest Years.* London: DES/ Sure Start.

Department for Education (DfE) (2010) *The Importance of Teaching: The Schools White Paper 2010.* London: DfE.

Department for Education (DfE) (2012) *The Teaching Agency Website* (Active from 01/0412). London: DfE.

Department for Education and Skills (DfES) (2004a) *Every Child Matters: Change for Children.* London: DfES.

Department for Education and Skills (DfES) (2004b) *Choice for Parents, the Best Start For Children: A Ten Year Struggle For Children.* London: HMSO.

Department for Education and Skills (DfES) (2007) *The Early Years Foundation Stage: Setting the Standards for Learning, Development and Care for Children from Birth to Five.* Nottingham: DfES.

Department for Education and Skills (DfES) (2008) *The Early Years Foundation Stage Guidance.* London: DfES.

DfEE (1997) *Excellence For All Children: Meeting Special Educational Needs.* Suffolk: DfEE.

EPPE (2004) *The Effective Provision of Pre-School Education [EPPE] Project 1997– 2004.* Nottingham: DfES.

Giddens, A. (1998) *The Third Way: Renewal of Social Democracy.* Cambridge: Polity.

Hargreaves, A. (2003) *Teaching in the Knowledge Society.* New York: Teachers College Press.

Moss, P. and Petri, P. (2002) *From Children's Services to Children's Spaces.* Abingdon: RoutledgeFalmer.

Nutbrown, C. (2012) *Nutbrown Review Final Report* [Online]. Available at: www.education.gov.uk/ nutbrownreview.

Papatheodorou, T. and Moyles, J. (2012) *Cross Cultural Perspectives on Early Childhood.* London: Sage.

Pence, A. and Moss, P. (1994) 'Towards an Inclusionary Approach in Defining Quality' in Moss, P. and Pence, A. (eds) *Valuing Quality in Early Childhood Services: New Approaches to Defining Quality.* London: Paul Chapman.

QCA/DfEE (1999) *The National Curriculum: Handbook for Primary Teachers in England.* London: TSO.

QCA/DfES (2000) *Curriculum Guidance for the Foundation Stage.* London: QCA/DfES.

Rawls, J. (1973) *A Theory of Justice.* London: Oxford University Press.

Sylva, K., Melhuish, E., Sammons, P., Siraj-Blatchford, I. and Taggart, B. (2008) *Final Report from the Primary Phase: Pre-school, School and Family Influences on Children's Development During Key State 2 (7–11).* Nottingham: DfE RR 061 The Department for Education (DfE).

Thomas, L. (2012) *Re-thinking the Importance of Teaching: Curriculum and Collaboration in an Era of Localism.* London: RSA Projects [Online] Available at: www.thersa.org/__data/assets/pdf_file/0008/570716/RSA-Re-thinking-the-importance-of-teaching.pdf (Accessed on 18 March 2013).

Tizard, B., Blatchford, P., Burke, J., Farquhar, C. and Plewis, I. (1988) *Young Children at School in the Inner City.* London: Erlbaum Associates.

Education in Finland

Mabel Ann Brown

Acknowledgements

I would like to thank the University of Derby for the opportunity they gave me in researching the Finnish Early Years system and the University and Nurseries in Finland that I visited during my research in 2008.

Introduction

The children in Finland do not start school until they are seven. They master several languages: Finnish, English and/or Swedish and a high proportion of them stay on for higher education or training, clearly demonstrating continued engagement with education. The Finnish children learn more by accident with the emphasis on raising interest rather than by prescribed teaching in their early years (5–7 year olds) and yet still succeed. This success, as Hausstatter and Takala (2008:122) pointed out, has 'aroused a great deal of interest' (e.g. Anderson 2006; Itkonen and Jahnukainen 2007).

In Finland there is a strong emphasis on nurturing and support for the parents and not on education. Its origins lie in supporting parents who wished or needed to work. The Finnish day care 'has been considered a part of the social and the family policy and only more recently as part of the educational policy' (Hujala et al. 1998:148) in Karila (2008:212). In the words of the Ministry of Education and Culture (2012) 'the pre primary, basic education and upper secondary education and training form a coherent path that supports child development and well being'. In addition, there are before and after school care facilities. There is a one-year voluntary pre-primary followed by nine years of basic education.

Culture

Finland from 1323 up until 1523 was part of a Union of Finland, Norway and Sweden under the auspices of Swedish law. In the 1700s the Russians invaded Finland and by the 1800s Finland had become separated from Sweden and more aligned with Russia. However, by the late 19th century Finnish nationalism was growing. By 1917 Finland was declared an independent republic, but with internal political unrest the Germans intervened in 1918, but by 1919 Finland had a new constitution and became a republic. In the Second World War Finland was invaded by Russia thus they sought support from Germany in 1941, but were forced to leave the war in 1943 and made a ceasefire with Russia in 1944.

Since this time the country has known both a booming economy and recession. In 2002 the Finnish currency was replaced by the euro after joining the EU in 1995.

For more information visit www.localhistories.org/finland.html.

The main industry and resource has been timber, although metalwork, engineering and electronics have grown since 1945. Nokia has also been a significant Finnish company which has been at the forefront of mobile telephone developments.

Finland has throughout its troubled past succeeded in maintaining both a language and an identity and is keen to see this continue; however, it is a country that also understands the need to be able to communicate with its neighbours for trade and political reasons.

Finland, although a large land mass, has a much smaller population, 5.3 million and only 3.8 per cent are foreign born (see the Pearson Foundation (2012) web site). Anckar (2000: 499) stated that in Finland '11 percent of the population are Swedish speakers and 89 percent are Finnish speakers, with many who are bilingual.'

Finland is a country with a close proximity to nature as there are numerous lakes and many trees. The people also have to deal with a much colder climate for a significant part of the year. Lindon (2000:79) claimed that most 'families have summer homes outside the towns', thus for many families there is still a close link with rural life even though many work in a more urban environment. There are opportunities for all irrespective of background or locality.

As the Ministry of Education and Culture (2012) clearly state on their website,

> The welfare of Finnish society is built on education, culture and knowledge. All children are guaranteed opportunities for study and self-development according to their abilities, irrespective of their place of residence, language or financial status. All pupils are entitled to competent and high-quality education and guidance and to a safe learning environment and well-being. The flexible education system and basic educational security make for equity and consistency in results.

The number of mothers working in Finland is comparable with Britain. According to Thomson (2008), Finland had 56.9 per cent of working women (aged 15 and older) whilst the United Kingdom had 55.2 per cent, however a more recent survey in the OECD PISA (2012: 2) puts the maternal employment rate in Finland as approximately 75 per cent and the United Kingdom at approximately 70 per cent. Thus the day care provision in Finland is designed to support working families. There is one trained adult to four under threes in Finland and one to seven for the over threes within the childcare provision.

The Finnish voice

The system is as follows: government-funded nurseries (*paivakoti*) are very popular because they are everywhere and heavily subsidised. The most you pay is somewhere between 200 and 300 euros a month. Most families pay less. The year the child turns six most children (about 90 per cent) go to pre-school which is not, however, mandatory. The role of pre-school (*esikoulu*) is to build the child's confidence, learn by playing games and spend lots of time out of doors with lots of free play and minimal guidance from teachers to let the children's imagination develop. The idea is also to spot and tackle potential problems by preventing them through early intervention. The group sizes are small, up to 20 children but often less.

The year the child turns seven they start primary school (*ala-aste*) where they learn with the help of a class teacher who teaches most subjects apart from music, art and physical education. Often you have the same teacher for two years at a time. School dinners are free. Every lesson is 45 minutes long after which there is a 15 minute break. During primary school the school week is about 25 hours, in the first year I believe it used to be 20 hours. You start learning a foreign language at the age of nine (class 3) – I myself had to choose between Swedish and English. The amount of choice varies school to school. Outdoor play is very important throughout primary school, and children take outdoor clothes, including shoes and trousers, off before they go to class. Wet play does not really happen because all children generally wear waterproof clothing.

At the age of 13 (class 7) children go up to senior school (*yla-aste*) for three years. After that more than half of pupils go into doing their matriculate examinations (*lukio*). *Lukio* lasts three years after which you are able to apply to go to university.

Hoffman and Zhao (2008:1) point out that 'even a cursory glance at early childhood education and development programmes in universities and educational training institutes around the world reveals a startling emphasis on a few major theorists such as Piaget, Dewey and Vygotsky.' Thus in Finland, practitioners are trained and familiar with the theories that pervade childhood and educational development. The Pearson Foundation (2012) web page notes that 'Finland recruits its teachers from the top 10% of graduates.' In fact all teachers in Finland are required to have a Master's degree.

Hancock (2011) noted that:

> Finland has vastly improved in reading, math and science literacy over the past decade in large part because its teachers are trusted to do whatever it takes to turn young lives around.

Read more at: www.smithsonianmag.com/people-places/Why-Are-Finlands-Schools-Successful.html#ixzz24BWzGKuJ

Community and the curriculum

Moriarty (2000) explored the professionalism of educators in Finland and England and two aspects of culture can be observed in her paper. The first is that in Finland municipalities or local areas help to determine their own curriculum. The second is that parents contribute to this arrangement, thus the partnership with parents is much more equal than in England where the curriculum is pre-determined and teachers share this with parents in order to encourage their support. In Finland from the outset parents know what they wish for their children and teachers deliver a curriculum that meets their criteria, thus there is no question of gaining parental support as it is already there. Moriarty (2000:237) describes this as 'shared authority and power'. More importantly the settings in Finland 'reflect the values of parents' (Moriarty 2000:239). However, since 2003 the curriculum has become more structured although it is only a set of guidelines in Finland with the introduction of the National Curriculum Guidelines on Early Childhood and Care in Finland.

The Ministry of Education and Culture (2012) claim that 'the Finnish education and science policy stresses quality, efficiency, equity and internationalism. It is geared to promote the competitiveness of Finnish welfare society.'

The municipalities in Finland (these are similar to counties in England) are responsible for their areas, thus the settings meet local needs and organise themselves. An example of this is pupil progress: there are no national league tables; instead a record is kept of pupil progress. 'Schools in Finland are focal centres for their communities' (Pearson Foundation 2012).

Individual pupil records

In Finland the day care and pre-school settings in 2008 were maintaining individual pupil records in a structured manner where previously there was only teacher assessment.

Community

Marion Dowling (2005) reflects on Steiner (1861–1925) schools and their sense of community, use of natural materials and protection from the outside world. All this enables children to strengthen their inner resources. However, in England some schools have become more like fortresses rather than part of the community. Yet the nursery or school in England is generally, or should be, at the heart of the community. (Brown 2009.)

Thus Finland has a community system that engages parents from the outset and the schools and day care settings are very much a part of that community.

Another significant difference in Finland is that either the parent or the day care centre receives the financial allowance. A parent cannot expect to receive the money and then take their child for a free nursery place.

Special needs

Children in Finland are given additional support whenever it is observed as being required, but children are not labelled as 'statemented'. The view is much more that all children have needs and different potentials. As Hausstatter and Takala (2008:121) say, 'special needs education forms a part of the national goal of high quality education and inclusion is not mentioned.' In line with the Finnish National Board of Education 2004 the children needing support are identified early and then support is provided in 'cooperation with the parents' (Hausstatter and Takala 2008:123). Support is a child's right and is provided for children with 'learning problems' and 'social and emotional problems' (Hausstatter and Takala 2008:125). Pearson Foundation (2012) refers to the 'special teacher' as identifying students who need support and then providing it so that the children can keep up with the rest of their cohort.

World rankings

OECD PISA

In 2009 Finland was third in the OECD PISA for reading, yet the teaching of reading is generally more structurally facilitated once the children turn seven. However, children are offered opportunities to witness adults reading to them and books are available for children to handle and begin to appreciate and enjoy. In addition, many adults in Finland read a newspaper at home as one Finn told me. The OECD PISA results have been considered in many articles, from which one is included below.

> Hancock (2011) noted that:
>
> By 2006, Finland was first out of 57 countries (and a few cities) in science. In the 2009 PISA scores released last year, the nation came in second in science, third in reading and sixth in math among nearly half a million students worldwide.
>
> Read more at: www.smithsonianmag.com/people-places/Why-Are-Finlands-Schools-Successful.html#ixzz24BWzGKuJ

Pearson Foundation (2012) claim that 'Finland was the top performer in the PISA 2000 tests and in 2009 the number of Finnish students reaching the top level of performance in science was three times the OECD average.' A recent newspaper article (Boyes 2012:41) however suggests that this is no longer quite so outstanding. In his article *How a Country Was Built the Nokia Way*, Boyes says 'For years Finland boasted two great national assets; its education system which topped all international league tables; and Nokia the mobile phone company that gave it global reach', however, he goes on to imply that both may be slipping away but only time and further statistics will make this truly apparent.

Age and school systems

TABLE 5.1 Comparing childcare facilities in Finland and England in 2008

Finland	England
Population: 5.3 million (UN, 2007)	**Population:** 60.7 million (UN, 2007)
■ The day care fees are based on family size and income level. For low income families day care is free. Client fees cover about 15 per cent of the total day care costs. Allowances are paid directly to the service provider.	■ Free entitlement for three and four year olds of 15 hours of childcare a week.
■ Child home care allowance is an alternative.	■ 15 hours free entitlement offered to two year olds in disadvantaged communities.
■ Day care centres are open from 6.30am–5pm for children age 1–6 years inclusive.	■ Parents can pay for nursery care available 8am–6pm.
■ Fluid groups – the children are not in one ability group.	■ Can be organised into mixed age groups known as family grouping – this is evident in some settings but more frequently children are placed in a room of one age group, for instance all the three year olds together.
■ Focus on whole child development.	■ Education oriented to some extent.
■ Pre-school for six year olds is free and available.	■ Children commence school the term before they turn five.
■ Children start school at seven.	■ Pupil profile – assessment – individualised learning.
■ Teacher/parent/child all contribute to an assessment folder.	■ Graduate Leader Fund Early Years Professional Status (EYPS).
■ Kindergarten teacher or class teacher qualification.	■ Every Child Matters and Early Years Foundation Stage (EYFS) requirement.
■ Curriculum guidelines.	

Source: Adapted from Brown (2009)

The most significant detail in Table 5.1 is that children in Finland officially start school at age seven unlike England where they start at age five. In terms of success this factor does not appear to make a significant difference, in fact it seems to lead to greater achievement by the time children are 15. Perhaps this is because in general society in Finland views education as important or it may simply reflect long cold winter evenings and more time spent reading. The schools are central to the communities with libraries located next door in some cases. Parents and children can visit the library either on their way to school or after school. The teaching staff are well respected and recognised for their sense of responsibility and professionalism.

Language and literacy development

Layard R. and Dunn J. (2009:9) said that 'Children flourish when they have a sense of meaning in their lives, which comes both from social engagement and from enthusiastic development of their own interests and talents.'

FIGURE 5.1 Handwriting practice in Finland (2008)

If the children in Finland wish to draw or write, paper and pens are available. In addition to this, children who are ready for learning have opportunities to write about what they enjoy or what they have done.

A Finnish teacher's response in 2008

'On Monday the children bring toys or have a book day when they bring a book. It could be a specific toy. The children write their own name each day in the register.'

Another teacher in Finland went on to say, 'They have tasks once in two weeks at a table. More play, physical activity, things with your hands, drama and painting.'

Sue Palmer, the author of *Toxic Childhood*, wrote in the *Guardian* that

> The curriculum for under-sevens in Finland – which has the best literacy results in the world – is based on these 'natural' foundations for social, emotional and cognitive development, but is also carefully structured to prepare children for formal learning with the emphasis on social skills, language and listening (including phonics).
>
> (Palmer 2008)

In a global society, children need to be able to communicate both orally and on paper; in Finland oral communication is encouraged through play, rhymes and song but when children demonstrate an interest in writing, this is nurtured through playing with letters. This is also encouraged in nursery and in reception classes in England.

One practitioner in Finland 2008 said, 'We do rhymes, when the children are four they should hear the rhymes, when six they need to hear the first letter of a word'. Yet another said, 'There are more expectations from pre-school, they can start reading at three but we look at what is needed.'

FIGURE 5.2 Children's ice skating drawings, Finland (2008)

Another criteria for writing is experience; the children need to know what it is that they are writing about, thus the ice skating drawings (see Figure 5.2) were illustrating what the children had had direct experience of in the winter.

When teaching, the author once asked a child to write about the fairground and the child said 'How can I, I have never been.' Thus it is essential that children receive some first-hand experiences.

Ofsted (2003) produced a comparative study between England, Denmark and Finland and point 116 suggests,

> The real test of these differences of expectation, however, is not whether the reading skills of a typical six year old in England are 'ahead' of or 'behind' … but where the different versions of curriculum lead in terms of the developing child's capacities and predispositions and indeed in terms of later outcomes in the individual's school career and adult life.

Clearly the development of children's potential is the important element.

Lindon (2000:79) described the Finnish system as 'following a Froebel approach' with 'publicly funded centres and family care provision'; there are usually mixed age groups and there is an emphasis on experiencing the outdoors, thus in 2008 staff indicated that children spend one hour outside in a morning and the same in the afternoon.

Waller (2005:103) reflects that many writers, including Bailey et al. (2003), Fjortoft (2001) and Rickinson et al. (2003), all recognise the special place of education out of doors. Their studies indicated that playing in the natural environment had a positive effect (Waller 2005:103). The children in Finland are outside far longer each day than children in England and the day care provisions are set up with drying facilities so that children can be outside no matter what the weather is. Perhaps this is the reason why Finnish children do so well.

Brown 2009:6–7

Sharing books is a positive experience in Finland as children do not need to demonstrate that they can do it on their own, thus it encourages a positive feeling towards books and this forms part of the daily practice in Finland for the early years. A reading scheme is not used until children are seven when the 'Aapinen' is introduced – this is a book used by all the children but with each page divided into four graded sections so children appear to be at the same level but are in fact working at their own stage of development.

If children are ready for writing, two languages are introduced at the same time, thus children refer to calendars that are written in both English and Finnish or Swedish. The month and the day of the week are in both languages.

Maths was introduced to the children as a physical activity in Finland, thus the children went into a space or hall in Finland to undertake active maths. As there were restricted number cards the children themselves worked out that if the seven had been used they could put a three and four together to make seven. Applied maths is important for the individual and for society as a whole.

Readiness

Piaget is quoted in Macleod-Brudenell and Kay (2008:148) as stressing 'the readiness idea: a child cannot achieve certain skills until ready to do so. His or her readiness depends upon his or her stage of development'.

A class teacher in Finland (2008) said: 'We start when they come in but we don't teach them how to read we read to them and tell them stories, rhymes, we give them the experience of language. We give them experiences.'

One member of staff in Finland (2008) said: 'We use playful methods they play with letters reading things in the environment we don't teach reading we encourage it if they want to know.'

A class teacher in Finland (2008) said: 'We assess what they can do already and then organise the lessons to meet their needs – the more able go to the library to choose a book or bring a book from home.'

Day routines and curriculum

The daily routines in Finland are slightly different to those in England. The number of hours children undertake in school was gradually increased with the child's age as depicted in Table 5.2.

TABLE 5.2 The number of hours in the school day in Finland

The school day in one school in Finland	
Time in school: 20 hours per week Year 1 (age seven) 20 hours per week Year 2 (age eight) 24 hours per week Year 3 (age nine) 24 hours per week Year 4 (age ten) 26 hours per week Year 5 (age 11)	There is a phased start and end to the day for Year 1: Half the class start at 8am and finish at 12pm Half the class start at 9am and finish at 1pm

Source: Adapted from Brown 2009

Bangs (2009:16) stated that in Finland 'schools are expected to adapt the curriculum to the needs of their students'.

In Table 5.3 it is the allocation of time for English and maths that is interesting as there is very much a focus on language acquisition primarily as it is viewed that these skills are necessary for maths achievement.

TABLE 5.3 The allocation of curriculum time in Finland

The allocated time in one school in Finland (per week/per subject)		
Year 1 (age seven)	Year 2 (age eight)	Year 5 (age 11)
■ 7 hours reading and writing ■ 3 hours maths ■ 2 hours plus 2 hours art and craft ■ 2 hours music ■ 2 hours gymnastics/sports ■ 1 hour religion ■ 1 hour combined biology/ the environment/geography	■ 6 hours reading and writing ■ 4 hours maths	■ Children with an additional language do an extra 2 hours a week

Variants in terminology

Day care centre and pre-school in Finland are equivalent to a nursery in England. Municipalities are equivalent to counties in England.

> ## Reflective questions
>
> When should children start school?
>
> Does starting school at seven make a significant difference?

Creativity

The Ministry of Education and Culture (2012) emphasises creativity and culture with an abundance of cultural provision and the Finns as very much participating in these opportunities,

> Altogether 52 theatres, 25 orchestras and 132 museums receive government funding. The annual number of museum visitors is five million; the National Opera and orchestras have an annual audience of over 900,000 and the annual number of theatre-goers is 2.5 million.

Current challenges and issues

The main current challenge for Finland is to maintain their standards when people in other countries are observing their practice. Their very success has brought the Finns substantial interest which means that the focus moves from the children to the international arena; where once the day job was the main and only focus there is now great pressure to maintain the international lead.

Since 2004 there has been greater curriculum guidance with the introduction of the National Curriculum Guidelines on Early Childhood and Care in Finland. It will take time for this to demonstrate any significant changes in children's success.

Conclusion

Finland and the United Kingdom have 'the same goal of creating workers for a global future' (Hausstatter and Takala 2008:122), but each culture adopts its own style to achieve this. The curriculum, as Hausstatter and Takala (2008:122) point out, is 'running towards a target'. However, that target cannot be fixed as competencies continue to change and develop in society. An example of this is the continuing changes in information technology.

Finland is a successful country educationally but as Waller (2005:135) points out, 'quality is a problematic concept', and is meaningless without 'clarity about values and beliefs that underpin a service' (Penn 1999 cited in Waller 2005:134). Thus the Finns philosophy is successful within their society as it meets the needs and values of their people but there is much to consider for other countries that aspire to achieve in the OECD PISA.

The OECD PISA results are based on an input that has spanned the children's childhood up to the age of the PISA survey. Thus the early years practice may have been very different in 1987 to 2012.

It may not be the early years that are making a difference; it could actually be the entire school experience.

Practice is continually developing; there may be changes in practice that are not referred to in this chapter. The author would be pleased to hear about these with a view to them being included in any future editions of this book.

Areas for further consideration

Qualifications

Qualifications are important in Finland; all staff are qualified, with the exception of students who are in practice gaining experience.

> One teacher in Finland (2008) said, 'There are no assistants but we do have students, some schools may not have anyone else. … In the schools many teachers achieve their doctorate and masters qualifications.'

Writing and mark making

The Finns believe that children need to mark make first before they can begin to read – mark making is the very early experimental stage of holding a pencil, brush or crayon and making marks on a paper or flat surface is the initial stage of writing; the children are beginning to recognise in this phase that marks have meaning. There is no pressure on children to write until they are seven, when the necessary support is provided for those who have not already mastered the art of writing. There is no sense of failure as children commence writing when they are ready. The adults encourage any child who demonstrates an interest in writing, but until then they have access to paper and pens but it is the child's choice to engage with them. As Hancock (2011) quotes below, the emphasis is not on tests and measured statistics but on children achieving when they are ready and having the skills to learn rather than learning facts.

> Hancock (2011):
>
> 'I think, in fact, teachers would tear off their shirts,' said Timo Heikkinen, a Helsinki principal with 24 years of teaching experience. 'If you only measure the statistics, you miss the human aspect.'
>
> 'We prepare children to learn how to learn, not how to take a test,' said Pasi Sahlberg, a former math and physics teacher who is now in Finland's Ministry of Education and Culture. 'We are not much interested in PISA. It's not what we are about.'
>
> Read more at: www.smithsonianmag.com/people-places/Why-Are-Finlands-Schools-Successful.html#ixzz24BWzGKuJ

Independent learning

In Finland children are encouraged in the pre-school phase to choose their own activities and develop at their own rate. The idea is to develop independence from a very early age. In contrast to this, a nursery nurse in England observed the following:

A nursery nurse in England 2012 said, 'We have introduced a free structure into the Nursery and children choose their own activities during the day but now parents are complaining because the children want this freedom at home as well.'

In Finland children independently choose their activities and move on to something else when they are ready, but they are encouraged to responsibly put games and toys away afterwards.

Finally, the Finnish culture values education, the pre-schools and schools, and the staff within them are respected by society, thus there is neither public criticism nor failing schools. The professionalism of the well-trained staff is respected and they work to achieve the success of all children.

Further reading

www.pearsonfoundation.org/oecd/

www.minedu.fi/OPM/Kulttuuri/?lang=en

www.minedu.fi/OPM/Koulutus/koulutuspolitiikka/?lang=en

www.localhistories.org/finland.html

www.smithsonianmag.com/people-places/Why-Are-Finlands-Schools-Successful.html#ixzz24BWzGKuJ

References

Anckar, O. (2000) *University Education in a Bilingual Country: The Case of Finland* Higher Education in Europe, Vol. 25, No. 4, pages 499–506.

Anderson, F.Ø. (2006) *Finsk Pædagogikk – Finsk Folkeskole [Finnish Education – Finnish Elementary School]*. Frederikshavn: Dafolo.

Bailey, R., Doherty, J. and Jago, R. (2003) 'Physical Development and Physical Education' in Riley, J. (ed.) *Learning in the Early Years: A Guide for Teachers of 3–7*. London: Paul Chapman Publishing.

Bangs, J. (2009) *Lessons From Finland* Education Journal for Professionals in Children's Services and Learning at Every Stage, Issue 114, Devon: The Education Publishing Company.

Boyes, R. (2012) 'How a Country Was Built the Nokia Way' in *The Times*, 9 February, page 41.

Brown, M.A. (2009) *Rethinking Early Education and Health – the Finnish Perspective ECER 2009 Vienna*, The European Conference on Educational Research, Post-Graduate and New Researchers Pre-Conference, 28–30 September.

Dowling, M. (2005) *Young Children's Personal, Social and Emotional Development*, 2nd edn. London: Sage.

Fjortoft, I. (2001) *The Natural Environment as a Playground for Children: The Impact of Outdoor Play Activities in Pre-primary School Children* Early Childhood Education Journal, Vol. 29, No. 2, pages 111–117.

Hancock, L.N. (2011) *Why Are Finland's Schools Successful?*, in *Smithsonian* magazine, September 2011 [Online]. Available at: www.smithsonianmag.com/people-places/Why-Are-Finlands-Schools-Successful.html#ixzz24BWzGKuJ.

Hausstatter, R.S. and Takala, M. (2008) *The Core of Special Teacher Education: A Comparison of Finland and Norway* European Journal of Special Needs Education, Vol. 23, No. 2, pages 121–134.

Hoffman, D. and Zhao, G. (2008) 'Global Convergence and Divergence in Childhood Ideologies and the Marginalization of Children' in Zajda J., Biraimah K. and Gaudelli W. (eds) *Education and Social Inequality in the Global Culture*. Milton Keynes: Springer.

Hujala, E., Karila, K., Nivala, V. and Puroila, A.-M. (1998) 'Towards Understanding Leadership in the Finnish Context of Early Childhood' in Hujala, E. and Puroila, A.-M. (eds) *Towards Understanding Leadership in Early Childhood Context*. Ouluensis. Series E 35. Oulu: Oulun yliopistopaino, pp. 147–170.

Itkonen T. and Jahnukainen M. (2007) *An Analysis of Accountability Policies in Finland and the United States* International Journal of Disability, Development and Education, Vol. 54, No. 1, pages 5–23.

Karila, K. (2008) *A Finnish Viewpoint on Professionalism in Early Education* European Early Childhood Education Research Journal, Vol. 16, No. 2, June 2008, pages 210–223.

Layard, R. and Dunn, J. (2009) *A Good Childhood: Searching For Values In a Competitive Age*. London: Penguin.

Lindon, J. (2000) *Early Years Care and Education in Europe*. Bristol: Hodder & Stoughton.

MacLeod-Budenell, I. and Kay, J. (2008) *Advanced Early Years: For Foundation Degrees and Levels 4/5*, 2nd edn. London: Pearson Education.

Ministry of Education and Culture (2012) *Education System in Finland* [Online]. Available at: www.minedu.fi/OPM/Koulutus/koulutusjaerjestelmae/index.html?lang=en (Accessed on 17 May 2012).

Moriarty, V. (2000) *Early Years Educators in Finland and England: Issues of Professionality Educateurs Pre 'Scolaires en Finlande et en Angleterre: Questions de Professionnalite' Los Educadores de Menores en Finlandia e Ingaterra: Temas de Profesionalidad* International Journal of Early Years Education, Vol. 8, No. 3, pages 235–242.

OECD PISA (2012) *LMF1.2: Maternal Employment Rates* [Online]. Available at: www.oecd.org/els/family/38752721.pdf (Accessed on 19 March 2013).

Ofsted (2003) *The Education of Six Year Olds in England, Denmark and Finland: An International Comparative Study* HMI 1660.

Palmer, S. (2008) 'Letters' in the *Guardian*, 5 February [Online]. Available at: www.guardian.co.uk/education/2008/feb/05/letters.educationguardian2?INTCMP=SRCH.

Pearson Foundation (2012) [Online]. Available at: www.pearsonfoundation.org/oecd/ (Accessed on 13 February 2012).

Rickinson, M., Dillon, J., Teamey, K., Young Choi, M., Morris, M. and Benefield, P. (2003) *A Review of Research on Outdoor Learning: Summary of Interim Findings* Reading: NFER.

Thomson, A. (2008) 'A Career Woman? No, a Mother Who Works' in *The Times*, 15 July 2008 [Online]. Available at: www.thetimes.co.uk/tto/opinion/article2036955.ece.

Waller, T. (2005) *An Introduction to Early Childhood: A Multidisciplinary Approach*. London: Paul Chapman.

6

Education in Greece

Penelope Louka and Angeliki Papangeli

Acknowledgements

We would like to thank the teachers, the principals and the students of the two schools that agreed to participate in this study. We dedicate this chapter to our family members and the 'educators' among them.

Introduction

This chapter provides a description of the Greek educational provision and focuses on current changes and issues as they are seen through 'children's eyes'. According to the constitution, education is a basic mission of the State, aiming at the moral, intellectual, professional and physical promotion of all children. Education is a means for the promotion of national and religious awareness and the formation of free and responsible citizens (Papagueli-Vouliouris, 1999). The current Greek education system targets to provide general skills with particular emphasis on humanities. The development of the Greek education system as it is nowadays reflects considerably the socio-economic development of the country. Given today's economy and quality of life, it is important for Greece to invest in education. The future of the economy will depend on improving education quality and performance while maintaining commitments to equity and social justice (OECD, 2011).

Greek culture and education

The significance of education has always been valued in Greece. From ancient times, Greeks valued all sciences (e.g. mathematics, astronomy, rhetoric) as well as art; knowledge which they considered would make children valuable citizens. Elementary schools in ancient Greece, which were predominately attended by boys of affluent families, covered seven years of teaching (from ages 6–7 to 13–14), after which adolescents could either end their education and follow a trade or continue under the tutoring of teachers-philosophers.

The value of education is also seen during periods when education was not allowed (e.g. during the Ottoman period), where Turks prohibited formal education in Greece, in several geographical areas. The term 'hidden school' (*krifo scholio*) in Greek literature and folklore denotes the social representation of the educational significance as a means of keeping alive the Greek identity, language and religion.

The emphasis on education is also evident in Greek society nowadays, as to some extent one's value is judged on the basis of his/her educational achievements and chosen profession.

Reflective tasks

Think about how the concept of education has changed throughout the years and the social, cultural, political, historical and financial factors that contributed to its current form.

Think about how the concept of childhood has changed and how this is reflected in education nowadays.

Description of the Greek educational system

Historical background

Greece has been involved in more than four wars, foreign occupation, long-lasting dictatorships and civil war and has accepted in the last few decades large inflows of refugees and immigrants. The history of this independent state has weighed heavily on national development, affecting consequently the educational system. Until an important reform of the education system that took place in 1964, the years of compulsory education were six; i.e. only primary education was compulsory. After that reform they rose to nine, only to be reduced again to six during the period of the military dictatorship (1967–1974) (Gouvias, 1998). Reforms that were implemented after the restoration of democracy in 1976 increased the years of compulsory education to nine, thus making primary as well as lower secondary education compulsory.

The contemporary educational system in Greece

Nowadays pre-school, primary and lower secondary education is compulsory for all children 5–15 years old and it is provided free at all levels. Nowadays school life, for most children, starts from the age of approximately 2.5 years. Compulsory education includes kindergarten (*nipiagogeion* (sg)), which lasts one year, primary (*demotiko* (sg)), which lasts six years and lower secondary (*gymnasio* (sg)) education, which lasts three years (in total ten years of compulsory education).

Non-compulsory education includes: upper secondary education, Vocational Training Institutes (IEK) and higher education. Upper secondary education can be distinguished into the unified upper secondary school (*eniaio lykeio* (sg)) and the Technical Vocational School (TEE), both lasting three years. The IEK are part of post-secondary education offering scientific, technical, vocational and practical knowledge and developing the students' skills in order to ease their entrance into the world of work and their adaptation to the ever-changing needs of production processes. Higher education is divided into universities (*panepistimio*) and Technological Educational Institutions (TEI). Admission to tertiary education is based on a student's performance in national level examinations taking place at the end of the third year of upper secondary education.

Along with the mainstream schools of primary and secondary sducation, special *nipagogeia* (pl), *dimotika* (pl), *gymnasia* (pl), *lykeia* (pl) and upper secondary classes are in operation, which admit students with special educational needs. Musical, ecclesiastical and physical education *gymnasia* and *lykeia* are also in operation.

The following graph presents concisely the structure of the Greek education system, as it consists of institutions of the formal, classified or unclassified education.

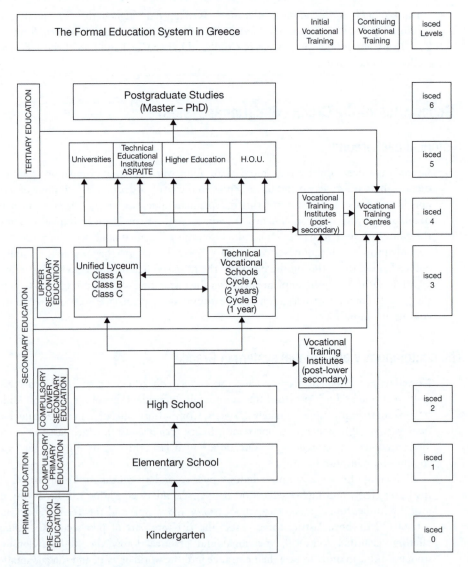

FIGURE 6.1 The Greek educational system

Source: www.ekep.gr/english/education/diagramma.asp

Early childhood provision

The early childhood setting can be distinguished into two settings: early childhood education (*nipiagogeion*) and early childhood care (*pedikos stathmos*). *Nipiagogeion* is the first formal pre-primary educational stage and, since 2006, it is compulsory for children aged 5–6 years old. Either private or public, early childhood education comes under the supervision of the Ministry of Education. Kindergartens operate between 8.00am and 12.30pm and the whole-day kindergartens until 4.00pm (Petrogiannis, 2010). Early childhood care centres, namely day care centres or nurseries, are run by the private sector and mainly through municipalities by the public sector. Services are provided to children aged 40 days (or seven months for the public sector nurseries) up to five years of age. Their supervision comes under the Ministry of Interior Affairs (for the municipalities' centres), Health and Welfare or the Ministry of Education (for the cases of licensing of a kindergarten class).

The new socio-economic conditions in Greece have created new demands for early childcare and education provision. According to a relatively recent estimation 110,000 children aged between five months and five years attend nursery school (Tsoulea and Kaitanidi, 2005). Despite some improvements recorded in the last decade (i.e. legislation including kindergarten to the obligatory education), the existing early childcare services have only been minimally altered in the last decades (Anagnostopoulou and Papaprokopiou, 1998).

Primary education

Attendance at primary education (*dimotiko*) lasts for six years, and children are admitted at the age of six. All-day primary schools are in operation, with an extended timetable and an enriched curriculum. The obligatory subjects in primary education are: religion, modern Greek, maths, history, environmental issues, geography, physics, social and political education, music, gymnastics and two foreign languages. In secondary education (*gymnasio*), in addition to those subjects, ancient Greek, chemistry, biology, computer science, technology and educational orientation are taught. As a consequence of the classification of the education institutions, a title (school-leaving certificate, degree, etc.) is compulsory for students at each education level in order to continue to the next. Compulsory primary and secondary education operates from 8.00–8.10am until 1.30pm and all-day schools last until 3.30pm.

The academic year lasts 175 days for primary education and 150 for secondary education. School starts on 11 September and lasts until 15 June for primary education and 31 May for secondary education. Each teaching session lasts 40–50 minutes and schools are open five days of the week. Teaching hours vary according to level: 25 hours for the first two years in primary school, 30 hours for the next four years and 35 hours for secondary education. According to the Ministry of Education, the number of students in each class in primary education should not be more than 25. In secondary education this number can increase by 10 per cent. In primary education, there is one teacher per class who teaches all subjects apart from gymnastics, music and foreign languages. In secondary education all classes are taught by specialised teachers.

'My day is busy because I go to school'

Case study 1

Thirteen 4th grade children (five boys and eight girls) were given the three open-question questionnaire in class, in the presence of their teacher, and were asked to answer all three questions as best as they could. The questions asked were the following:

Question 1: Describe one day at school.
Question 2: What do you like about your school?
Question 3: What do you want to change in your school?

Question 1: One school day

The students were given this statement to describe as best as they could one typical day at school.

'We are taught history, math, reading, language, religious studies and gymnastics … in order to speak I need to be given permission to do so, by raising my hand … we also have small intermissions between classes' (Boy 1).

'At school we are taught many kinds of lessons … during intermissions we play and we eat what our mothers have prepared for us' (Girl 4).

'…after the typical day is over, we stay at school longer ("all day school") to prepare our lessons so we do not have to do them at home' (Boy 2).

'Before our lessons start we say Grace and then we have our lessons and then we prepare our homework' (Girl 8).

The majority of them mentioned the time of arrival and departure and the lessons they are taught during the day. Taking into account that this particular school is an all-day school, which means that children remain longer in the school's premises, the majority of students also mentioned this, indicating that this extra time was spent as a means to prepare their homework so that they could have more free time at home and also play some more with their friends.

Question 2: Things I like about my school

'I like history because we watch it (cartoon-based learning)' (Boy 1).

'I like gymnastics because it is play time, I like music because we sing and I like reading because I know all the countries' (Girl 2).

'I like the things we are taught because we get smarter but I also like our play time, because we get to run and play hide-and-seek' (Girl 3).

The above sample of student responses indicates a clear distinction between the school as a building and what a school stands for and is all about, i.e. primarily a place to learn new things. Also a means of making friends as well as a place to play games which they could not play anywhere else (taking into account that they live in the capital, near the centre of Athens, where play zones are scarce, if not non-existent). Thus, students' emphasis was placed on the latter (the meaning of school) as the majority of them commented on the different aspects of learning and their taught units as well as the time given to have fun and play.

Question 3: Things I want to change in my school

'I would like for my school to have two floors … the 1st, 2nd and 3rd grade to be located on the 1st floor and the 4th, 5th and 6th grade to be located on the 2nd floor. I would also like for our school to have a big back garden and for the trees to grow so we can have some shade' (Girl 2).

'I would like to change the gymnastics facility because it has no roof and when it rains we have to go inside and draw … but drawing is also good! I would also like to have lockers so we could safely store our things so they are not stolen … I would like for us to have a digital board to have more fun' (Girl 3).

'I would like more green' (Girl 4).

'I would like to go to school 2 days and the remaining 5 not to go … I would also like for our school to have 2 floors' (Boy 2).

'I would have liked for our school to have a swimming pool because I love to swim' (Girl 5).

'…I would like for our school to be more secure so no one could come in…' (Girl 6).

'I would like cleaner toilets' (Boy 3).

'…I would like for our school to be repainted blue and yellow…' (Boy 4).

'I would like my school to have three floors, a swimming pool and toys' (Girl 8).

It comes as no surprise that the students had a lot to say, especially taking into account their answers in the previous question ('things I like about my school'). Four students mentioned their wish not to go to school that often. This, on the one hand, could be explained as an aversion and a resistance to being compelled to read, study and having to do homework that some students may experience. On the other hand, it could also be seen as a wish of spending less time at a place that they do not consider student friendly. This argument could be further substantiated by the fact that almost all students mentioned that they would appreciate a cleaner and larger school, more greenery, extra facilities and enhanced security. This illustrates the picture of a large number of public schools near the centre of Athens: schools that lack space, that are not surrounded by greenery and have only the basic facilities compared to other schools such as private ones located in the more affluent Athenian suburbs.

Case study 2

Thirty-two 3rd grade students (17 boys and 15 girls), 19 5th grade students (nine boys and ten girls) and 22 6th grade students (ten boys and 12 girls) were asked to answer the same questions as in Case study 1.

Question 1: One school day

'I wake up, I eat my breakfast, I brush my teeth and I go to school. At school the bell rings, we say Grace and then we start our lessons. I like math, history and language. When school finishes, I go home and eat my lunch and then I do my homework. After that I play with my toys, I eat dinner, brush my teeth and go to bed' (Girl 11, 3rd grade).

'Everyday I wake up, drink my milk and go to school … I like math, religious studies and history. When I go home I eat and then study. When I finish I play on my computer, I watch TV, I draw and I play with my toy soldiers, I talk with my sister and my parents … at night I drink my milk and go to bed' (Boy 3, 3rd grade).

'I wake up, eat my breakfast and go to school. When school finishes, I go home, eat, and do my homework and then play. Around 18.00 I go to my English class and at 22.00 I go to bed. My day is busy cause I go to school and I have to read a lot … I wish there was a law not to have classes at school' (Girl 2, 5th grade).

'I wake up and go to school. When I come home I eat and then study. After that I go to my English class, come home, watch some TV, eat and then sleep. This is the typical day of every child my age' (Girl 9, 5th grade).

'I wake up at around 07.00 and I go to school. When I go home I do my homework and then I go to my English class' (Boy 3, 6th grade).

'…after the school day is over I am involved in other activities such as tennis and guitar lessons, English and chess' (Boy 8, 6th grade).

The majority of 3rd and 5th graders not only described what they typically did at school, but from their answers it was evident that they also considered their school-related activities at home (i.e. homework) to be part of their school day. This was more evident in the answers provided by the 3rd graders whereas the 5th and 6th graders apart from this also mentioned other extracurricular activities such as swimming, guitar and football classes.

Question 2: Things I like about my school

'I like my school because it has nice colours and big classrooms and I also like the plants out in the playground' (Girl 2, 3rd grade).

'I like history and math' (Boy 4, 3rd grade).

'I like all the lessons and I also like to play' (Girl 8, 3rd grade).

'At school I like the fact that we are taught many things, especially history and math, and I also like playing with my friends' (Girl 10, 3rd grade).

'I like math because I like calculations and solving problems and I like language studies' (Girl 3, 5th grade).

'I like everything because we learn many things and when I grow up I will have a very good job' (Girl 4, 5th grade).

'I like everything about my school because we learn many things and also have fun … if I stayed at home I would be bored!' (Girl 2, 6th grade).

'I like it because you are educated and you see your friends … it is much better than spending all day in front of a computer and having to wear glasses!' (Girl 4, 6th grade).

As in the previous study, the clear distinction between the school as a building and the meaning of school was evident once more. A small minority of 3rd graders mentioned that they liked their school as a building whereas the remaining students (all grades) commented upon the different things they are taught at school. Similarly with the previous study's findings, students subdivided the things they liked about their school, not only on the basis of the different lessons but also as a chance to see their friends and play with them.

Question 3: Things I want to change in my school

'I do not like the mark D and 0' (Boy 4, 3rd grade).

'I do not like it when we have too much homework, but I know it is for our own good, but I do not like it' (Boy 6, 3rd grade).

'I do not like fighting with my friends' (Girl 6, 3rd grade).

'I do not like English because they are yelling and when I go home I have a headache' (Girl 8, 3rd grade).

'I do not like English at all, I wish someday that it (English) will be removed from our school … I hope and I wish it!' (Girl 10, 3rd grade).

'I do not like that I have to wake up early every morning to go to school' (Boy 11, 3rd grade).

'I do not like any lesson that we have to learn by heart, but I have to read them as I do not want to be unintelligent … I will try!' (Girl 3, 5th grade).

'I do not like the theoretical lessons and I do not like when children fight' (Boy 2, 5th grade).

'I do not like the English class, because the teacher gives us many photocopies to translate' (Boy 3, 6th grade).

'I do not think that any child likes going to school, you have to wake up in the morning and study, then you have homework … at least I play with my friends' (Boy 9, 6th grade).

'I do not like Friday's tests; Friday should be a fun day…' (Girl 8, 6th grade).

'I do not like tests, they make me anxious … I also do not like the queue for the canteen!' (Girl 9, 6th grade).

Contrary to the answers provided by the 4th graders in case study 1, which were primarily concentrated around the changes in their school as a building, here 3rd graders provided more varying answers; from marks and fighting to homework and specific lessons. The 5th graders were more concerned about their theoretical lessons, which they have to learn by heart. The 6th graders did not like more solid aspects, such as tests. Also, the majority of 3rd grade students and some 6th grade students did not like English, not specifying if it is a matter of difficulty learning a second language or if it is due to the way they are taught English at school. Evaluation of teachers is considered to be a weak point in the Greek education system (Papagueli-Vouliouris, 1999). This may be indicative of the need to develop a teacher's and school's evaluation system and listen to children's views.

Children from a young age appreciate the importance and meaning of school. They do acknowledge the value of their taught lessons and some are able to provide initial thoughts and connect these to their life opportunities on the basis of their educational level and career prospects. On the other hand, it is only logical to show and express their frustration regarding their homework, perhaps making a distinction between the things they *have* to do and the things they *want* to do.

The Greek social representations regarding the educational system are that in order to be successful you have to be educated (Karatzia, Stamelos and Lambropoulos, 2006). On the basis of this, it comes as no surprise that adolescents are encouraged to follow 'high status' professional careers, such as a Managing Director, lawyer, professor, etc. Obviously this was not evident in the findings of these studies as they included a younger sample. What was evident though was the students' clarity regarding the school's aim.

Reflective questions

How would you help a child change his/her school?

Do you think that children's opinions are heard macro- and micro-socially in your country?

Have a discussion with the children in your classroom to start making their proposed ideas into reality. Do not forget that children's voices are equally important as adults'!

Pedagogic practices

According to the Greek educational curriculum guideline (DEPPS, 2002), the teacher creates the right conditions using an attractive, safe, friendly and rich-in-stimuli environment in order to ensure motivation and learning conditions for all children. The educator is responsible for organising attractive learning experiences that are meaningful and interesting for the children, supporting learning through play, investigating, using a variety of sources, i.e. new technological means, and utilising prior knowledge and experiences of children to build new knowledge.

Table 6.1 illustrates the weekly distribution of teaching time per subject and grade, indicating the emphasis of both art-related topics as well as science-related ones. The contemporary Greek educational system cannot 'escape' the nation's heritage, since history, geography, religious studies as well as social-political sciences seem to have a prominent place in the curriculum. As shown in Table 6.1, the Greek educational system follows the Flexible Zone program, a cross-curriculum approach, where students and teachers can materialise projects in which they deal with issues and problems of everyday life, using cooperative, problem-solving and synergistic methodologies.

Approaches to assessment and achievement

Assessment is a key step in any organised and systematic process of education in practice. The main purpose of assessment is to improve the educational process. In kindergarten there is no standard way of learning and/or assessment. Evaluation is ongoing, incorporated

TABLE 6.1 The weekly allocation of teaching time per subject and grade

Subject	Grades in primary school (age 6–12)					
	Grade 1	Grade 2	Grade 3	Grade 4	Grade 5	Grade 6
Greek language	9	9	8	8	7	7
Mathematics	4	4	4	4	4	4
Environmental studies	3	3	3	3	—	—
Art and Music	3	3	3	3	2	2
Gymnastics	2	2	2	2	2	2
Religious studies	—	—	2	2	2	2
Physics	—	—	—	—	3	3
History	—	—	2	2	2	2
Geography	—	—	—	—	2	2
Social and Political studies	—	—	—	—	1	1
English	—	—	—	3	3	3
Flexible Zone program	4	4	3	3	2	2
TOTAL (hours)	**25**	**25**	**27**	**30**	**30**	**30**

in the daily process, and based on the total progress of the program. During the evaluation process individual characteristics of each child, differences in the way and the pace of each student's learning, perception, abilities and opportunities, as well as the family, the social background and special features – such as foreign language speaking children, children with special educational needs and special abilities and inclinations – will be taken into account (DEPPS, 2002).

In kindergarten the emphasis of assessment is given in three different domains:

a. The course and outcomes of work plans
b. The assessment from the children collectively as a team
c. Each child's portfolio

The portfolio is a record of the learning process containing material revealing what interests the child, what has been learned, samples of work that are original productions of children (e.g. plans, paintings, handicrafts, writing samples, construction) and not pre-designed worksheets for assessment. It should also contain other records such as photographs, the child's participation in activities, recordings, narratives of children, etc. It also contains notes of the teacher. The portfolio should be accessible to parents and parents should have frequent communication and be informed at regular intervals by the kindergarten teacher for the overall progress of the child.

In primary schools, the assessment process is distinguished in:

– ***Diagnostic.*** The diagnostic evaluation involves the exploration on the part of the teacher at the beginning of the school year or at the beginning of a section, through conversation and appropriate oral and/or written questions in order to determine the degree of achievement on the relevant section, the level of skills that the student has acquired from previous years of study or the modules that are taught during the same school year, the usual 'mistakes' and the overall problematic areas regarding the taught module.

– **Formative.** The formative evaluation is a continuous and daily process during which teachers seek information about the student's progress during the last teaching subject. Depending on the outcome of this assessment, the teacher decides and plans possible interventions in order to improve the process and achievement of the learning objectives.

– **Final.** The final evaluation, carried out with the completion of a module or at the end of the school year, systematically evaluates the outcome of the teaching process and the personal effort of the student. The results of this evaluation help both the teacher and the student to progress further.

Means of evaluation, which are used as appropriate, are: written tests, oral and written comprehension questions, short written essay questions, short answer questions, oral or written, discussion on certain topics, orally or in writing, creative work, etc.

The above indicative forms of assessment that take place in all courses where appropriate.

Reflective question

Think about how new technological means are used to extend knowledge.

Consider how technology is or could be incorporated into your school in order to advance teaching and learning.

Conclusion

In the last few years, a number of socio-economic changes have taken place in Greece, such as the loosening of family ties, the change in values and the increase in divorce rates, influencing the need in improving educational policy (Bagavos, 2005). The current chapter attempts to illustrate children's views on the educational system. The need to raise quality in education is constant and considering children's voices should be a priority in terms of improving school effectiveness.

Current changes to the system

In light of the short- and long-term economic pressures on the country, the Greek government has established a bold agenda pursuing significant changes involving reforms of compulsory education, upper secondary education and the administrative structure of the education system within an overarching framework, 'The Student First – New School' (Νέο Σχολείο), in order to strengthen finance and accountability mechanisms. Current issues that must be addressed are: the unsustainable cost-structure of the system and the inefficiencies that are inherent in an out-dated, ineffective centralised education system. The changes involve transforming governance and management structures; eliminating, consolidating or merging small inefficient units; making significantly better use of human resources; improving quality-assurance and information systems for accountability; and establishing far more effective capacity to lead and sustain the implementation of changes in governments.

All the changes, choices and actions that are launched reflect the best practices in OECD countries and converge in a perspective for the overall restructuring of Greek education which will guarantee the quality, meritocracy, equal opportunities and possibilities, so as to trigger creativity, imagination and the initiative for innovation, and which will promote collegiality, solidarity and respect of others. This action takes time, perseverance and patience. (Anna Diamantopoulou, 'We Change Education, We Change Greece,' March 2011) (OECD, 2011).

References

Anagnostopoulou, L. and Papaprokopiou, A. (1998). *Crisis in the Welfare System and Young Children's Quality of Life in the Preschool Settings*. In I. Konstantopoulou (ed.), *Family-Europe-21st Century: Prospects and Institutions. Proceedings of the European Forum for Child and the Family*. Athens: Foundation for Child and the Family/Nea Synora Livanis (in Greek).

Bagavos, Ch. (2005). *Demographic Dimensions of Families and Households Changes in Greece – A First Approach*. In L. Moussourou and M. Stratigaki (eds). *Issues of Family Policy*. Athens: Gutenberg (in Greek), pp. 31–72.

Diathematiko Eniaio Plaisio Programmatwn Spoudwn (DEPPS) gia to nipiagwgio (2002). Athens: YPEPTH (equivalent of DfES).

Gouvias, D. (1998). *The National Examination's System of Greece and Its Function as A Mechanism of Social Selection*, Paper Presented at the "European Conference on Educational Research", Ljubljana, Slovenia 17–20 September 1998.

Karatzia, E., Stamelos, G., Lambropoulos, H. (2006). *Higher Education Quality and University Evaluation: European Political Discourse and Localized Practice: The Case of Greece*. In XXII CESE Conference "Changing Knowledge and Education: Communities, Information Societies and Mobilities", 3–6 Granada 2006.

OECD (2011). *Strong Performers and Successful Reformers in Education: Education Policy Advice for Greece*, OECD Publishing. [Online]. Available at: www.oecd-ilibrary.org/education/education-policy-advice-for-greece_9789264119581-en (Accessed on 16 January 2012).

Papagueli-Vouliouris, D. (1999). Evaluation of Teacher Education in Greece – A Political Demand of Our Time. TNTEE Publications, 2(2), pp. 129–137.

Petrogiannis, K. (2010). Early Childhood Care and Education in Greece: Some Facts on Research and Policy. International Journal of Early Childhood, 42, pp. 131–139.

Tsoulea, R. and Kaitanidi, M. (2005). Lottery Ticket Is To Find a Place In a Day Nursery. *Ta Nea*, 13 June (in Greek).

Useful links

Ministry of Education, Lifelong Learning and Religious Affairs: www.minedu.gov.gr
National School Network: www.sch.gr

7

Education in Japan

Yukari Iguchi

Acknowledgements

This chapter would not have existed without a tremendous degree of help provided by Naoko Ito, who provided a depth of information of current policies and practice and her valuable insight of the Japanese primary education. I also would like to express my gratitude to Kanako Ishida who helped me with data collection, and Shinichi Goto and his family for providing their thoughtful views on primary education from parents' perspectives. At last but not least, I also would like to thank Leonard Cseh for his continuous moral support throughout research.

Introduction

This chapter discusses the policies and practices of Japanese primary education by highlighting some routines and events in order to illustrate how philosophies of compulsory education are embedded into curriculum and extracurricular activities, and then presents some of the issues the Japanese primary education system currently faces.

This chapter largely consists of two sets of data: government publications and the actual voices of primary school children, parents and teachers. Publications of the Ministry of Education, Culture, Science and Technology (MEXT) were researched in order to establish a clear picture of education policies and systems. Much information of actual practice was obtained through interviews via electronic communication tools (emails and VoIP) between August and September 2011. In total five school teachers, four children and parents participated in this research from Osaka city, Kobe city and Ikoma city, all in the Kinki region in western Japan. The limitation of geographical spread may impact on generalisability as educational policies and practices are varied depending on regions; therefore, additional information or corrections, if needed, by the readers of this chapter will be hugely appreciated.

Pre-school years

Types of childcare provisions

Compulsory education starts at six years of age although the majority of children attend kindergartens or nurseries. Two national ministries govern the early years childcare/education provisions in Japan: the Ministry of Health, Labour and Welfare controls nurseries from social welfare perspectives and the MEXT controls kindergarten from educational perspectives.

Kindergartens (*yochien*) provide non-compulsory early years education for children from the ages of three to six. Nurseries (*hoikusho*) accept children from the age of a few months old to compulsory school age. In addition to them, there are new types of childcare institutions called *kodomoen*: the childcare centres that integrate provisions of *yochien* and *hoikusho,* which do not require parents to be unable to provide daytime childcare (which is a main requirement for admission to *hoikusho*), accept children at the age of 0–5 years and offer flexible hours (Cooperation Promotion Office, 2006).

Impacts of childcare types

The type of early years childcare depends on the family circumstances rather than preference, mainly due to the nurseries' relatively strict admission criteria. One may expect that the type of childcare may result in a difference in children's behaviour and skills due to the differences in hours and philosophies. However, from the perspectives of primary school teachers interviewed in this study there were no notable differences between kindergarten and nursery graduates. This may be mainly because there is no prerequisite for the primary schools, but also because children in kindergartens develop social behaviour through structured activities while children in nurseries naturally learn those behaviours by spending long hours away from home.

Primary school

Background

The compulsory education in Japan originates in 1872 when the new government established the Government Code of Education, adopting the American and French systems. In the 20th century, following Japan's defeat in WW2, the Allied Powers reformed the government systems including education. The Basic Act on Education was established in 1947 followed by the School Education Law and the Courses of Study.

Today, the MEXT determines the Courses of Study as broad standards for all schools, from kindergarten through upper secondary schools, in order to ensure consistencies throughout the country. The Courses of Study are normally revised every ten years and the latest version for primary schools was revised in 2008 and has come into effect in 2011.

The aims of compulsory education are defined as:

1. fostering the next generation which will be responsible for forming the nation and society; and
2. building a foundation to enable each child to lead a happy life.

(Elementary and Secondary Education Planning Division, 2005)

In 2010 there were 22,000 primary schools in Japan, of which 21,713 were run by local educational authorities, 213 run privately and 74 run by the government (Bureau of Life Long Learning Strategy, 2010). National primary schools deliver the same curriculum with the public primary schools and in addition, play roles as teacher-training institutions where education students at university train, as well as to run pilot schemes in order to develop national curricula. Since the national schools are not representative of the primary school in general, this chapter focuses on public primary schools.

Philosophy of primary education: a brief history of the Courses of Study

The current Course of Study aims to nurture the 'Zest for Life' (*ikiru chikara*), based on the educational principles expressed in the revisions of the Basic Act of Education. Table 7.1 summarises a history of the Courses of Study. The 'Zest for Life' philosophy was first introduced in 2002, which emphasised on importance of a level of 'latitude' (*yutori*). It comes from the lesson learnt from the 1971 version, which is often referred to as 'compressed education (*tsumekomi kyoiku*)'. It emphasised much on conveying knowledge rather than children's overall development and resulted in a high failure rate, collapse of classroom discipline, increased rate of vandalism and a number of 'successful' graduates who were only good at exam techniques but lacked a range of skills such as applications, critical thinking and interpersonal skills.

TABLE 7.1 History of the Courses of Study (Japan)

Year	Key points	Criticism
1947	The first Course of Study after WW2; restoration of education system; introduction of democratic philosophies; set class hours for each subject.	Written in a short period of time; interrelationship between subjects not thoroughly planned.
1951	'Independent study' integrated into extracurricular activities; revision of moral study; raising awareness of international views.	Over-reliance on experiential learning and modular system; flexible hours caused geographical gaps of children's academic skills.
1961	Aims to raise awareness as citizens of an independent country who contribute to cultural enrichment and building a democratic society; emphasis on basic academic skills; more weight on math and science.	Rapidly became outdated due to fast-changing political, cultural and social environment.

1971	'Modernisation curriculum'; corresponding to the 'Modernisation of Education' movement in the U.S.; updated to suit social and political changes and technological advancements; increased syllabus to teach within similar class hours.	Too much emphasis on conveying knowledge rather than overall development of children (knowledge, moral, physical); a high failure rate due to intensive curriculum.
1980	'Latitude' curriculum; emphasis on developing balanced persons; reduced syllabus through revision on core knowledge; reduced class hours.	Created only minimum 'latitude' due to ineffective reduction of syllabus; gaps in achievement rate between public and private schools (as many private schools did not reduce hours/syllabus); competition became too high.
1992	New definition of 'academic achievement'; emphasis on building a foundation of life-long learning; merging general science and sociology into 'Life Environment Study' (*seikatsu ka*); focus on individual character; further reduction of class hours.	Reduced hours resulted in lower academic achievements represented by the lower ranks in OECD/PISA in 2003.
2002	Emphasis on developing the 'Zest for Life' within 'Latitude'; further reduction of syllabus and class hours; introduction of 'General Study' from Year 3.	Reduced hours resulted in lower academic achievements represented by the even lower ranks in OECD/PISA in 2006; 'Zest for Life' not demonstrated by pupils/youngsters.

The 1980 version of the Course of Study reduced the syllabus and class hours; however, the reduction was kept to a minimum and it did not create the expected level of 'latitude'. The 1992 version redefined the main aim of education as developing individuals' skills to support themselves in the fast changing world. The syllabus and class hours were reduced and all schools were closed on every other Saturday – in the 2002 version, class hours were further reduced to close schools on every Saturday. This significant reduction aimed to encourage children to spend more time within communities, participating in extracurricular activities and volunteer work for self-development purposes.

However, critiques were concerned that this significant reduction in class hours (over 100 hours a year) would result in lower academic achievements (Fujita, 2005). This concern was widely supported by public when the ranks of OECD/PISA dropped significantly in 2003 and 2006 (see Table 7.2).

TABLE 7.2 OCED/PISA results (ranks of Japan)

Year	Mathematics	Reading	Science
2000	1st	8th	2nd
2003	6th	14th	1st
2006	10th	15th	5th
2009	9th	8th	5th

One parent interviewed shared this concern on the 'latitude' education concept:

> It was before my daughter started school, but even then I didn't see a clear vision in the 'latitude' curriculum. I only felt children were given more free time without any guidance. Young children were still in the process of learning how to be independent, and when they were simply given more free time they would do nothing constructive. It seemed to me that the concept of 'freedom' was confused with 'neglect', and this created a generation of youngsters who are very impatient and do not persevere.
>
> (A mother of a Year 2 pupil, Ikoma city)

The Course of Study 2011

The 2011 version of the Course of Study continues to aim to nurture 'Zest for Life' based on the educational principles expressed in the revisions to the Basic Act on Education. The new Course of Study increases class hours for the first time in 30 years and emphasises on balancing the attainment of thinking skills, decisiveness and expressiveness under a slogan, 'the future of education is neither "latitude" nor "compressed" (MEXT, 2010). This seems a positive change and the introduction of a foreign language (English in most schools) at Year 5 would be regarded as a good move in the increasingly internationalised society. This new Course of Study seems to be generally welcomed by teachers interviewed in this study, perceiving the increased syllabus and curriculum as a major improvement. One teacher also stated that there are clearer guidelines in regards to indicative contents of certain subjects.

However, another teacher perceived that it has created additional workload and uncertainty due to a lack of support and direction by the government:

> The new Course of Study increased class hours but not at all levels, and in some cases we have to teach increased syllabus in the same number of hours. Also, English became compulsory for the first time so we have to teach English without sufficient knowledge. Currently there is no formal system of allocating external native English speakers and there is no uniformed approach to the syllabus. For these reasons, English education has become a burden for us.
>
> (A teacher, Osaka city)

While teachers had clear views of the new Course of Study, most parents interviewed in this study did not perceive major changes in children's learning experience except for increased class hours. One parent commended the end of 'latitude' education and more teacher-led learning activities in the current Course of Study, however, she was sceptical that it would not necessarily resolve the problems due to her perception that many parents today are not mature enough to raise children (as they studied the 'latitude' curriculum). Indeed, this concern is shared widely in today's Japanese society and this may explain why the MEXT emphasises on 'balancing attainment of knowledge and skills with thinking capacity, decisiveness, and expressiveness', developing a good personality along with academic achievement (Elementary and Secondary Education Bureau, 2011).

Primary school curriculum and OECD/PISA

Although Japan's decline of ranks in OECD/PISA caused much debate and the 'latitude' curriculum was to be blamed upon, there was only a low level of awareness of OECD/PISA among children, teachers and parents in this study. One teacher commented:

> I hardly ever think about OECD/PISA when I teach children. Of course I am concerned with each test result, but I am also aware that it depends on whether children are taught techniques to achieve higher grades, or whether the design of a test suits children's traits. If we set a target to achieve full marks in OECD/PISA tests, we would have to teach much more than the current syllabus.
>
> (A teacher, Osaka city)

Another teacher stated:

> I know about OECD/PISA, but it is just information to me and I am not concerned about it when I teach my children. This is because I believe the aim of the Japanese education system is different from other countries. Our aim is to 'build good individual characters'.
>
> (A teacher, Kobe city)

These comments indicate that the decline in OECD/PISA ranks was merely used as quantifiable evidence for the failure of the 'latitude' curriculum. The main reason for unpopularity of the curriculum was a perceived failure to develop good individuals. There is a general consensus among the Japanese that anything can be achieved if one works hard enough; therefore, not educating children to persevere was the serious shortfall of the 'latitude' curriculum.

In addition to the main purposes of compulsory education, it is generally considered that three types of education should be provided to children:

1. Intellectual education: developing skills to learn new knowledge;
2. Moral education: establishing an identity as a member of society through developing a sense of responsibility, ability to cooperate with others and developing communication skills;
3. Physical education: learning how to look after oneself through developing physical and mental strength, i.e. learning about food and nutrition, having regular exercise and learning how to maintain self-hygiene.

Most teachers in this study considered the latter two aspects as the strengths of the Japanese education system, in addition to equality of admission. The next section describes a typical day at primary school and discusses how these types of education are provided to children.

Reflective questions

How is OECD/PISA perceived in your country? Does it have influence on teaching practice?

A day at primary school

Whitburn (2003) describes in detail the life of Year 1 (age six) children in Japanese primary schools, which is comparable to the life of the participants of this research. A typical day of a Year 1 child is shown in Table 7.3.

Children from Year 1 usually travel to and from school independently of parents either individually or in groups of friends. Children are expected to come in between 8:00 and 8:20am and when they arrive at school they are free to play in classrooms and the school playground, often unsupervised. Dodgeball and football are always popular sports in the playground, and in classrooms children often draw, read or just chat in small groups until the first bell.

As the example timetables (Tables 7.4 and 7.5) show, different activities take place before the first class. In the example timetables, children have a 'story time' on Wednesday and are given a short calculation test on Thursday morning, after which they check the answers among peers.

TABLE 7.3 A typical day of a six-year old child (Japan)

6am	Wake up
8am	Go to school
3–4pm	Finish school
After school	Swimming lesson (Monday 4–5pm), calligraphy lesson (Wednesday 5–6pm), snack 4pm, reading books, watching TV, homework 4.30–5pm (other days)
7pm	Dinner
9pm	Go to bed

TABLE 7.4 Year 1 (age six) timetable (Japan)

	Mon	Tue	Wed	Thu	Fri
8:00–8.20	Coming in to school				
8:30	General assembly	Class assembly	Story time	Calculation time	Class assembly
8:45	Life environmental study	Class activities	Life environmental study	Japanese	Music
9:30			Break		
9:40	PE	Japanese	Japanese	Math	Math
10:25			20-minute break		
10:45	Math	Math	Math	PE	Japanese
11:30			Break		
11:40	Japanese	Library	Life environmental study	Music	Japanese

12:25	Lunch				
13:15	Cleaning	Cleaning	Break	Cleaning	Cleaning
13:30	Break	Break	Crafts (13:30–14:15)	Break	Break
13:50	Crafts	PE		Life environmental study	Moral study
14:35	Class assembly	Class assembly	Class assembly (14:15–14:25)	Class assembly	Class assembly
14:45–16:30	Going home	Going home	Going home (14:25)	Going home	Going home

TABLE 7.5 Year 6 (age 11) timetable (Japan)

	Mon	Tue	Wed	Thu	Fri
8:00–8:20	Coming in to school				
8:30	General assembly	Class assembly	Story time	Calculation time	Class assembly
8:45	Class activities	Japanese	Sociology	Japanese	English
9:30	Break				
9:40	Japanese	PE	Math	Math	General science
10:25	20-minute break				
10:45	Math	Math	Japanese	Sociology	Math
11:30	Break				
11:40	General study	Sociology	General science	Domestic science	Japanese
12:25	Lunch				
13:15	Cleaning	Cleaning	Break	Cleaning	Cleaning
13:30	Break	Break	Moral study (13:30–14:15)	Break	Break
13:50	Music	General science		PE	Crafts
14:35	Break	Break	Briefing (14:15–14:25)	Break	Break
14:45	Committees/societies	General study	Going home (14:25)	Music	Crafts
15:30	Class assembly	Class assembly	—	Class assembly	Class assembly
15:40–16:30	Going home	Going home	—	Going home	Going home

Class leader (*nitchoku*)

Each class has a rota with which a pair (usually a boy and a girl) performs the class leader's roles for a day. The duties include arriving at school early and unlocking the classroom, writing down on the blackboard the date and their own name, chairing the morning and afternoon class assembly, giving a command to bow at the teacher at the beginning and end of class, erasing the blackboard clear before each lesson, filling in the class journal and switching off the light and locking the classroom at the end of the day. This role is rotated in a class therefore all children have regular opportunities to be in this position and develop a sense of responsibility and leadership, as well as some skills such as public speaking.

Emphasis on reading

Many schools emphasise the importance of reading as a basis of literacy and communication skills development, and have a morning session where a teacher or community volunteer reads stories to younger children. The older children may individually read a book of choice in silence and this is perceived to have positive effects on children's behaviours, such as higher concentration levels.

This emphasis on developing reading skills is also reflected through the allocation of 'library hours' in timetables. This does not appear in the Year 6 timetable but some hours in general study are allocated to this activity. One teacher describes her school's practice as:

> We want to develop children's vocabulary and expressions. Now most schools require each child to have their own 'reading cards', which they read out every day as homework. It is aimed to develop their skills to express their own idea by reading them out loud. Children who are weak in this aspect often cannot understand questions asked in other subjects such as science, so we are aiming to develop overall academic achievement through reading. Also, children with limited vocabulary often end up fighting with other children as they cannot communicate their own feeling clearly.
>
> (A primary school teacher, Osaka City)

Children also spend some hours practicing traditional brush-and-ink calligraphy in Japanese classes from Year 4 (age nine) onwards. As the activities in Japanese classes diversify and class hours for the subject decreases, there is less emphasis on reading in the later years. This may indicate a belief on the importance of developing appropriate literacy skills at an early stage.

Lunchtime

Primary and secondary schools normally do not have dining rooms and lunch is served in the classroom. Each class organises a group rota and a group of children in aprons and hats collects lunch from the meal store (see Figure 7.1). Each child has a role to play in laying up dining tables by combining four to six desks together and laying luncheon mats or a table cloth. When the food arrives, a group of children serve to each table (see Figure 7.2) while the others are supposed to wait quietly.

When everyone is served, a pair of class leaders read out the menu and ingredients to the class, with some nutritional information from an information leaflet provided. In some

FIGURE 7.1 Children transporting lunch to their classroom

FIGURE 7.2 Serving lunch in the classroom

cases, children play a regular quiz about important food groups and tastes (Caterer and Hotelkeeper, 2007). Then everyone starts eating at the same time after calling out '*itadakimasu*' ('I humbly take this') with both hands put together (as if praying). This is a Japanese custom before each meal, showing gratitude to those who produced, cooked and served the meal.

Exactly the same meal is served for everyone in a school. Having school meals in the classroom is usually included in a teacher's job description as a part of 'food education' activities. Children are encouraged to eat everything served at each meal to show respect to the others and avoid waste, based on the traditional Japanese value and health perspectives. According to a teacher interviewed, this is becoming harder as more children have food allergies or behavioural problems in recent years, however, a series of activities to serve lunch is aimed to educate children about the importance of food from moral and physical perspectives.

Usually children are not allowed to leave the table until everyone in the group has finished, therefore there is often a degree of peer pressure to eat everything served even when they do not like it. When everyone finishes, the class leader calls out '*gochisousama deshita*' ('I enjoyed the feast') with both hands put together, followed by the rest. Tables are cleared and the group on rota returns all pots, crockery and cutlery, then everyone starts cleaning the classroom and communal areas.

Cleaning time

It is a norm in Japanese schools (from primary to secondary school) that pupils or students perform general cleaning duties every day. In primary schools all children clean classrooms and communal areas together. Children are divided into small groups to clean the assigned areas such as classrooms, corridors, toilet, playground or sports hall. Large communal areas, such as the playground, are often cleaned by children from all years, where older children teach and supervise younger ones.

Children are initially taught how to clean the area while supervised by a teacher, however, as they become familiar with the routine they often perform duties without the teacher's presence and the group leader usually reports to the teacher when the task is completed. It is a common consensus in Japan that through performing cleaning duties, children develop an identity as a member of society and a mindset to perform volunteer work and learn the importance of handling equipments and facilities with care. There is a set time (usually 15 to 20 minutes) for cleaning, therefore children also learn how to complete all tasks in a set time.

Committees and clubs

After the lunch break classes take place for another hour for lower grades and two hours for the higher grades. As shown in the Year 6 timetable, usually there is a time slot for the clubs and committees every week for the higher grades (usually Years 5 and 6). Each child belongs to specific committees and clubs to perform duties or practice their interests. Some examples of the committees and clubs are shown in Tables 7.6 and 7.7.

As Table 7.6 indicates, the committee activities are often embedded in the daily school life. These duties also foster children's sense of responsibility and professionalism, as well as some technical skills, while clubs are to develop and share personal interests and develop social and technical skills.

After school

When the class assembly (a session to reflect on the day and check the next day's plan, usually chaired by the class leaders) ends children go home, although they are usually allowed to stay in the classroom or playground to play with friends. However, many children leave school soon after the class assembly and attend various courses and lessons. A study found that 85 per cent of children in Years 1 to 3 attend a lesson or course after school and the most popular lesson was swimming, followed by music and singing (Benesse Corporation, 2007). In this research the popular lessons were swimming, calligraphy and abacus.

TABLE 7.6 Examples of committees (Japan)

Committee	Duties
Health	Helping the school nurse during the break; promoting hygiene, i.e. washing hands by designing posters around the school; refilling soap dispensers; accompanying unwell classmate to the medical room, etc.
Broadcasting	Operating the school PA system to support general assemblies and other school events {-} producing and broadcasting the school programmes in the morning, lunchtime and after school in order to ensure communication between different year groups and classes as well as to enrich school life.
Library	Maintaining the library resources, e.g. mending damaged books and tidying up shelves; staffing the library loan desk in lunch break; promoting the use of the library through planning events or campaigns.
Horticulture/animal keeping	Looking after plants and animals within the school during term time and break.
Newspaper	Publishing the school newspaper and posters to raise children's awareness of the social and school affairs.
Physical exercise	Ensuring the smooth operation of PE classes and sports clubs by maintaining school's sports facilities and equipments, e.g. inflating all balls regularly, tidying up equipment storage spaces, etc.

TABLE 7.7 Examples of clubs (Japan)

Cooking/hand craft	Computer	Manga (Japanese comic)
Music	Reading	Basketball
Gymnastics	Track and field	Tennis
Table tennis	Badminton	Football

A child's voice

When asked about her school life, a Year 2 child stated:

> The subjects I enjoy the most are PE and music, but what I look forward to the most is travelling to and from school with my best friends. What I enjoy the least is math. My teacher always asks 'who can answer this question?' I sometimes don't know the answer, but because everyone puts hands up I also do so. I always feel so stressed and hope I won't be picked!

Similarly to this comment, some other children stated that playing with friends during breaks is what they enjoy the most in school life. This may suggest that a large part of primary school activities emphasise on social elements.

A year in primary school

School events

An academic year starts in April and children take part in a series of school events throughout year. The Course of Study (MEXT, 2008, p.103) sets the purpose of the school events as: 'developing desirable human relationships, deepening a sense of belonging, solidarity, and public welfare, and voluntary and proactive attitudes to build the better school life cooperating with others'. It sets five types of events to take place at primary schools as shown in Table 7.8:

The following section highlights some of the school events to discuss against the above typology and the value fostered through them.

TABLE 7.8 Types of school events (Japan)

Ceremonial events	Add meaningful changes and milestones, provide children with sombre and fresh feelings and motivate them to start a new life.
Cultural events	Provide opportunities to present outcomes of learning, raise motivation to learn and familiarise them with culture and arts.
Health, safety and physical activities	Develop interests in building a healthy mind and body, learn safe behaviours and discipline, familiarise them with physical activities, foster a sense of responsibility and solidarity and improve physical strength.
Excursions and group overnight trips	Enable children to see the wider world and familiarise them with the nature and culture in the environment different from their daily life, and have positive experiences of the appropriate ways of group living and public manners.
Production and volunteer work	Provides children with opportunities to learn the value of labour and joy of production through experience, and fosters the mindset to participate in social welfare activities such as volunteer work.

Source: MEXT, 2008

School event calendar

A life in Japan consists of a series of ceremonies and rituals. As shown in the school events calendar (Table 7.9), children start and graduate from school with a ceremony, and each term starts and ends with a ceremony. It is considered that ceremonies help children integrate into the school and develop a sense of membership. They also serve as milestones with which children switch between 'on' and 'off', which is considered to be an important skill in Japanese value.

At the end of each term, children and teachers perform deep-cleaning tasks such as scrubbing and waxing the floor, cleaning windows, erasing small scratches and drawings on desks and walls. The deep cleaning at the beginning of term is to clean dust that accumulated during the long break and start the new term in a fresh and clean environment. These activities help children develop a sense of responsibility and learn how to handle things with care and respect.

TABLE 7.9 School events calendar (Japan)

Month	Events
Term 1	
April	Entrance ceremony; the beginning-of-term ceremony and deep cleaning; 'welcoming the first year' assembly; health check
May	Day excursion; Year 6 overnight trip; class tutor visits each child's home
June	Swimming lessons begin in PE class; Year 5 summer camp
July	Morning-only classes; extra swimming lessons; deep cleaning; the end-of-term ceremony; summer break begins
August	Summer break; swimming pool opening days supervised by volunteer parents
Term 2	
September	The beginning-of-term ceremony and deep cleaning; swimming lessons end in PE
October	Sports day; day excursion
November	Evacuation drill; Year 5 professional visit; class tutor meets each parent individually
December	Deep cleaning; the end-of-term ceremony; winter break begins
Term 3	
January	The beginning-of-term ceremony and deep cleaning; parents observe a class
February	—
March	'Farewell' assembly for Year 6; graduation ceremony; deep cleaning; the end-of-year ceremony; the academic year ends; spring break begins

Twice a year a school excursion takes place per year group, often one for cultural experiences such as visiting temples and museums, and the other as a social/professional visit, e.g. visiting local council water plants. Children usually bring their own lunchbox and a pack of snacks. Figure 7.3 shows the lunch break on a school excursion, after which children need to make sure they do not leave any waste behind. Years 5 and 6 usually have an overnight trip, a summer camp in Year 5 and another trip in Year 6, which is termed as study completion trip'.

Sports day is a major event; in addition to a range of competitions, each year group practices a mass-game type of performance for weeks in advance. It could be fairly simple group dancing (see Figure 7.4) for earlier years but it becomes more disciplined and highly skilled in the later years (see Figure 7.5). In the latter, children do not only need physical abilities and skills but also to trust each other. Synchronised move is also crucial in this type of performance, hence children need to be able to work with others and perform their roles as expected.

The results of competitions are announced at the closing ceremony (see Figure 7.6) and the winning team receives the trophy and certificate.

FIGURE 7.3 Lunchtime during a school excursion

FIGURE 7.4 Year 2 performance on sports day

FIGURE 7.5 Year 5 performance on sports day

FIGURE 7.6 Children celebrating their victory at the closing ceremony

Current issues

Learning to cooperate = not to compete?

Evidence presented in this chapter highlights the emphasis of Japanese primary education on developing communication skills and identity as a member of a community with a sense of respect, care and cooperation. Some teachers interviewed stated that the strength of the Japanese primary education system is the equal opportunity for education, which leads to diversity of children's skills, traits and personal circumstances within a classroom. One teacher stated:

> Because children are not divided into classes according to their ability, the stronger performers in the class are aware of weaker ones who need some help and the weaker ones know there are stronger performers whom they may be able to catch up with should they work hard enough. This creates a culture of cooperation based on recognising each other's abilities. We also have children with special educational needs studying together; I heard it is very rare in the overseas schools and children could grow up to be self-centred.
>
> (A teacher, Kobe city)

However, it is perceived by some parents and critiques that the efforts to develop a sense of cooperation have gone too far and there are not enough opportunities for competition and subsequent achievement or learning from lessons:

I feel the school is discouraging children to compete; this may be a good thing, but children would not develop competitive spirit and may forget the fact perseverance would reward them. In my child's school they still don't give a score for each test at Year 3. I want teachers to trust children that they can achieve something if they make enough efforts.

(Parent of a Year 3 child, Kobe city)

This practice of not grading the tests seems to be a practice in some regions. While this comment was made by a parent in Kobe city, a teacher in Osaka city commented that they provide a grade to each test from Year 1, but they do not rank children in the sports day competitions except for the winner. This is often described as 'the equal opportunity that has gone too far'; the emphasis on harmony and cooperation gradually transformed to the overprotection of weaker performers. The main purpose of this practice is not to harm the feelings of the weaker performers, however, parents are concerned that children would grow up without learning the importance of perseverance and would develop rather fragile mentalities. There is a general concern that those children who have been 'wrapped up in cotton wool' may not be mentally strong enough to face a competitive world, similar to the past critiques against the 'latitude' curriculum.

Reflective questions

How is creating competition among children perceived in your country? What long-term effect would it have on children's development?

Teachers' workload and skills shortage

The common agreement among all teachers interviewed was that their workload was too heavy, due to a lack of qualified teachers. A class size of up to 40 children seems to be a norm in city schools; one teacher commented that due to a range of issues her school experienced in recent years, the class size was reduced to 35 children per class, which made a positive change. One parent in a less-populated area commented that she liked the small class size in her daughter's school, while there are still 30 children. A large class size affects the level of personal attentions, and one teacher commented that he is unable to make most out of his expertise as he has to teach so many subjects and plan a wide range of activities.

It is also commonly discussed that the quality of teachers has declined over past decades, and some again blame this on the 'latitude' curriculum. As the younger teachers grew up in a non-competitive environment studying much-reduced curriculum, they are sometimes regarded as incompetent and not strong enough to teach children discipline. One parent interviewed in this study felt there was a need for training and development of younger teachers in her child's school. This is indeed an urgent matter, as statistics show that the number of primary school teachers retiring will increase in the next five years while the number of the newly qualified teachers is declining (MEXT 2007, cited by Benesse Corporation, 2008). In an effort to keep the decline to a minimum, the MEXT has increased the number of places available to be qualified and is currently reviewing the teaching qualification framework, however, the main concern is on quality rather than quantity of teachers, hence would be harder to resolve.

Conclusion: developing the right values and attitudes

This chapter discussed the systems, policies and procedures of preschool and primary education in Japan. It became evident that the policies and practices are mostly aimed to develop individuals who cooperate with others to achieve a common aim, largely reflected on Japanese tradition that emphasise the value of harmony. Most academic activities in the early years seem to be directed to develop communication skills through reading and a sense of community through various learning activities inside and outside classrooms, but other daily routines such as the class leader system, lunchtime and cleaning duties, and committee activities all enable children to foster a sense of responsibility, to play a role in a larger group and skills to coordinate activities with others.

The actual voices of children, parents and teachers suggested that OECD/PISA has little influence on Japanese primary education since people do not consider it as a measure of educational success. Many comments made by parents and teachers indicated that people largely believe that children's academic success is a result of developing the right values and attitudes towards oneself and society, hence the results of OECD/PISA are also an indication of children's non-academic skills. This may be the reason why the main concerns expressed were somewhat skewed efforts to develop children's skills and teacher's skills shortage.

These two issues are complex and closely interrelated. Since a large part of primary education is about personal characteristics, resolving these issues is a significant challenge to the government and there may be a need for a drastic change of the teaching qualification framework and curriculum.

Further reading

MEXT (2008) *Course of Study for Kindergarten* [Online]. Available from: www.mext.go.jp/component/english/__icsFiles/afieldfile/2011/04/07/1303755_002.pdf

Whitburn, J. (2003) 'Learning to Live Together: The Japanese Model of Early Years Education', *International Journal of Early Years Education*, Vol.11 No.2, pp.155–179.

Unfortunately the Courses of Study for primary schools are not available in English; however, purpose and contents of each subject is available from the MEXT website:

www.mext.go.jp/english/elsec/1303755.htm

References

Benesse Corporation (2007), 塾・習い事 ～第2回～ [Online]. Available from: http://benesse.jp/berd/data/dataclip/clip0006/index2.html (Accessed on 25 September 2011).

Benesse Corporation (2008), 学校・教員 ～第2回～ [Online]. Available from: http://benesse.jp/berd/data/dataclip/clip0006/index2.html (Accessed on 25 September 2011).

Bureau of Life Long Learning Strategy (2010), 学校基本調査—平成22年度(確定値)結果の概要 [Online]. Available from: www.mext.go.jp/b_menu/toukei/chousa01/kihon/kekka/k_detail/__icsFiles/afieldfile/2010/12/21/1300352_1.pdf (Accessed on 28 September 2011).

Caterer and Hotelkeeper (2007), 'School Food in Japan' [Online]. Available from: www.catererandhotelkeeper.co.uk/Articles/25/04/2007/313302/school-food-in-japan.htm (Accessed on 25 September 2011).

Cooperation Promotion Office (2006), こども園パンフレット, Tokyo: Cooperation Promotion Office for Ministry of Education, Culture, Sports, Science and Technology and Ministry of Health, Labour and Welfare.

Elementary and Secondary Education Bureau (2011), *The Revisions of the Courses of Study for Elementary and Secondary Schools* [Online]. Available from: www.mext.go.jp/english/elsec/__icsFiles/afieldfile/2011/03/28/1303755_001.pdf (Accessed on 29 August 2011).

Elementary and Secondary Education Planning Division (2005), *Reform of Compulsory Education* [Online]. Available from: www.mext.go.jp/english/elsec/1303526.htm (Accessed on 15 August 2011).

Fujita, H. (2005), 教育の未来にとって真の課題とはなにか 「誤った問題設定による改革の推進は更なる混乱を招く」BERD, No.1, June 2005.

MEXT (2008), 小学校学習指導要領, Tokyo: Ministry of Education, Culture, Sports, Science and Technology.

MEXT (2010), 生きる力, Tokyo: Ministry of Education, Culture, Sports, Science and Technology.

Whitburn, J. (2003) 'Learning to Live Together: The Japanese Model of Early

Years Education', *International Journal of Early Years Education*, Vol.11 No.2, pp.155–179.

Education in Latvia

Mara Dirba

Acknowledgements

I would like to acknowledge support of the colleagues from the University Educational Circle.

Introduction

The goal of this chapter is to provide an insight into the situation and problems of education in Latvia. The chapter presents a broad overview on early years and primary education in Latvia. It begins by providing an insight into some background on the historical, social and cultural influences that have shaped the education system. Further on, general information about how the phases of education are divided (early years, primary, secondary, etc.) and variance in provision between public/private, etc. are described. Areas of the curriculum, teaching and learning, and assessment in pre-school and primary education in Latvia are explored. In conclusion, challenges of the educational system in Latvia are discussed.

Education in post-communist Latvia has undergone considerable change from a Soviet totalitarian educational system based on communist ideology to a democratic educational system in the European Union (EU). It has been a long step-by-step process and has been reflected in pre-school and primary education curricula, teaching and learning, and assessment. The situation in Latvia can be characterized by constant changes, complex language issues (reform, bilingual education, referendum) and historical wounds (16 March, 9 May) that are difficult to deal with in education. Latvia is one of the poorest states in the EU and this fact is reflected in financing of education as well as growing up in families where sometimes there is just grandmother/grandfather left to take care of the child, as both parents are earning money outside Latvia.

Latvia is a small country in the eastern part of Europe on the coast of the Baltic Sea. Its territory is 64,589 sq. km. Currently the number of inhabitants of Latvia is 2 million. According to Hazan (2011) at least 200,000 people have left Latvia during the last five years and 100,000 people in total will keep emigrating from Latvia for yet another three to four years (Hazan, 2011). In addition, the birth rate has decreased in Latvia.

Due to its good geographical position on the crossroads of the trade routes between the East and the West, Latvia has a very complicated history. As the results of different wars, the territory of Latvia was taken over by Germans, Poles, Swedes and Russians.

The Republic of Latvia was founded on 18 November 1918 and after just 22 years it was occupied by the Soviet Union (in 1940). It managed to regain its independence after more than 50 years (in 1991). Thousands of Latvians were deported to Siberia between 1940–1942 and 1945–1949. In 1935 the proportion of Latvians was 77 percent of the population, but in 1989 only 52 percent. During the Soviet rule, as the result of the immigration of about 1.5 million Russians, Belorussians and Ukrainians, the ethnic composition drastically changed.

According to the Population Census (Population Census, 2011) major ethnic groups in Latvia are: Latvians 57.7 percent, Russians 29.6 percent, Belorussians 4.1 percent, Ukrainians 2.7 percent, and Poles 2.5 percent. In reality, basically two languages are used: Latvian and Russian, because the majority of Belorussians and Ukrainians speak Russian. Both the Latvian and Russian languages are Indo-European languages, but while Latvian is Baltic, Russian is a Slavic language. Latvian writing uses a Latin alphabet, but Russian uses a Cyrillic alphabet. Thus, we can see that both languages are rather different. On the one hand it is a challenge, on the other hand it might be used as a good resource for developing meta-linguistic competences of the inhabitants of Latvia. In reality, the language situation has become tense and the politicians provoke people to conflicts. It is reflected also in education. Minority school teachers have reported many cases when the pupil refuses to learn the Latvian language. The official language in Latvia is Latvian (one of the two Baltic languages), but on 18 February 2012 there was referendum on the question: "Are you for the draft law – *Amendments to the Latvian Republic Constitution* – which provides for the Russian language to be established as a second state language?" The referendum results showed that the majority of people in Latvia prefer to have only Latvian as the official language.

Childhood is conceived as an important period of life and much effort is invested in promoting manifold development of the child at pre-School and primary school. Education, as such, is valued highly in the society of Latvia. Parents believe that getting quality education is crucial for the future competitiveness and quality life of the child. Therefore, most parents are searching for the best pre-school and primary school for their child.

The system of education in Latvia

Due to the history and ethnic composition, the language situation in Latvia is complex and tense. Language is a symbol of identity and provokes strong emotions. The language of instruction is Latvian in most schools, but Latvia has also state-financed ethnic minority schools or classes at primary through upper secondary level where lessons are partially presented in Belorussian, Estonian, Hebrew, Lithuanian, Polish, Roma, Russian and Ukrainian.

There have been significant changes in education management, financing and evaluation after regaining independence. Education Law (1998; last amended in January 2007) and the National Education Standards envisage the strategic goals and main tasks of compulsory curricula. It took a long time to shift from the centralized decision-making characteristic during the Soviet era to democratic decision-making processes.

The levels of education are: pre-school and early childhood care, basic (primary and lower secondary), upper secondary education and higher education. Educational standards and regulations regarding assessment of learning achievement for the compulsory school are drafted by the National Centre for Education. It is a national administrative body reporting directly to the Minister of Education and Science. It develops curriculum for pre-school and basic school, and develops subject standards and sample teaching-learning programs that are approved by the Cabinet of Ministers. Learning achievements of students are assessed through examinations, organized both at school level and centrally at national level.

TABLE 8.1 Education in Latvia

Education Levels	Students' age	Funding	Organizing learning process
Pre-school education – up to five years	Children aged 1–5	State organized and private	Free play and structured activities
Pre-school education – two years compulsory Preparing for basic school Environment: pre-school or basic school	Children aged 5–7	State organized and private	Integrated program for six year olds
Basic education – nine years	Students aged 7–16	State organized and private	Basic school programs, standards
Secondary education – three years	Students aged 16–18	State organized and private	Secondary school programs, standards
Higher education – three years (Bachelors degree) plus two years (Masters degree) plus three years (Doctorate)	Students starting from 19	State organized and private	Study programs according to the area of studies

The educational system is administered on three levels – national, municipal and institutional. The Parliament, Cabinet of Ministers and Ministry of Education and Science are the main decision-making bodies on the national level. Public primary and secondary general education in Latvia is free of charge and is financed from the municipal budget. However, there are also some private pre-schools and primary schools. It should be taken into consideration that before regaining independence, Latvia was part of the Soviet Union where private schools were not allowed and there are no long-standing traditions and experience of opening and managing a private school. Thus, the majority of pre-schools and basic schools are public.

The goal of education is that young people would be able to build a knowledge-based society that is integrated and inclusive.

As there are not enough municipality pre-schools and the parents have to wait in a long queue to get the place in the municipality pre-school for their child, especially in Riga, the number of private pre-schools is increasing. The municipality is organizing competition, so that private pre-schools might receive co-financing and as a result parents can afford to send their children to private pre-schools.

World ranking PISA

Latvia has been involved in the Programme for International Student Assessment (PISA) since 2000. PISA 2012 research results will be known only in December of 2013. Thus, the most recent data available at the moment are from PISA 2009.

According to Geske et al. (2010, p.106), in 2009 the average achievements of Latvian students in mathematical competence did not statistically differ from the achievements of students from Hungary, the USA, Ireland, Portugal, Spain, Italy and Lithuania (ibid., p.107). The average achievements of Latvian students in mathematics (482 points) are below OECD states average level (496 points); only in a few European countries were the achievements worse than in Latvia (Greece, Rumania, Bulgaria and Balcan states). From all 65 countries participating in PISA 2009, the rank of Latvia is between the 32nd and 37th place.

The average achievements of Latvia, according to the combined reading scale, are 484 points which is statistically significantly lower than the average achievements in OECD countries.

According to achievements in reading (ibid., p.54) Latvia is in the group of eight countries that take the 27th–34th place in the reading achievement scale with the achievements in reading being not statistically different from Portugal, Makao (China), Italy, Slovenia, Greece, Spain, the Czech Republic and Slovakia.

According to Geske et al. (2010, p.127) average achievements of Latvian students in sciences do not differ statistically from students of the USA, the Czech Republic, Norway, Denmark, France, Iceland, Sweden, Austria, Portugal, Lithuania, Slovakia, Italy, Spain and Croatia. The average achievements of Latvian students (494 points) are statistically significantly below the average level of OECD countries (501 points), but the difference is not big (it is only seven points). From all 65 countries participating in PISA 2009, the rank of Latvia is between 25 and 35. It is higher than in mathematics.

The PISA ranking results show that much improvement is needed in pedagogical processes and practices in Latvia to ensure the competitiveness of Latvian students in the world.

Pedagogic practices

The goal of pre-school education is to promote the general development of a child and his/her readiness to start primary education. It is compulsory for five and six year olds to be prepared for primary school by attending pre-school or by attending preparatory groups in the primary school.

Basic education is compulsory and lasts for nine years. The content of primary education is determined by the state standard of basic education.

The full basic education programme is realized by educational institutions called basic schools. The first four grades' programme is realized by educational institutions called basic schools. The first four grades' programmes can be realized by primary schools that can be separate or as part of a basic school.

Educational content

The content of education is adjusted more and more to suit the needs of the individual and society, to prepare children for life in the 21st century.

TABLE 8.2 Indicative subjects for a child aged six in Latvia

		1A	1B	1C	2.a	2.b
MONDAY	1.	Music	The Latvian language	Housekeeping and technology	Matemātika	Matemātika
	2.	Mathematics	The Latvian language	Visual arts	Ētika/Kristīgā mācība	Dabaszinības
	3.	Natural sciences	Music	Mathematics	Sports	Latviešu valoda
	4.	The Latvian language	Visual arts	Music	Latviešu valoda	Sports
	5.	—	Visual arts	Social sciences	—	Ētika/Kristīgā mācība
TUESDAY	1.	The Latvian language	The Latvian language	Mathematics	Matemātika	Matemātika
	2.	The Latvian language	Social sciences	Ethics/Christian education	Dabaszinības	Latviešu valoda
	3.	Ethics/Christian education	Matemātika	The Latvian language	Latviešu valoda	Sociālās zinības
	4.	Visual arts	Ethics/Christian education	The Latvian language	Mūzika	Latviešu valoda
	5.	Visual arts	Natural sciences	—	Latviešu valoda	Mūzika
WEDNESDAY	1.	Mathematics	The Latvian language	Sports	Mājturība un tehnoloģijas	Matemātika
	2.	Sports	The Latvian language	The Latvian language	Mājturība un tehnoloģijas	Latviešu valoda
	3.	The Latvian language	Mathematics	Mathematics	Latviešu valoda	Mājturība un tehnoloģijas
	4.	Housekeeping and technology	Sports	The Latvian language	Latviešu valoda	Mājturība un tehnoloģijas
	5.	Social sciences	—	Housekeeping and technology	Sociālās zinības	—
THURSDAY	1.	Sports	Music	Natural sciences	Matemātika	Klases stunda
	2.	The Latvian language	Mathematics	Music	Vizuālā māksla	Sports
	3.	Music	The Latvian language	The Latvian language	Vizuālā māksla	Latviešu valoda
	4.	Mathematics	Natural sciences	Mathematics	Latviešu valoda	Vizuālā māksla
	5.	Class teachers' lesson	Class teachers' lesson	Class teachers' lesson	—	Vizuālā māksla
FRIDAY	1.	Housekeeping and technology	Sports	The Latvian language	Mūzika	Matemātika
	2.	The Latvian language	Housekeeping and technology	Natural sciences	Sports	Latviešu valoda
	3.	Mathematics	Housekeeping and technology	Sports	Matemātika	Dabaszinības
	4.	Natural sciences	Mathematics	Visual arts	Dabaszinības	Mūzika
	5.	—	—	—	Klases stunda	—

Source: www.zalisaskola.lv/main.php?lapa=sko

Note: This is a real 1st grader's timetable at Rīga Valdis Zālītis Basic School in 2012. There are three parallel 1st grade classes at the school: 1A, 1B and 1C.

New subjects have been included in the learning content: civil sciences, economics and ethics. At the moment, learning the first foreign language (English) starts at the 3rd grade, but in future it will start from the 1st grade. Most parents want their children to start learning English at pre-school.

On the other hand, not enough is done at pre-school and primary school to facilitate creativity of children. There are discussions in focus groups at the moment in Latvia on the issue of promoting creativity of children at school. We have excellent possibilities, especially in Riga, to attend different extra classes after school in art, dance, music, sports, in making cartoons, languages, mathematics, science and technical exploration and design, etc.

ICT

Developing ICT skills at basic school is topical; there has been a European Union project to improve the technical basis and learning materials in sciences and mathematics at the basic schools in Latvia. On the other hand, even children who attend pre-school may have learned basic ICT skills at home at the age of four.

Sometimes teaching of ICT is too theoretical at primary schools. Latvian translations of different parts and elements of the computer screen and software are rather bizarre and not used in everyday life. Most people of Latvia use English terminology instead. Thus, Latvian terminology learned at schools is not very useful for life. There is a lack of modern, effective computers in many schools, especially the ones that did not receive financial help from the EU project mentioned above. The supply with the most recent technology and interactive boards depends also on the municipality that the school belongs to and the number of students at school. Some municipalities are richer than others and can afford to give more financial aid to their schools.

Literacy

The literacy level is rather high in Latvia and a variety of teaching/learning materials have been created for promoting reading and writing skills. Child-centred constructivist approaches, cooperative learning methods, are used.

The International comparative study PIRLS (Progress in International Reading Literacy Study) 2006 results (Mullis et al., 2007, p.37) show that from 45 countries participating in the research, reading achievements of Latvian students average scale score was 541 points which put Latvia in 17th place and was significantly above the average score of 500. Thus, the results of Latvian students were above the ones of students from the USA, England, Austria, Canada and France. On the other hand, this result is lower than Latvian students had in PIRLS 2001 (PIRLS, 2006, p.44). In 2001 the reading achievements of Latvian students average scale score was 545 points. The difference is just four points; still, two years after joining the EU it should have been higher, not lower. It will be interesting to see the results of PIRLS 2011 that should be published soon.

As to students' attitude towards reading (see Mullis et al., 2007, p.141), in Latvia in 2006 there was a decreased percentage of students at the high level of SATR (Students' Attitudes Toward Reading). Chart 4.1 (ibid.) shows that the percentage of students with high SATR in Latvia in 2006 was 33 percent and the country was in last place among 45 countries with a significantly below international average of 49 percent.

Further reading

Students' Attitudes Toward Reading (SATR)

Read chapter 4 "Students' Reading Attitudes, Self-Concept, and Out-of-School Activities" (pp.139–156) from Mullis, I.V.S., Martin, M.O., Kennedy, A.M. and Foy, P. (2007) *PIRLS 2006 International Report: IEA's Progress in International Reading Literacy Study in Primary Schools in 40 Countries*. TIMSS & PIRLS International Study Center. Boston: Lynch School of Education, Boston College. Available from http://timss.bc.edu/PDF/PIRLS2006_international_report.pdf

In addition, the percentage of students with low SATR had increased in Latvia significantly since 2001 (by 6 percent). Only the percentage of students with medium SATR (52 precent) had increased by 3 percent since 2001. It was above the international average of 44 percent. The PIRLS Index of Students' Attitudes Toward Reading shows students' views on reading for enjoyment and appreciating books. The majority of students from Latvia tend to have rather negative attitudes towards reading. This tendency can bring a decrease in reading achievements in future and can negatively influence the achievements in other school subjects. Thus, we can conclude that it is necessary to improve the situation and find innovative and enjoyable ways for increasing students' appreciation of reading.

Low results in SATR might be also explained by the fact that many primary school teachers do not pay enough attention to the language and speech problems that children have, such as dyslexia, and do not identify in time the possible language problems that a child might have. Teachers need to identify possible language problems early (in the 1st grade) and help students by using interactive methods, involving a speech therapist and special pedagogue, using ICT (electronic texts and multimodal ways of presentation) for developing reading skills, and using exciting and curiosity stimulating reading content.

Mathematics

Developing mathematical competence in students is one of the priorities in primary education. The results in mathematics have not been improving much since 2004, though a lot of financing has been invested to work out efficient learning materials and strategies for teaching/learning mathematics at basic school. Between 2008 and 2011, an ESF project "Sciences and Mathematics" team has been working out and approbating innovative printed and electronic teaching and learning materials for schools such as films, animations, activities for interactive boards, etc. This material has been available since September 2011 in more than 750 schools in Latvia and also on the project website (www.dzm.lu.lv). It will, however, take a long time to see real results of the project and its influence on students' motivation and achievements.

There is a sample programme for teaching mathematics from grade 1 to grade 9 available at the homepage of the National Centre for Education (http://visc.gov.lv/en/). It deals with aims, learning outcomes, content, sequence and time allocated for learning each mathematical concept and mathematical actions. The learning/teaching content is divided in three groups: grades 1–3, grades 4–6 and grades 7–9. From grade 7 the content of mathematics is divided in two areas: algebra and geometry. The teachers can be rather autonomous in choosing particular teaching/learning activities and text-books for their students. Still, sometimes the inspectors who come to school to check the situation are too bureaucratic and demand too much paperwork instead of being interested in the school environment and what students have learned.

At the moment lots of attention is devoted to facilitating students' and teachers' creativity, to using generative/imaginative activities and to using problem-finding/problem-solving activities.

Approaches to assessment and achievement

At primary school, children are not evaluated by grades, just a description is written about the performance of each child. Starting from grade 5, students' knowledge and skills are evaluated according to a ten-point scale, where ten points signify an excellent performance and one point signifies an extremely weak performance. After graduating from basic school, students are supposed to take centralized examinations. The number and content of the examinations is determined by the Ministry of Education and Science. Students that have positive evaluation in all school subjects, tests and examinations receive a certificate of basic education and an achievement sheet. The documents acknowledging students' basic education grant them the right to continue learning at secondary school. The students that have a negative evaluation in any of their school subjects or examinations receive an attestation that grants them a right to learn in basic level vocational schools.

Curriculums

The content of education is determined by the National Centre for Education. It has developed an integrated learning programme for six-year-old children. The programme has been approbated in a pilot project from 1 September of 2010 until 31 May 2011.

The pre-school education programme prepares children for primary school and includes: the formation of personality, mental, physical and social development; strengthening health; developing creativity, initiative, curiosity and basic Latvian language skills. It is done by playing games.

The standards of basic education are determined by the Regulation No 1027 of the Cabinet of Ministers from 19 December 2006.

Since 1 September 2002, preparatory programmes are compulsory for children from the age of five. According to the Law of Education, the state grants the salaries of the pedagogues who realize education programmes for children from the age of five, both in public and private educational institutions.

In order to ensure the necessary competences according to the findings of pedagogical science and constructivist approaches to curriculum, the Ministry of Education and Science has worked out, and the Cabinet of Ministers has affirmed in 2010, the Regulations on State Guidelines for Pre-school education. The Guidelines are compulsory for everybody who designs pre-school education programmes. According to the normative acts, pedagogues working with pre-school children should have higher education and corresponding professional pre-school qualifications.

The Law on Local Authorities and the Law of Education determine that any local authority has the responsibility to grant the children living in its administrative territory the possibility to receive education in the nearest educational institution to their home.

The local municipality, in coordination with the Ministry of Education and Science, finds, finances, reorganizes and liquidates pre-school institutions and helps parents apply to ensure their child has a place in a pre-school education institution.

Current challenges

At the moment, the problem is that more and more young people cannot find a job in Latvia and move to other countries. School education in Latvia does not prepare them for life and does not develop entrepreneurial competences for improving the economic situation in Latvia. As the birth rate is low and lots of families emigrate from Latvia, the number of pupils is decreasing and the demand for teachers, too. From the school year 2005/2006 the number of pupils in mainstream schools has decreased by 24 percent.

A reform in education is needed. To achieve this goal, the Minister of Education is inviting a variety of stakeholders to a dialogue, organizing round tables and focus group discussions with parents, teachers, policy makers, school principals, teacher education providers, employers, representatives of teacher associations and municipalities, etc. The Minister of Education accepts and is ready to carry out effective innovative and creative ideas for improving the educational system in Latvia. He informs Latvia society about topical issues and activities in education on his video blog. Discussions are about education content, learning and teaching methods; the amount of learning load for students and the length of the school year; financing education; and promoting students' and teachers' innovations and creativity.

Diversity as a resource

Another current challenge is about developing diversity in education; about developing an inclusive attitude and the ability to collaborate with all kinds of people and to view diversity as a resource. Diversity can be viewed as a problem and it can be also viewed as a resource. Inclusive education is when every child is welcomed and valued regardless of family background, ability or disability or any other factor. Inclusive education cannot be implemented without creating an inclusive school environment where all school staff act as a team, where inclusion is a school mission, where special policy and methods are worked out to prevent bullying, to manage peer mediation programmes. The awareness that we are diverse ourselves (our inner diversity, complexity) (Dervin and Dirba, 2006) might help us to understand and manage diversity between people more effectively. Diversity in education deals with different strategies of diversity management that children can start learning from an early age.

One of the ways diversity in education is implemented in Latvia is through bilingual education, which focuses on the integration of pupils from minority families in Latvian society by using the Latvian language as a tool in learning different subjects, for example, physics, chemistry, history, geography and music. One of the main problems with the bilingual education in Latvia is that many Russian-speaking families are not psychologically ready for their children to learn the Latvian language. In addition, many teachers of the Russian schools do not know the Latvian language well enough, so they cannot teach in Latvian. There are also not enough teaching materials for the bilingual education.

The Latvian government has worked very hard to solve these problems by improving the Latvian language skills (Latvian language courses), providing methodological preparation of the teachers (courses of bilingual methodology) and introducing new teaching and studying materials. During the introduction of the bilingual education in Latvia there were many protests (huge demonstrations in Riga with the slogan "Hands off Russian schools!") against the school reform. Different models of the bilingual education have been developed and schools can choose the model that fits their students and teachers. The schools also have the possibility to develop their own bilingual model.

Special educational needs

Another challenge is that many teachers and school principals in Latvia refuse to admit that they have students with disabilities; sometimes it becomes clear that in their understanding, the image of a student with functional disorders is only a student with severe disabilities. There are also still lots of cases of bullying at schools in Latvia and many school principals are trying to hide these cases of bullying and also the fact that they have students with functional disorders, such as learning disorders or language disorders, because they think that otherwise their school would be considered bad; a place where teachers do not teach students effectively. Thus, many students do not receive help early enough when it is most needed in reading, writing and mathematics. Some even are afraid to go to school.

The World Report on Disability stresses that disability refers to difficulties encountered in any or all areas of functioning (World Health Organization, 2011, p. 5). According to the Report, environmental factors (the natural and built environment, support and relationships, attitudes, and services) can facilitate the wellbeing and development of the persons with functional disorders or can become barriers to their effective functioning. Negative attitudes and actions can lead to low self-esteem and reduced participation (ibid., p.6).

More interactive materials and methodological materials to work with students of different kinds of special needs in mainstream schools are needed in Latvia. In order to improve the support for students with disabilities and their parents and teachers, a ESF project "Forming the system of support for students with functional disorders" was launched in Latvia in 2011. The goal of the project is to create a support system for ensuring qualitative education of students with functional disorders and enhancing their inclusion in society. Educational institutions will be provided with methodological and support material for students with special needs who learn both in mainstream schools and special education schools; the material for developing active speech, language and mathematical skills will be worked out.

Conclusions

The situation of education in Latvia is complex due to cultural, historical and economical reasons. Latvian society is almost divided into two communities: Latvian-speaking and

Russian-speaking and the situation with language use is tense at the moment. It is reflected also in education.

Educational reforms are needed as there are lots of problems and challenges. As the new Minister of Education is ready to solve the problems and to carry out the Educational Reform, the situation in education might change dramatically in the next three years.

In order to have really inclusive education in Latvia, much work still has to be done. School principals and teachers need to attend seminars and courses on how to create an inclusive school environment. Effective support systems for pupils with special needs should be established. This process has been started by the ESF project and the ways to ensure profound long-term influence of the project should be found.

Reflective tasks

1) Download the following articles, read them and find some more sources on the Educational Reform in Latvia in 2004. Use any research methods to explore the attitude of pupils, parents and teachers from Latvia towards bilingual education. Express your opinion about the Educational Reform of 2004 and bilingual education in Latvia (write an essay). Do you think it is effective? What might be done differently?

www.mfa.gov.lv/data/visit/12-education.pdf

www.academia.edu/302964/Bilingual_Education_Theater_Behind_the_Scenes_of_Latvian_Minority_Education_Reform

2) Download the following articles on the reform ideas and activities of the Minister of Education. Express your views on his ideas. Do you find them innovative and meaningful? What would you do if you were the Minister of Education of your country?

http://bnn-news.com/survey-29-55-reforms-kilis-47058

http://bnn-news.com/kilis-2012-key-challenge-agree-45694

Please note, since May 2013, Latvia has a new Minister of Education, Vjačeslavs Dombrovskis.

Further reading

Ministry of Education and Science (2008) The Development of Education: National Report of Latvia. [Online]. Available from: www.ibe.unesco.org/National_Reports/ICE_2008/latvia_NR08.pdf (Accessed: 7 January 2011).

Dervin, F. and Dirba, M. (2008) "Figures of Liquid Strangeness: Blending Perspectives from Mobile Academics" from Byram, M. and Dervin, F. (eds) *Students, Staff and Academic Mobility in Higher Education*. Cambridge: Cambridge Scholars Publishing, 237–261.

Dirba, M. (2007) "Intercultural Learning and Language Education" from Krūze, A., Mortag, I. and Schulz, D. (eds) *Sprachen- und Schulpolitik in Multikulturellen Gesellschaften*. Leipzig: Leipziger Universitatsverlag, 101–109.

Nīmante D. Perceptions (2008) Perceptions, Possibilities and Implementation of Inclusive Education in the Latvian Context. Paper presented at the European Conference on Educational Research, University of Vienna, 28–30 September 2009. [Online]. Available from: www.leeds.ac.uk/educol/documents/186702.pdf (Accessed: 5 January 2011).

References

Dervin, F. and Dirba, M. (2006) "On Liquid Interculturality: Finnish and Latvian Student Teachers' Perceptions of Intercultural Competence" from Pietilä, P., Lintunen, P. and Järvinen, H.-M. (eds). *Language Learners of Today. Suomen Soveltavan Kielitieteen Yhdistyksen (AFinLA) Julkaisuja* no.64. Jyvaskyla, 257–271.

Geske, A., Grīnfelds, A., Kangro, A. and Kiseļova, R. (2010) *Ko skolēni zina un prot – kompetence lasīšanā, matemātikā un dabaszinātnēs Latvija OECD valstu Starptautiskajā skolēnu novērtēšanas programmā 2009*. Latvijas Universitāte, Pedagoģijas, psiholoģijas un mākslas fakultāte Izglītības pētniecības institūts, Rīga.

Hazan, M. (2011) Hazan: Another 100 000 People to Leave Latvia. LETA, 21 November. [Online]. Available from: http://bnn-news.com/hazan-100-000-people-leave-latvia-41665 (Accessed: 19 March 2013).

Mullis, I.V.S., Martin, M.O., Kennedy, A.M. and Foy, P. (2007) PIRLS 2006. *International Report: IEA's Progress in International Reading Literacy Study in Primary Schools in 40 Countries*. TIMSS & PIRLS International Study Center. Boston: Lynch School of Education Boston College. [Online]. Available from http://timss.bc.edu/PDF/PIRLS2006_international_report.pdf (Accessed 16 January 2012).

Population Census (2011) [Online]. Available from: www.csb.gov.lv/en/statistikas-temas/population-census-2011-key-indicators-33613.html (Accessed: 3 January 2011).

World Health Organization (2011) *World Report on Disability* [Online]. Available from: http://whqlibdoc.who.int/publications/2011/9789240685215_eng.pdf (Accessed: 8 January 2011).

Education in the Netherlands

Jan Dekker and Jon White

Acknowledgements

I would like to thank the participants in the interviews and discussions for their honesty and patience. To have the real voices of children and young people has brought life to this chapter.

Introduction

The Netherlands is a small country in the north of Europe with a rich and interesting history. A former colonial power, the Dutch navigators travelled the world, taking Dutch culture to the Far East and bringing back spices and other wealth. The relatively recent social and political developments in the European Union have seen the Dutch consolidate their economic strength and become a powerful player in the development of a new Europe.

With a population of just under 17 million, the Dutch have a high percentage of citizens of non-Western origins (11 per cent), reflecting their former colonial status and their openness to immigration. The total population continues to grow steadily.

While Dutch is the native language, the language of Frisian is spoken in the Province of Friesland. English is widely spoken by the majority of Dutch citizens, many of whom also have some fluency in German and French. With a literacy rate of 99.3 per cent, the Dutch can confidently identify themselves as one of the most literate societies in the world.

Successive governments have made education a priority, with the education budget being 11.5 per cent of government expenditure in 2009 (see http://search.worldbank.org/data?qterm=education+budget&_topic_exact%5B%5D=Education for public spending on education 2013). This has allowed the development of not only a solid infrastructure of high-quality buildings and materials, but also a very low pupil: teacher ratio in both primary and secondary education. The Programme for International Student Assessment (PISA: co-ordinated by the OECD) ranks education in the Netherlands significantly higher than the OECD average (OECD 2012).

The Dutch education system is different from that seen in most countries as there is a fundamental choice for 'freedom of education', as stated under the constitutional law. The consequence of this has led to an education with a rich variety of school types. This choice caused another consequence: the impossibility to choose and develop a single National Curriculum. However, within this variety, Dutch education is very well organised and well equipped. It possesses a variety of well-developed teaching methods in all subjects as instruments for teachers and has a very good success rate. The pedagogical aspects of education are well integrated in today's primary education and more or less integrated in secondary education (Letschert et al. 2005).

Nowadays, with a changing society, the shift in Western European countries from production economies to high-tech service economies and the fast moving era of ICT, the context of new Europe is one in which the Dutch people will all face challenges.

Social/cultural influences

Since the national system of education was introduced in the 1800s, the Dutch government has been open to the ideas of change and being flexible in its education provision. The revolution within the Batavian Republic began a series of reforms, leading to the establishment of primary schools in all regions. These had a basic curriculum that the schools were expected to follow. However, in 1848, the constitution was changed to provide 'freedom of education' allowing them to respond to local needs and the social and economic modernisations that were sweeping through Europe. By 1901, education had become compulsory for all children aged 6–12 and there were well-established pathways in secondary education.

The different forms of secondary education were streamlined in 1963, which introduced four differentiated pathways for education. By the 1990s, these had become the three pathways we see today (VMBO – preparation for professional education, HAVO – higher general continued education and VWO – preparatory scientific education), each reflecting the interests, aptitudes and abilities of the students enrolled. Great emphasis is placed through all pathways in the value of information management, autonomy and personal responsibility.

So the underpinning drivers for these changes are the recognition that each student needs to be on the pathway which feels right for them. This 'respect' and 'ownership' characterises the experience of Dutch learners, from early years to the end of their formal education. It is this confidence and resilience that Dutch students take into the workplace, making their individual contribution to the success of the Dutch economic model.

Childhood in this country

Dutch people see themselves as hard-working. This attitude partly comes from the work that has been undertaken to reclaim land from the sea. Controlling water in this way requires many parties to meet and plan together. It has forced them to learn how to work as a team and adopt pragmatic solutions.

This spirit of co-operation is imbedded in the Dutch psyche at an early age. It has resulted in a society that is egalitarian, individualistic and modern. Education, hard work and ambition are valued. Excessive consumption and greed are seen as unpopular and inappropriate.

In order to instil these values in children, the Dutch have invested heavily in providing well for their children. This care begins at home, with both parents contributing to the care of their children. In spite of this, there is still a strong demand for high-quality childcare, recognised as one of the most expensive in Europe. There are long waiting lists for the best places in nurseries, toddler groups and playgroups. An increasing number of 'host parent groups', child-minders and babysitters are seen as a solution to the lack of preschool provision. These services are allowing mothers to remain at work. It is an area where there is likely to be change in the future.

There are significant numbers of Dutch citizens from the former Dutch colonies and other parts of the world. This includes Surinam, Aruba, the Dutch Antilles, Turkey, Indonesia and Morocco. The attitude of the Dutch government has been quite liberal and open towards the provision of citizenship, but in recent years there has been a narrowing of the criteria. This has made it more difficult to gain Dutch citizenship, a reflection of the social and economic pressures all countries are experiencing.

As a consequence, the experience of some minority communities has not been as inclusive as it might have been and there is recognition by government that more needs to be done to support the children of minority groups. This is a typical Dutch approach, to recognise and deal with a problem in a practical and organised way.

Reflect on these two childhoods

Case study 1: Mirjam

I grew up in a little village called Twisk in the west of the Netherlands. My mother and father considered my brother and I to be little adults so we were taught to take responsibility at an early age. We lived on a farm. There were animals – including a pony and some chickens, rabbits, ducks and fish. We played a lot outside. When the weather was bad, we had some computer games – nothing like the ones today!

When I was 2 years old I went to nursery. I loved to play with the other children and to sing songs. When I was 4 years old, I went to Primary School. This was a public school in the village – about 170 children. I now know that there were 10 teachers and 8 classes. It was a traditional school with lessons "from the books".

All the children were from our village. There were no immigrants.

We were able to play outside on the swings and the slide and the climbing frame.

What I remember best are the music lessons where the teacher played his accordion and taught us songs.

There were "reading mothers" who came in to help the children with their reading; they helped all the children – not just those who found reading hard.

When I finish at school, I will stay and work on the farm.

Case study 2: Ahmet

I was born in Almelo in the east of the Netherlands. My father came to the Netherlands in the 1960s. My oldest sister was born in Turkey and when she was 1 year old, she and my mother came to the Netherlands to join my father. My other sisters and my brother and I were all born here. The rest of our family – uncles and aunts and cousins – all live in Turkey.

I have attended kindergarten, primary school, HAVO and accelerated high school. I have worked hard and been a good student.

In my primary school, there were 12 children whose parents came from Turkey. They all did well because they had to make sure that they were able to get a good job and not just be "another immigrant". When I finish being a student, I will be a teacher and so knowing Dutch, Turkish and English means I will be able to work with children and adults to help their language improve.

Primary provision – assessment and achievement

Between the ages of four and twelve, children attend elementary school (*basisschool*). This school has eight grades or groups, called groep 1 through to groep 8. School attendance is compulsory from groep 2 (age five), but almost all children start school at age four (in groep 1). Groeps 1 and 2 used to be held in a separate institution like a kindergarten (*kleuterschool* – or toddlers' school) until they were merged with elementary schools in 1985.

From groep 3 onwards, the children will learn to read, write and do arithmetic. Most schools teach English in groeps 7 and 8, although some start in groep 4.

The school day begins at 8.30am and has a lunch break in the middle of the day. The children leave at 3.30pm, although some may stay longer if there are special activities for them.

One point to notice here is that the teachers usually have lunch with the children and all will eat the typical Dutch lunch of bread, eggs, cheese and ham. There is a tradition of this simple food and eating together that is not always seen in other countries.

In groep 8, the vast majority of schools will administer an aptitude test called *Cito Eintoets Basisonderwijs* developed by the *Centraal Institute voor toetsontwikkeling*. The outcome of this is to be able to recommend the type of secondary education best suited for a pupil. In recent years, this test has gained authority, but the recommendations of the groep 8 teacher, along with the opinions of the pupil and their parents, remain a crucial factor in choosing the right type of secondary education.

The Cito test is not mandatory. Some schools administer the *Nederlandse Intelligentietest voor Onderwijsniveau* (NIO – *toets*) or the *Schooleindonderzoek*.

A considerable number of elementary schools are based on a particular educational philosophy, including Montessori, Pestalozzi Plan, Dalton Plan, Jena Plan or Freinet. Most of these are public schools, but some special schools also base themselves on one of these educational philosophies. They receive funding from the government if they meet the inspection standards.

Pedagogic practices

The Dutch education system is organised to teach young citizens how to read, write and do sums as well as to transfer cultural history. These are core values for Dutch society as there is an expectation that children from a very young age will look at the past and learn from it. There is a general sense of co-operation that exists in most schools, where generic competencies are encouraged to develop. The teachers are the best examples of this and are expected to be good role-models for the children.

When you consider how the different types of schools have flourished, it is interesting to see that it is the openness of Dutch society that values difference. It is a foreign notion to Dutch teachers to have an imposed National Curriculum, although some teachers welcome recent guidance from the government that has given stronger policies regarding the content of what is taught.

But it is a strength of the Dutch system that there is a strong emphasis on active learning. Children are involved in the classes and listened to by their teachers. Dutch children are recognised by UNESCO (United Nations Educational, Scientific and Cultural Organization) as some of the 'happiest' children in the world and so it is important to ask how that has happened. One mechanism that might help explain this is the concept of 'social pedagogy'.

This a phrase used in some northern European countries to describe the work of a wide range of professionals who work in the community. They may embrace health workers (occupational therapists), social workers in residential settings and work with young offenders. It can extend to faith communities and may be considered to represent co-ordinated engagement with the complexities of childhood and children's services (Galuske 2009).

The underpinning tradition of the social pedagogue is that they are primarily concerned with the happiness of the person. This is expressed through understanding them in a holistic way. This has been described as the 'Continental tradition' and recognises the importance of social cohesion and a sense of belonging to a community (Eriksson and Markström 2003). The three features of this approach are a concern with

1. The nature of mankind – a sense of belonging and the need for social interaction and inclusiveness.
2. The social context – a sense that it is essential to consider the impact of inequalities and to recognise their potential for damaging people, families and communities.
3. The pedagogical influences – how people, policy makers and academics have their thinking challenged.

The interpretation and continued development of these features draw on modern writers (such as Peter Moss and Iram Sirij-Blatchford) as well as the classics from Rousseau, Dewey, Pestalozzi and Freire.

Activity

Consider the phrase 'where care and education meet'.

What defines the difference between *care* and *education*?

If you were writing a job description, what are the key characteristics you would look for in a potential new member of your team?

The history of social pedagogy goes back a long time, to ancient Greece. Castle (1961) explores this tradition, noting that the first pedagogues were probably educated slaves, expected to supervise the children of the boys of the household. They taught them manners and courtesy as well as reading, writing and traditional customs. They were part of the household and must have been good all-rounders in order to maintain their position.

Karl Mager (1810–1858) is said to have first used the term *sozial padagogik* in 1844, but it is the Prussian philosopher Freidrich Diesterweg (1790–1866) who brought the term into common use. He advocated the connection of theory and practice generally, as well as the belief in learning by doing. Throughout the nineteenth century, German, French, English and Dutch writers continued to explore this notion, but it was in the twentieth century that it gained a political momentum with the rise of national socialism. The state was in a position to take the social elements of this inclusive philosophy and use it to break down the influence of grouping such as family, community and church, leading to an atomisation of the individual. The state penetrated the most intimate parts of life, perhaps illustrated by the popularity of *Volk* camps for young people where the state could strengthen the bonds of comradeship – creating an 'us' and 'them' social construction (Schiedeck and Stahlman 1991). It is now recognised that, while any education philosophy can be taken to an extreme and abused, the principles *behind* this approach have much to commend them.

While this strategy has been a great influence in the Dutch view of education, it continues to make only slow progress in the English speaking world. However, the Scottish Executive (2003) issued a discussion paper to explore community learning and to promote discussion on the 'best' ways of engaging communities in their own development, leading to the creation of a 'new profession' – the Scottish pedagogue (Children in Scotland 2008). This has become a strand of Dutch government policy as the economic needs of some communities have become strikingly high. It is hoped that this approach, which has been so successful in the Netherlands and a range of European countries, will be explored critically in the future and may find a place in other societies as well.

Brief systems in older age groups

As discussed previously, there is a strong belief in the Netherlands that education is important. So we have different routes for students of different aptitudes. A balanced society needs a range of skilled citizens, so the education system needs to prepare children for the right work for them as individuals.

This is achieved in two ways. The first way is to put together the opinion of the teacher with the results of the (optional) Cito test to give an indication of the right form of secondary education. The second way is for the children to be encouraged to think about where they see themselves going and to reflect on their own strengths and weaknesses.

This is not something that is just done in the final year at school, but something that is developed over time and involves great discussion with the child, their parents and the teachers. It reflects the openness of Dutch teachers to listen and to respect the children and their decisions. After all, whether a practical route (VWO) or a more academic route (VMBO) is chosen, they will all have the same opportunity to enter master's level at university.

At the age of 12, pupils enter a transition period of two years in secondary education to find out what kind of follow-up education would fit to their situation. So a choice for

VMBO (preparation for professional education) leads to MBO (literally: middle level professional education); HAVO (higher general continued education) leads to HBO (higher professional education); and VWO (literally: preparatory scientific education) leads to university.

In the Netherlands many students take a longer route to higher education; after primary school they enter VMBO and MBO (highest level 4) and then continue to a related HBO bachelor education that offers a shorter route for students with this MBO level 4 diploma. After this, they can continue to a university level. The system of reasonable grants provides for these longer routes.

The government gives final terms for each stage in the educational system but the schools are free to choose in which way they will meet the criteria described by the government. However, at the end of secondary education there are exams on a national level for each type of school.

When a school succeeds in demonstrating this ability to meet the criteria, they will be funded by the government, so all schools, public and private, have to use the same goals and are all paid by the government in the same way.

Primary and secondary education in the Netherlands is free of charge. Professional education and scientific education are charged with a contribution of the parents or student themselves. For higher education, this annual tuition fee is around €1,500, considerably lower than in most other European countries.

Until the age of 18, part time (at least two days a week, including on-the-job-training) schooling is compulsory.

Assessment matters

The Dutch educational system has a complex structure of monitoring learning progress and testing. Although not compulsory, many schools made the choice to use the monitoring and evaluation system of Cito, a 'former governmental' system for monitoring and evaluation of education. This is not only for reasons to please the educational inspectorate, but also for

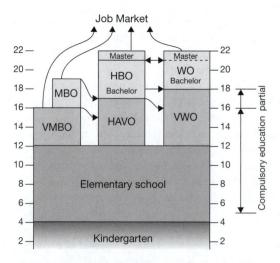

FIGURE 9.1 Schematic representation of the Dutch educational system

economic and public relation reasons. For example, both parents and secondary educators tend to use the Cito results of the final test at the end of primary education to classify the quality of the school and to predict the chances of successfully passing the chosen school for secondary education.

When pupils enter primary education at the age of four they are diagnosed on various aspects of development, but the language learning is the most important aspect. During the primary school period, the monitoring structures on development of reading, writing and mathematics are systematically used. At the end of primary education, schools have to provide an educational report in which the development on the prime subjects is described and an adviser is given for follow up education. Almost 85 per cent of the Dutch primary schools use the final test of Cito for this. The scores of this test give access to a certain type of secondary education.

In secondary education, students first have to enter a basic period of two years and then have to choose for a 'content profile'.

At the end of secondary education there is a structure with both school exams and a final exam; an average of school exams and final exams leads to the final grade for a subject.

However, not all subjects of the chosen profile are assessed in the final examination and this reflects the flexibility in the system that is available to individual schools.

International comparisons

'God made the world, but the Dutch made Holland' is a popular folk saying from the Netherlands. It is clear that the Netherlands has made a great impact on the world for such a small country. Dutch people have a track record of success in a range of areas from sport (football in particular), business (Shell, Philips and pharmaceuticals) and culture (van Gogh and Vermeer are two well-known Dutch painters).

The government has invested heavily in all levels of education, but it is the higher education sector that has really made a difference to the economic success of the Netherlands. The country is peppered with good educational provision and this is typical of the Dutch commitment to equality. The 'tall poppy syndrome' (where to stand out is seen as bad manners) has led to a prevalence of good team players.

The Times Higher Education World University Rankings confirms this, with 12 out of the 13 Dutch universities making the top 200 world ranking. However, no Dutch university was in the top 50. As a result, the government is hoping to sharpen the focus of the university sector and there is serious competition between the leading institutions to become the national leader for research and development.

Reflect

What do you see as the key purpose of higher education and a university degree? Is it to ensure that you have good prospects in the job market OR is it for you to develop your interests and personal education?

However, not all Dutch citizens will go to university. Some will enter the job market at the age of 18. Here, it is clear that they are still good employees. PISA (2011) comparisons suggest that the Netherlands is a strong international performer in a wide range of areas. For example, the mathematics level is 16th out of 66 and reading is 10th out of 66 in the world.

Further skill analysis suggests that when it comes to 'reading and reflecting', Dutch students are even higher at 5th in the world, with 'reflecting and evaluating' not far behind.

Whatever the Dutch teachers are doing, it is working – and there is a co-ordinated national strategy that presents a culture of applied practical knowledge to drive a successful economy.

Consider

While many Dutch children are doing well and getting good grades, what help is there for those children who come from homes where Dutch is not the first language? Are they able to be part of the Netherlands success story?

Current challenges

The key challenge for early years is to have enough high-quality childcare at prices that ordinary families can pay. This is a long-term objective. It is seen as important for all children to have access to this but in some of the big cities and some of the rural communities it is a challenge.

Another challenge is to raise the levels of education in some of the minority communities. This applies in particular to girls, many of whom do not complete their formal education. To invest in this area of provision, through the mechanisms of the social pedagogue, is a long-term objective. This is, of course, not only a problem in the Netherlands; but the Dutch are going to look at this and solve this problem in the usual way – by discussing and planning and then by doing.

Our final challenge is to continue the growth of the Dutch economy. There is competition with other countries and economic blocks, where people will not have such a high cost of living. With lower wages, it is possible to make things cheaper and this is powerful competition for Dutch companies working abroad. Therefore, we will go back to the basic idea that we are innovators and hard-working people who look at problems and work together to find answers.

Conclusion

As we have seen in this review, the Dutch education system is doing well. We are nurturing our young people in ways that reproduce the culture that we have known and developed for many years.

From the early years, there is a balance of care between both parents who both play their part traditionally. When in school, children are given challenges, but also they are listened to and given the time they need to develop knowledge and understanding. Then they go through to secondary education where there is again a listening to the children and encouragement for them to follow pathways that are felt to be right for their future.

However, it is in the training of teachers and the wide range of adults who work with children that the Dutch provision is able to pass on the secrets of success.

References

Castle, E. B. (1961) *Ancient education and today*. Harmondsworth: Pelican.

Children in Scotland (2008) *Working it out: developing the children's sector workforce*. Edinburgh: Children in Scotland.

Eriksson, L. and Markström, A.-M. (2003) 'Interpreting the concept of social pedagogy' in Anders Gustavsson, Hans-Erik Hermansson and Juha Hämäläinen. *Perspective and theories in social pedagogy*. Göteborg: Daidalos.

Galuske, M. (2009) *Flexible sozialpadagogik*. Weinheim und Munchen: Juventa Verlag.

Letschert, J., Thijs, A. and Paus, H. (2005) *The learner in the centre: trends in Primary Education in the Netherlands*. Enschede: SLO.

OECD (2012) *Education at a glance: OECD indicators 2012*. Available from: www.keepeek.com/ Digital-Asset-Management/oecd/education/education-at-a-glance-2012_eag-2012-en (Accessed on 19 March 2013).

Schiedeck, J. and Stahlman, M. (1991) *Education to the community, read by the community: the disciplining of the people in Nazi Germany*. Bollert: K T Verlag.

10

Education in Australia and New Zealand

Simon Brownhill

Acknowledgements

The author would like to dedicate this chapter to Carolyn Randell for her incredible help, support and advice during the writing of this chapter. He would also like to offer his sincere thanks to Daniel Green, Jane Keeling, Adam and Penny McQuilkin, and Graham Crews.

Introduction

There are many words which can be used to describe Australia and New Zealand: diverse, isolated, breathtaking, friendly, unusual, green, dynamic, desolate, majestic, warm, fresh, and independent are but a few. Located in the Southern Hemisphere, Australia is one of the largest countries in the world by total area, being made up of the mainland Australian continent, the island of Tasmania and numerous smaller islands in the Indian and Pacific Oceans. New Zealand, which is located to the south-east of Australia, comprises of two main land masses known as the North Island and the South Island, along with numerous smaller islands. Populated by approximately 22 million people (Australia) and 4.5 million people (New Zealand) both countries may be considered 'unique' when one reflects on their respective climates, animals, natural landscapes, flora and fauna, and cultural traditions which stem from the Aboriginal and Torres Strait Islander peoples in Australia and the Māori and Polynesian population in New Zealand.

This chapter focuses its attention on select aspects of educational provision and practice which is offered to children in Australia and New Zealand. Discussions will be based around two Cs, these being *curriculums* and the notion of *'world class'*. The chapter begins by exploring ways in which educational provision for children in Australia and New Zealand is highly regarded on the 'international education stage'.

'The culture of the countries'

There are many other aspects which contribute to Australian and New Zealand culture; these include: sports (**very** important to the Aussies and Kiwis!), music, literature and art. In an effort to develop a personal understanding of these aspects, particularly in relation to the contribution made by the indigenous peoples found in each country, consider visiting the following websites:

Australia

- www.indigenousaustralia.info
- www.creativespirits.info/aboriginalculture/education
- www.aussieeducator.org.au/tertiary/subjects/history/australian/culture.html

New Zealand

- www.mch.govt.nz
- http://activenewzealand.com/resources/new-zealand-culture.php
- www.educationalleaders.govt.nz/Leading-change/Manaakitanga-leading-with-moral-purpose/Creating-Culturally-Safe-Schools-for-Maori-Students

Reflect on the influence of culture on educational provision for children as you engage with these websites and with the remainder of this chapter.

The notion of 'world class'

On a worldwide scale including 65 countries, evaluation findings of the Programme for International Student Assessment (PISA) (OECD, 2009) ranked the Australian education system as 9th in the world for reading, 10th for science and 15th for mathematics; the New Zealand education system was ranked even higher; for reading it was ranked 7th in the world along with science (7th) and 13th for mathematics. In comparison, the UK was ranked 25th for reading, 16th for science and 28th for mathematics.

World rankings – 'getting an overview'

Visit www.guardian.co.uk/news/datablog/2010/dec/07/world-education-rankings-maths-science-reading for a visually comprehensive summary offered by Shepherd (2010) about the OECD's (2009) comprehensive world education ranking report, PISA. Alternatively, download a copy of the *PISA 2009 Results: Executive Summary* which is available at www.oecd.org/dataoecd/34/60/46619703.pdf.

By reflecting on the statistics above, one is likely to question what it is that settings and schools in Australia and New Zealand are doing which result in children acquiring these 'world class' literacy and numeracy skills. This section will offer a response to this consideration by focusing its attention on two key factors which contribute to these impressive world rankings: *pedagogic practices* and *approaches to assessment and achievement*.

Pedagogic practices

ICT and literacy in Australia

In 2008 the Department of Foreign Affairs and Trade reported that the Australian government was investing $1 billion 'to deliver access to world class information communication technology (ICT) based teaching and learning in Australian schools' (A.S Edugroup, 2011). This initiative, based on a promise made by the Labour government, was purposefully designed to 'support students to acquire the skills and knowledge needed to participate in society and employment in a digital world' (ibid.: 6). Provision of this nature is clearly designed to capitalise and build on the seemingly developed ICT skills of Australian children (see Ainley, 2010: 4–6).

Through the use of ICT applications and multimedia resources, children in Australia are able to attend classes which operate as a 'digital classroom' – access to small personal computers allow children to communicate with others and complete coursework both at school and at home; video conferencing and multimedia learning resources enable distance learning for some students and schools. The use of various ICT hardware and software in Australian classrooms supports a wealth of development in relation to children's literacy skills: from speaking and listening skills using webcams, microphones and Dictaphones, to reading e-books and writing with a purpose through e-mail, wikis and blogs. Kunyung Primary School in Victoria, Australia (visit www.kunyung.vic.edu.au), for example, proudly offers children access to the Information Technology Centre which has a computer laboratory with 16 stations with internet access to facilitate research activities; in the UK many children have similar access to computers which are located in an ICT suite in their primary school. It should be noted, however, that this is common in most schools.

Mathematics in New Zealand

Anthony and Walshaw (2009: 148) identify ten principles of effective pedagogy in mathematics that 'develop mathematical capability and disposition within an effective learning community'. These principles (all of which are explained in more detail in Anthony and Walshaw's research paper) range from *teacher knowledge and care* and *mathematical communication* to *an ethic of care* and *building on students' thinking*. Of particular interest is the principle of *making connections* where it is argued that 'making connections across mathematical topics is important for developing conceptual understanding' (Anthony and Walshaw, 2009: 156):

> For example, the topics of fractions, decimals, percentages, and proportions, while learning areas in their own right, can usefully be linked through exploration of differing representations (e.g. ½ = 50%) or through problems involving everyday contexts (e.g. determining fuel costs for a car trip).
>
> (Anthony and Walshaw, 2009: 156)

The practice of making connections to real life experiences is also advocated: 'When students find they can use mathematics as a tool for solving significant problems in their everyday lives, they begin to view the subject as relevant and interesting' (Anthony and Walshaw, 2009: 156). Practical examples of this are offered by the author in Table 10.1.

TABLE 10.1 Examples of 'real life' activities and how these relate to key mathematical knowledge and understanding for children of different ages in New Zealand

Age group	Example of a real life activity	Links to mathematical knowledge and understanding
0–5	Sorting and matching freshly laundered socks.	Identifying similar characteristics, concept of a pair (two of the same), matching skills.
5–9	Pulling empty cardboard packaging apart ready for recycling.	3D objects are made from flat shapes, 2D shapes, the notion of 'nets' and 'solids'.
10–13	Playing an 'end of term' board game with a dice.	Concepts of probability and chance.

The New Zealand curriculum for mathematics

Visit www2.nzmaths.co.nz/frames/curriculum/index.aspx and engage with the 'interactive' New Zealand curriculum for mathematics. Identify any ideas, strategies or approaches to learning and teaching which you could adopt as part of your own provision and practice to enhance and enrich the learning experiences of the children you work with.

Approaches to assessment and achievement

Digital learning portfolios in Australia

An exciting approach to the recording of children's school achievements relates to the discussion offered about ICT and literacy provision for children in Australia where there is evidence of literacy based work contributing to individuals' *digital learning portfolios* (electronic collections of students' work). O'Rourke (2004: 1) reports on how Australian teachers working with the Australian National Schools Network have used these portfolios 'that richly represent the learner and provide authentic evidence of learning. They demonstrate evidence of the student's efforts, progress and achievements in one or more areas, and illustrate a learning journey.' The State of Victoria (Department of Education and Early Childhood Development) (2010: 17) asserts that in the past 'students have used flash drives or USB memory sticks to transfer work, which can result in work being lost or files being incompatible with other computers'. E-portfolios alleviate this issue as work saved within a school's learning platform means that it will be securely stored in the one place and can be accessed at any time. Some Australian schools are also using online quizzes and tests, written by older students for younger students, as an innovative approach to assessing children; these have been shown to provide instant and automatically generated feedback to students, the outcomes of which can be added to their digital learning portfolio.

Reflective questions

Download a copy of O'Rourke's (2004) article *Digital Learning Portfolios: A Critical Look* (available from http://edpartnerships.edu.au/image/file/Digital%20Portfolios_A%20critical %20look.pdf) and critically reflect on its content. Consider your response to the following questions:

- Do you use digital learning portfolios with the children you work with?
- What do you consider to be the benefits or limitations of these?
- How might you be able to use these to enhance the provision in the setting/school you are placed in/employed at?

Formative assessment in New Zealand

Whilst tests and examinations are considered by many practitioners and teachers to be 'classic' *summative* ways of measuring student progress, it is argued by OECD (2005: 1) that 'assessment should also be *formative* – in other words, identifying and responding to the students' learning needs'. The benefits of this approach to assessment for teachers are strongly advocated:

- Teachers are able to adjust their teaching to meet individual student needs;
- Teachers are better able to help all students to reach high standards;
- Teachers who actively involve students in the formative assessment process help children to develop skills that enable them to learn better.

(Adapted from OCED, 2005: 1)

Teachers at Long Bay Primary School in Auckland have clearly embraced formative assessment as part of their quality provision and practice. Their website (www. longbayprimary.ac.nz/index.html) emphasises 'the importance of children receiving high quality feedback and feed forward information that helps them to better understand their own learning needs and strengths and to set goals for continuous improvement.' A wonderful presentation for parents and carers (available at www.longbayprimary.ac.nz/documents/ formative_assessment_at_lbp.pdf) shows how the school uses five different 'formative strategies' to assure high standards; these include *learning intentions, success criteria, goal setting, self-assessment strategies* and *written 'feedback/feed forward'*.

Independent research

Select one of the five 'formative strategies' identified above and undertake a web search of professional information to develop your personal subject knowledge and professional practice in the application of this strategy with children. Reflect on the value of this as part of the 'suite of assessment provision' you offer children you work with.

The use of formative assessment strategies clearly supports teachers in ensuring that the work they plan for children is appropriate to their individual capabilities. This is evident in the practice of Carolyn Randell, a part time teacher of 30 years, who works in a decile 10 school (which means the children are from middle to upper income families, the school is well resourced and parents take a big interest in their child's education) on the North Shore of Auckland. Mrs Randell describes her 'reading practice' with the six year old children she works with:

> Reading lessons are taken every day, usually a child will get a new graded reader to take home each night. Children are grouped according to ability and they have lots of fun activities to do before and after reading with the teacher.

These 'fun activities' include reading books from an individual class browsing box that the children have seen or read before, reading independently, reading with a buddy, going on the computers with a buddy and playing a reading or spelling game, completing alphabet puzzles, using whiteboards, and engaging in word matching games like *Go Fish*. Children clearly favour this variety of activities:

> My favourite reading activities are using the computers and writing on small whiteboards. (Child A)
> Computer stories are fun and interesting and I can choose what story or activity to do. (Child B)
> I like using whiteboards because I try to write more words than my friends. (Child C)

This 'daily experience' is considered to be one of the key reasons as to why standards in children's reading in New Zealand are so high (Ministry of Education, 2010). This practice is likely to be shaped and informed by the curriculum which teachers like Mrs Randell use to plan for effective provision in their classroom. It is to select 'curriculums' in Australia and New Zealand to which this chapter now turns its attention.

Curriculums

Australia: the Australian curriculum

> Over the next few years, teachers and school leaders will be engrossed in realising a significant milestone in our nation's [Australia] educational history – the development and implementation of a world-class Australian curriculum that will prepare young people for life in the 21st century.
>
> (Hill, 2009)

The Australian curriculum is an ambitious and exciting new national curriculum which 'sets out what all young Australians are to be taught, and the expected quality of that learning as they progress through schooling' (ACARA, 2011: 1). Guided by the *Melbourne Declaration on Educational Goals for Young Australians* (MCEETYA, 2008) and *The Shape of the Australian Curriculum* (ACARA, 2010), the Australian curriculum is a national approach to schooling and describes a learning entitlement for each Australian student that provides a foundation for successful, lifelong learning and participation in the Australian community. This is to be achieved by clearly setting out the core knowledge, understanding, skills and general capabilities important for children from Foundation* (five year olds) to Year 10 (15 year olds) with consideration to Years 11 and 12 (16–18 year olds) also being made.

Variants in terminology

In many UK settings the term *Foundation* is used to make reference to specific year groups in the 'early years' e.g. *Foundation One* (Nursery) and *Foundation Two* (Reception). The term *Foundation Year** has been used as a nationally consistent term for the year of schooling prior to Year 1 for the purpose of the Australian curriculum. It is important to appreciate that this does not replace the equivalent terms used in different states and territories in the country:

Kindergarten (New South Wales/Australian Capital Territory);

Prep (Queensland/Victoria/Tasmania);

Kindy/Pre-primary (Western Australia);

Reception (South Australia); and

Transition (Northern Territory) (ACARA, 2011).

Reasoning for the development of the national curriculum

There are a number of reasons as to why the Australian national curriculum has been developed:

1. School and curriculum authorities can collaborate to ensure high-quality teaching and learning materials are available for all schools;
2. Greater attention can be devoted to equipping young Australians with those skills, knowledge and capabilities necessary to enable them to effectively engage with and prosper in society, compete in a globalised world and thrive in the information-rich workplaces of the future; and
3. There will be greater consistency for the country's increasingly mobile student and teacher population (ACARA, 2011).

Reflective questions

Reflect on the three points offered above, considering how these apply to schools and settings you may have worked in:

1. In what ways have authorities worked together to produce materials you have used in your school/setting?

2. What skills, knowledge and capabilities do you actively promote in your school/setting with the children you work with to aid them now and for the future?

3. How does social mobility affect provision and practice in your school/setting?

Curriculum organisation

The Australian national curriculum is made up of a number of subjects and learning areas, many of which UK readers will notice are similar to those found in the national curriculum in England (DfE, 2013):

English	Mathematics	Science
Humanities and social sciences, specifically history, geography, economics and business, and civics and citizenship	The Arts, specifically dance, drama, media arts, music and visual arts	
Languages	Health and physical education	
Technologies, specifically design and technology and information and communication technology, while also providing for learning in other technology areas		

Adapted from ACARA (2010: 16–17)

The curriculum is published online and is being developed in various phases. Readers can explore the content of the first phase (English, Mathematics, Sciences and History) by visiting www.australiancurriculum.edu.au/Home and clicking on the *Curriculum* tab.

General capabilities

In an effort to help children to be lifelong learners, the Australian curriculum has embedded seven *general capabilities* into each learning area where appropriate and relevant; these encompass skills, behaviours and dispositions that children can develop and apply to content knowledge and that support them in becoming successful learners, confident and creative individuals and active and informed citizens. These include:

- Literacy;
- Numeracy;
- Information and communication technology (ICT) competence (e.g. typing skills);
- Critical and creative thinking;
- Ethical behaviour;
- Personal and social competence; and
- Intercultural understanding.

In an effort to explore these general capabilities further, this chapter will focus its attention on succinctly examining the notion of 'Ethical behaviour' in practice.

'Ethical behaviour' in practice

The ACARA (2011: 1) suggests that

> students develop ethical behaviour as they learn to understand and act in accordance with ethical principles. This includes understanding the role of ethical principles, values

and virtues in human life; acting with moral integrity; acting with regard for others; and having a desire and capacity to work for the common good.

So, how might this be translated into classroom practice in relation to English, mathematics and science? The examples offered below are given for the purposes of illustration:

English	Exploring how moral principles affect characters' behaviour and judgments – reading of extracts of Anna Sewell's *Black Beauty* by Year 5 children.
Mathematics	Selecting and interpreting data and statistics for different purposes – *is it morally right to compare and present the weight of individual Year 6 class members in a graph, displaying these for all to see?*
Science	Applying ethical guidelines in the gathering of evidence – *should Year 1 children 'make up' the animals they have seen in their 'mini beast walk' so that their observational findings are more interesting?*

Further information about the general capabilities can be found at www.australiancurriculum.edu.au/GeneralCapabilities/Pdf/Overview

Current challenges and criticisms

Whilst much progress has been made in the development of the national curriculum, delays, concerns and controversy have overshadowed this. For example, Italiano (2011) suggests that planning for the Australian curriculum will pose a number of issues for schools. These include:

- Determining how much time should be spent on each topic/learning area;
- The issue of combining 'small' school years together e.g. Years 4 and 5; and
- Establishing how the Australian curriculum will allow for differentiation in terms of learning abilities (e.g. students with disabilities and gifted and talented students).

Polster and Ross (2010), upon viewing the draft of the year-by-year syllabus for mathematics, were less than favourable with comments they made about it: 'What is proposed is little more than a cowardly version of current curriculums, a codification of the boring, pointless approach – which is "safe" but which has already failed a generation of students.' Malkin (2011) reported on how there was anger in Australia as school books 'write Christ out of history'. It was suggested that Australian Christians were furious over changes to the 'new politically correct curriculum' that would replace the terms BC (Before Christ) and AD (Anno Domini) from text books, replacing them with neutral, non-religious language.

The development of the Australia curriculum continues.

New Zealand: *Te Whāriki*

Te Whāriki (Ministry of Education, 1996) is a bilingual document which establishes the curriculum policy and framework from birth to five in New Zealand. It was developed in the 1980s in collaboration with practitioners, early childhood specialists and the government with the aim of developing a shared vision and a 'unified approach to early children care and education' (Pound, 2005: 67). Those coordinating the development of the curriculum wished to assure 'equitable educational opportunities and quality early childhood policies and practices into the framework' (Carr and May, 2000: 53), and so took into account the fundamental principles of the culture of its indigenous Māori people to create a bicultural document.

Exploring the curriculum

The curriculum is clearly holistic in its conception and underpinnings; in the introduction to the curriculum the following aspirations for children are clearly presented: 'To grow up as competent and confident learners and communicators, healthy in mind, body, and spirit, secure in their sense of belonging and in the knowledge that they make a valued contribution to society' (Ministry of Education, 1996: 9). The word *Whāriki* is a Māori word meaning 'woven mat' on which all can stand. This works as a metaphor for the curriculum as it allows the principles, strands and goals of *Te Whāriki,* appropriately differentiated for infants (babies), toddlers and young children, to be interwoven into diverse patterns of provision which different early childhood settings and services can embrace.

Aspects of diversity in early childhood settings in New Zealand

Te Whāriki recognises how '[d]ifferent programmes, philosophies, structures, and environments will contribute to the distinctive patterns of the [W]hāriki' (Ministry of Education, 1996: 11). Take a look at the list of differences identified on page 11 of the curriculum document (downloadable from www.dji.de/bibs/320_whariki.pdf) and reflect on if/how these considerations influence and affect provision and practice in early childhood settings that you work/have worked in.

The principles, strands and goals for the early childhood curriculum

Details regarding the principles, strands and goals of *Te Whāriki* are summarised in Tables 10.2 and 10.3; further details can be found at www.educate.ece.govt.nz/learning/curriculumAndLearning/TeWhariki/PartC/StrandsandGoals.aspx.

The strands and goals arise from the four principles in Table 10.2. The *Whāriki* is woven from these four principles and from the five strands, or essential areas, of learning and development shown in Table 10.3.

The principles and strands together form the framework for the curriculum. Each strand has several goals. Learning outcomes have been developed for each goal in each of the strands, so that the *Whāriki* becomes an integrated foundation for every child's development. The above can be summarised in diagrammatic form in Figure 10.1.

TABLE 10.2 Principles of *Te Whāriki*

Principle	Maori translation	Detail
Empowerment	Whakamana	The early childhood curriculum empowers the child to learn and grow.
Holistic development	Kotahitanga	The early childhood curriculum reflects the holistic way children learn and grow.
Family and community	Whānau Tangata	The wider world of family and community is an integral part of the early childhood curriculum.
Relationships	Ngā Hononga	Children learn through responsive and reciprocal relationships with people, places and things.

Source: Adapted from Carr and May, 2000

TABLE 10.3 Strands and goals of *Te Whāriki*

Strand	Maori translation	Summary of strand and the nature of the goals associated with it
Well-being	Mana Atua	The health and well-being of the child are protected and nurtured.
Belonging	Mana Whenua	Children and their families feel a sense of belonging.
Contribution	Mana Tangata	Opportunities for learning are equitable and each child's contribution is valued.
Communication	Mana Reo	The languages and symbols of their own and other cultures are promoted and protected.
Exploration	Mana Aotūroa	The child learns through active exploration of the environment.

Source: Adapted from Ministry of Education, 1996: 15–16

Te Whāriki: a five-piece fact file

1. The underpinning vision of *Te Whāriki* drew upon a sociocultural view of curriculum and childhood derived from Vygotsky (Soler and Miller, 2003: 59).
2. The *Te Whāriki* "curriculum" 'describes the sum total of the experiences, activities, and events, whether direct or indirect, which occur within an environment designed to foster children's learning and development.' (Ministry of Education, 1996: 10).
3. *Te Whāriki* has been 'widely acclaimed' in many countries which has fuelled interest in policies and practice which see 'children as central to their community and learning as a shared experience' (Nutbrown, 2011: 156).
4. Assessment of children's strengths and interests in relation to the five strands of the curriculum are made through *learning stories* (for more information, visit www.unisanet. unisa.edu.au/staff/SueHill/Learningstories.pdf).
5. '*Te Whāriki* is concerned with children as they are now. It is not aimed at preparing them for the next stage of schooling' (Pound: 2005: 68).

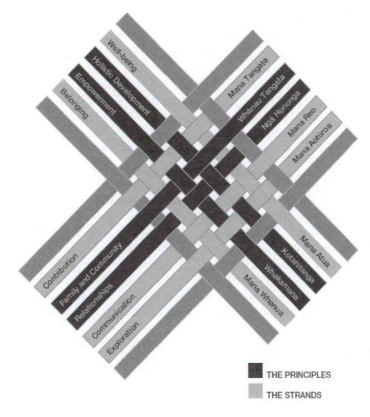

THE PRINCIPLES
THE STRANDS

FIGURE 10.1 *Te Whāriki*
Source: Adapted from Ministry of Education, 1996: 13

Te Whāriki: a short critique

Whilst there is much strength associated with *Te Whāriki* there are numerous criticisms and concerns which surround its delivery. Three key considerations are offered below under subheadings to highlight particular issues and tensions for the reader to reflect on:

The issue of practitioners and practice

Alvestad et al. (2009: 5) describe how *Te Whāriki* differs from other curricula in that it 'does not prescribe content or methods, but leaves it to the teachers to weave their own "Whāriki" (mat). In this way, each service can maintain its own "ways of working" with children and families which are in keeping with their setting.' This has been found to be both a strength and weakness of the curriculum due to the skill levels required by teachers to be able to make such professional judgements (Carr and May, 1993) and the risk that the challenges of the curriculum to traditional practices may be ignored (Cullen, 2003).

The issue of transitions

Peters (2000: 23) suggests that in New Zealand, as in many other countries, 'there is a degree of discontinuity between the ideas, philosophies and pedagogies of the early childhood and primary sectors'. This has had an impact on the smoothness of transitions of children from early years settings to school; whilst aspirations for continuity between sectors were implied in the Ministry of Education's (1994) proposed vision of a seamless education system, Holmes (1998: 51) noted that there was a 'sharp cut off' from the early childhood curriculum to the school curriculum.

The issue of subject knowledge

Ritchie and Rau (2009: 97) refer to 'a fundamental dilemma in the delivery of a "quality" early childhood curriculum' which arises from recognition of the limited extent to which non-Māori practitioners, the vast majority of whom lack an in-depth knowledge of the Māori language and culture, are capable of honouring authentically the indigenous content that is stipulated in *Te Whāriki*. Chapman (2011) reports how new guidelines – *Tataiako* – have been released by the government for teachers in schools and early childhood centres to increase their knowledge of Māori culture and improve their cultural awareness and skills. See www.minedu.govt.nz/theMinistry/EducationInitiatives/Tataiako.aspx for further information.

Conclusion

There is no doubt that there is much to commend in relation to the educational provision offered for children in Australia and New Zealand. Curriculum developments, both established and those currently being undertaken, demonstrate the real commitment educators, practitioners and policy makers have to ensure children have experience of a world-class education. There is growing evidence of teachers and practitioners from other countries looking to the educational provision offered in Australia and New Zealand and integrating/adapting elements of this within their own practice. It is hoped that the reader will be willing to embrace at least one strategy or idea presented in this chapter to strengthen/enrich their practice with children.

Areas for further consideration

There are many other areas for consideration which readers may wish to explore as part of their own private study. The suggestions below merely offer a select number of aspects which will help to develop their understanding of Australian and New Zealand education:

Australia	New Zealand
Promoting/sustaining effective parental partnerships	Addressing the issue of childhood obesity
The sufficiency of resources for Australian primary schools	Promoting positive race relations
Assuring internet safety in schools	Discipline in the classroom

When engaging with literature linked to one (or more) of these areas of consideration, reflect on how this relates to your own context. Consider any recommendations and implications for practice offered in your readings – how might these help to address concerns in your own school/setting? Is there provision and practice in your own school/setting which would be of benefit for Australian and New Zealand schools/settings?

Further reading

Australia

Anon (-) *Beyond harmony: rethinking intercultural learning for Australian primary schools.* [Online]. Available from: www.acsa.edu.au/pages/images/Beyond%20Harmony%20%20 G%20Toner%20ACSA%2009%20final.pdf (Accessed: 2 October 2011).

Baker, B. (2009) *Pedagogies and digital content in the Australian school sector.* [Online]. Available from: www.ndlrn.edu.au/verve/_resources/ESA_Pedagogies_and_Digital_ Content_in_the_Australian_School_Sector.pdf (Accessed: 2 October 2011).

New Zealand

Duhn, I. (2008) Globalising childhood: assembling the bicultural child in the New Zealand early childhood curriculum. *Te Whāriki International Critical Childhood Policy Studies*, 1(1), 82–105. [Online]. Available from: http://journals.sfu.ca/iccps/index.php/childhoods/article/ viewFile/5/8 (Accessed: 2 October 2011).

Smith, A. B. and May, H. (2008) Early childhood care and education in Aotearoa – New Zealand. IN: Huat, C. M. and Kerry, T. (eds) *International Perspectives on Education*. London: Continuum.

References

Ainley, J. (2010) What can Australian students do with computers? IN: *Research Developments*, 23. [Online]. Available from: http://tinyurl.com/chqch3g (Accessed: 15 March 2013).

Alvestad, M., Duncan, J. and Berge, A. (2009) New Zealand ECE teachers talk about *Te Whāriki*. *New Zealand Journal of Teachers' Work*, 6(1), 3–19. [Online]. Available from: www.teacherswork. ac.nz/journal/volume6_issue1/alvestad.pdf (Accessed: 4 September 2011).

Anthony, G. and Walshaw, M. (2009) Characteristics of effective teaching of mathematics: a view from the West. *Journal of Mathematics Education*, 2(2), 147–164. [Online]. Available from: http:// educationforatoz.com/images/_9734_12_Glenda_Anthony.pdf (Accessed: 25 September 2011).

A.S Edugroup (2011) *Study in Australia*. [Online]. Available from: www.asedugroup.com/study_ australia.html (Accessed: 15 March 2013).

Australian Curriculum, Assessment and Reporting Authority (ACARA) (2011) *A curriculum for all young Australians*. [Online]. Available from: http://ebookbrowse.com/a-curriculum-for-all-young- australians-2011-pdf-d347845383 (Accessed: 11 September 2011).

Australian Curriculum, Assessment and Reporting Authority (ACARA) (2010) *The shape of the Australian curriculum version 2.0*. [Online]. Available from: www.acara.edu.au/verve/_resources/ Shape_of_the_Australian_Curriculum.pdf (Accessed: 11 September 2011).

Carr, M. and May, H. (1993) *The role of government in early childhood curriculum*. Paper presented at What is Government's Role in Early Childhood Education? Conference, Wellington.

Carr, M. and May, H. (2000) *Te Whāriki*: curriculum voices. IN: Penn, H. (ed.) *Early childhood services: theory, policy and practice*. Buckingham: Open University Press. pp. 53–73.

Chapman, K. (2011) *Maori culture guidelines released for teachers*. [Online]. Available from: www.stuff.co.nz/national/education/5531063/Maori-culture-guidelines-released-for-teachers (Accessed: 1 September 2011).

Cullen, J. (2003) The challenge of *Te Whāriki*: catalyst for change? IN: Nuttall, J. (ed.) *Weaving* Te Whāriki: Aotearoa *New Zealand's early childhood curriculum document in theory and practice*. Wellington: New Zealand Council for Educational Research. pp. 269–296.

Department for Education (DfE) (2013) The school curriculum. [Online]. Available from: www.education.gov.uk/schools/teachingandlearning/curriculum (Accessed: 15 March 2013).

Department of Foreign Affairs and Trade (2008) *About Australia: our system of education*. [Online]. Available from: http://www.dfat.gov.au/facts/education_in_australia.html (Accessed: 25 September 2011).

Hill, P. (2009) *An Australian curriculum to promote 21st century learning*. [Online]. Available from: www.eqa.edu.au/site/anaustraliancurriculumtopromote21stcentury.html (Accessed 11 September 2011).

Holmes, T. (1998) Transition to school. *Childrenz Issues*, 2(1), 50–51.

Italiano, F. (2011) New Australian curriculum IN: *Circular, 2* (Term Two), pp. 14–15. [Online]. Available from: http://internet.ceo.wa.edu.au/Publications/Documents/Circular/2011/Circular%20Term%202_2011.pdf (Accessed: 15 March 2013).

Malkin, B. (2011) Anger in Australia as school books 'write Christ out of history'. *The Telegraph*. 2 September. [Online]. Available from: www.telegraph.co.uk/news/worldnews/australiaandthepacific/australia/8736932/Anger-in-Australia-as-school-books-write-Christ-out-of-history.html (Accessed: 15 March 2013).

Polster, B. and Ross, M. (2010) New maths curriculum a feeble tool calculated to bore. *The Age*. 4 March. [Online]. Available from: www.theage.com.au/opinion/society-and-culture/new-maths-curriculum-a-feeble-tool-calculated-to-bore-20100303-pivw.html (Accessed: 11 September 2011).

Ministerial Council on Education, Employment, Training and Youth Affairs (MCEETYA) (2008) *Melbourne declaration on educational goals for young Australians*. [Online]. Available from: www.curriculum.edu.au/verve/_resources/National_Declaration_on_the_Educational_Goals_for_Young_Australians.pdf (Accessed: 11 September 2011).

Ministry of Education (2010) *Supporting your young child's early learning*. [Online]. Available from: www.minedu.govt.nz/Parents/EarlyYears/SupportingYourYoungChildsLearning.aspx (Accessed: 8 October 2011).

Ministry of Education (1996) *Te Whāriki: early childhood education. He Whāriki Mātauranga mō ngā Mokopuna o Aotearoa*. Wellington: Learning Media.

Ministry of Education (1994) *Education for the 21st century*. Wellington: Learning Media.

Nutbrown, C. (2011) *Key concepts in early childhood education and care*. 2nd edn. London: Sage.

OECD (2005) Formative assessment: improving learning in secondary classrooms. *Policy Brief*. November. [Online]. Available from: www.oecd.org/edu/ceri/35661078.pdf (Accessed: 15 March 2013).

OECD (2009) *PISA 2009 results: what students know and can do: student performance in reading, mathematics and science*. [Online]. Available from: www.oecd.org/document/61/ 0,3746,en_3225 2351_32235731_46567613_1_1_1,00.html (Accessed: 25 September 2011).

O'Rourke, M. (2004) *Digital learning portfolios: a critical look*. [Online]. Available at: http://edpartnerships.edu.au/image/file/Digital%20Portfolios_A%20critical%20look.pdf (Accessed: 25 September 2011).

Peters, S. (2000) *Multiple perspectives on continuity in early learning and the transition to school*. Paper presented at 'Complexity, diversity and multiple perspectives in early childhood', The 10th European Early Childhood Education Research Association Conference, University of London, London, 29 August–1 September. [Online]. Available from: http://extranet.edfac.unimelb.edu.au/LED/tec/pdf/peters1.pdf (Accessed: 1 September 2011).

Polster, B. and Ross, M. (2010) New maths curriculum a feeble tool calculated to bore. *The Age*. 4 March. [Online]. Available from: www.theage.com.au/opinion/society-and-culture/new-maths-curriculum-a-feeble-tool-calculated-to-bore-20100303-pivw.html (Accessed: 11 September 2011).

Pound, L. (2005) *How children learn*. London: Step Forward Publishing Limited.

Ritchie, J. and Rau, C. (2009) Mā wai ngā hua? 'Participation' in early childhood in Aotearoa/New Zealand. *International Critical Childhood Policy Studies*, 2(1), 93–108.

Shepherd, J. (2010) *World education rankings: which country does best at reading, maths and science?* [Online]. Available from: www.guardian.co.uk/news/datablog/2010/dec/07/world-education-rankings-maths-science-reading (Accessed: 25 September 2011).

Soler, J. and Miller, L. (2003) The struggle for early childhood curricula. A comparison of the English Foundation Stage Curriculum, *Te Whāriki* and Reggio Emilia. *International Journal of Early Years Education*, 11(1), 57–67.

State of Victoria (Department of Education and Early Childhood Development) (2010) *Expanding horizons*. Digital Learning Platforms Research Series. 1. [Online]. Available from: www.eduweb.vic.gov.au/edulibrary/public/publ/research/publ/ExpandingHorizonsFinalforWeb.pdf (Accessed: 25 September 2011).

11

Education in Poland

Anita Gulczyńska and Monika Wiśniewska-Kin

Acknowledgements

The authors would like to offer their sincere thanks to Sylwia Grzegorzewska for her support during the writing of this chapter and to the authors of photos: Rafał Krzeszewski, Kuba Kulesza, Łukasz Lamecki, Rafał Nockowski and Przemek Nowakowski.

Introduction

In this contribution we assume that childhood is a social construction created and maintained by social actors in interactions (Blumer: 1954), (Berger, Luckmann: 1966). Even though each society in the course of its history develops the set of structures unifying the context of childhood experiences of its citizens (mainstream ideology, dominant 'concept of a child', educational system organization, etc.), it is the subjective perspective through the prism of which we attempt to explore childhood experience in the context of Polish primary education because childhood is always 'someone's'.

Hence the contribution presents first the normative picture of the Polish primary education. Then case studies are introduced which give us the picture of the Polish primary education from the narratives of the two 11-year-old students/pupils – Tomek (Tom) and Kasia (Kathy) – constructing their educational biographies in the context of objectively different social settings of Łódź – a city of 800,000 inhabitants in the centre of Poland. The narrative analysis of their school experiences explores the issue of unequal educational opportunities as one of the vital challenges we continually face.

Background on the historical socio-cultural influences on the education system

Poland had to create its educational system three times in the twentieth century: the first time after regaining independence in 1918 – in the Second Republic, the second time after World War II in the Polish People's Republic, and finally the third time after the transition of 1989 – in the Third Republic.

After regaining independence in 1918, on the Polish territory there operated varied school systems and educational traditions inherited from the invaders. In order to standardize the educational system in Poland during the period between the wars (1918–1939), the authorities successfully coalesced education that shaped the national consciousness, which allowed the Poles to survive and preserve the national culture and education during World War II.

During the war (1939–1944), teachers gathered in the Secret Teaching Organization (TON) and organized in the occupied territories secret teaching at all levels of education: primary, secondary, and university. They also took up various initiatives aimed at creating Polish educational centers abroad.

In the first postwar years (1944–1948) a belief was widespread in the Polish society that it became possible to create a democratic state of law. However, with the strengthening of the 'people's authority' imposed on the nation according to the Soviet model and the phenomenon of joining political parties together (1948–1953), it appeared that the 'people's democracy' regime imposed by the Soviets is far from the true liberal-democratic political system.

After the turn of the political system of 1989, Poland rejected the communist system and ideology and has been a sovereign democratic state of law. The '90s saw a number of key amendments in the law concerning schools: religion was introduced into schools as a subject, an opportunity was provided to implement teaching curricula designed by teachers, and legal possibilities were ensured to establish religious, social and private schools educating pupils and students at all levels.

Finally, in 1999, the Ministry of National Education began a general (structural, program, educational, evaluation) reform changing the education system. Its main purposes are to: equalize the educational opportunities for young people, improve the level of public education through the dissemination of secondary and higher education, and improve the quality of education understood as an integral process of education and upbringing (Wołoszyn: 1994, 2003).

The concepts of a child and childhood in Poland

The analysis of the image of a child and childhood in the Core Education Curriculum for Pre-School Education and Comprehensive Education for Primary Schools has been shaped by certain selected problems: where is education of a child supposed to lead to? How should a child's development be understood and how is a child's psychological profile presented? How are learning and a child's school activity understood? What educational activities are to assist a child in the learning process?

In the course of searching for answers to these questions, particular attention was paid to the changing political and socio-cultural climate in Poland determining the image of a child and childhood. Democratization of life, a political and social transformation, that our country has undergone, has brought about a new dimension to education. The time is now gone when education was subordinated to the existing social order. That subordination was manifested in the maintenance of a specific model of education, namely, adaptive education. This model restricted the development of an individual by limiting the powers of a critical overview of the reality.

In Poland, after 1989, this model was negated through the implemented subject educational model (in line with the reform) which focused on the individual, supporting a developing subject, the autonomy of the child and his/her independence in thought and action. The notion of a dialogue became particularly important, as well as agreement, cooperation and creative activity within the class community.

Nevertheless, the implemented reform is currently inducing a wave of discussions, controversies and protests, showing a deep discrepancy between the projects coined by education administration and social expectations. The criticism concerns certain assumptions of the subjective model of education in the Core Education Curriculum valid for junior classes, considering them to be superficial, inconsistent and not very relevant to the whole concept of education. Also, assumptions are challenged and the critics point to the development of educational practice in the junior classes according to the instrumental model (Klus-Stańska: 2009).

An introduction to the Polish education system

Understanding the Polish education system demands its contextualization through the reform of the law of the educational system introduced in 1999 which was the most vital for the current system of education (Śliwerski: 2004a, p. 392). The most significant changes cover: changes in the method of funding educational tasks, giving the school control over the content of education, changes in professional requirements towards teachers and introducing lower secondary schools (Konarzewski: 2000, p. 3). Structural changes were to create the conditions favourable to promote secondary and tertiary education and give equal educational opportunities to children and youth (mostly in villages), introducing new syllabi and reintroducing to schools their upbringing role (Śliwerski: 2004b, p. 290).

In the area of funding, units of territorial self-government were given the responsibility and right to set up and conduct practically all types of schools. Headmasters became more independent of the superintendent authorities.[1] Besides, 'local governments receive from the state a subsidy for educational tasks which are realized in primary schools and lower secondary schools […]thanks to which they can conduct local educational policy according to needs in the labour market' (Śliwerski: 2004b, p. 337).

This change with the transfer of decisions on educational content to schools became the foundations of the process of local diversification of educational institutions. The only tool to unify forms of educational content is the Core Education Curriculum.

The Core Education Curriculum determines that 'a supreme goal of school educational activities is student's holistic development' (Regulation of the Minister of National Education and Sport of 26 February 2002, annex no 2) and orders teachers to take up activities aiming at giving equal educational opportunities for students. One of the most important assumptions of the curriculum is the fact that it is to impose limits 'from the bottom' but not 'from the top'. It is an imperative not a ban indicating only what must be included in the school guidelines which give opportunities to individualize educational practice (Konarzewski: 2004, p. 16)

The curriculum stresses the significance of:

–   Understanding, not just learning educational contents by heart;

–   Developing perception of various relationships (cause/effect, functional, temporal, spatial, etc.);
–   Developing analytic and synthetic thinking skills [...]

(Regulation of the Minister of National Education and
Sport of 26 February 2002, annex no 2)

Teachers are obliged to encourage children to use acquired knowledge and teach the following skills:

–   Planning, organizing and assessing their own learning and taking more and more responsibility for it;
–   Effective communication in various situations [...];
–   Effective cooperation in a team and teamwork [...];
–   Creative problem solving;
–   Searching for, ordering and using information from various sources and effective IT use;
–   Referring acquired knowledge to practice and creating necessary experience and habits;
–   Developing mental skills and personal interests;
–   Acquiring methods and techniques of conflict and social problems solution through negotiations [...]

(Regulation of the Minister of National Education and
Sport of 26 February 2002, annex no 2)

Transformations in the field of funding and managing education, as well in aims and courses of educational process, go towards decentralization, which seems to be a natural direction of democratic social change in the state which experienced a socialist system.

Inner transformations of educational system organizations were supposed to promote equal educational opportunities. Their most significant example is the introduction of lower secondary schools (gymnasium). Figure 11.1 shows Polish educational systems at present.

Junior high school (gymnasium) shortened education in a primary school, at the same time prolonging common education by a year. In a new system of educating the youngest students, 'a child aged six is obliged to undergo a yearly pre-school preparation in a kindergarten or in a kindergarten unit organized in a primary school' (Dz.U. Nr 137 z 2003 roku, poz. 1304, Ustawa z dnia 27 czerwca 2003 r. o zmianie ustawy o systemie oświaty oraz o zmianie niektórych innych ustaw, art.14, ust.3). After a primary school which is shortened to six years students start their education in a three-year lower secondary school.

Pre-school education

Since 1993, in Poland, a continuous growth has been observed of the indicator concerning the dissemination of pre-school education, with a marked acceleration since 2009. In our country, since 2009, five-year-olds have had the right (and since 2011 it has been the obligation) to a year-long pre-school preparation in a kindergarten, a kindergarten department at a primary school or in other facilities providing pre-school education.

A separate discussion is required regarding the dissemination of education among the six-year-olds. In September 2004, an obligatory year-long pre-school preparation was introduced for children aged six.[2] This obligation is realized in a kindergarten or a kindergarten department organized at a primary school (commonly referred to as 'zerówka'). From 2014, in Poland there will be introduced compulsory education for children who are six years old. In recent years, the possibility of starting school education one year earlier has been used by about 0.7–1 per cent of six-year-olds. In 2009, this percentage rose to 4.5 per cent.[3] Nevertheless, in comparison with other EU countries, the education dissemination rate is still one of the lowest. Currently in Poland, 64 per cent of four-year-olds and 81 per cent of five-year-olds attend a kindergarten.

The purpose of pre-school

1) To develop children's social skills: communication with adults and children, being agreeable while playing and in situations involving various tasks.
2) To shape the self-care activities as well as cultural and hygienic habits. Instructing the children to maintain law and order.
3) To support language development.
4) To support children in developing intellectual activities which they apply while acquiring knowledge and getting to understand themselves and their surroundings.

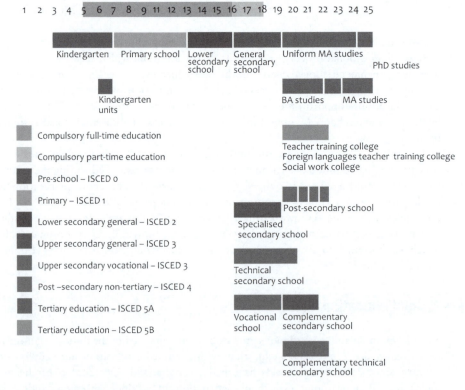

FIGURE 11.1 Structure of the Polish educational system

Source: www.eurydice.org.pl/sites/eurydice.org.pl/files/system2012.pdf

6) To instruct the children to care for their own safety and the safety of others.
7) Education through art – a child as an audience and an actor.
8) Education through art – music and singing, hopping and dancing.
9) Education through art – different forms of art.
10) To support the mental development of children through construction games and arousing the children's technical interests.
11) To help the children to understand the essence of atmospheric phenomena and to avoid various hazards.
12) To educate the children to respect the plants and animals.
13) To support the intellectual development of the children including mathematical education.
14) To shape the children's readiness to learn reading and writing.
15) Family, civic and patriotic education.

The recommended core curriculum for pre-school education

The Core Education Curriculum of Pre-school Education describes the process of supporting the development and education of children attending pre-school facilities. Kindergartens, kindergarten departments at primary schools and other facilities of pre-school education act in equal measures as care, education and training bodies. They ensure that children can play together and learn in an environment which is safe, friendly and tailored to their developmental needs.

This is designed to ensure the proper psychomotor development and course of upbringing and education of children of pre-school age. The following proportions of time spent in kindergarten are recommended (as presented in the weekly settlement):

1) At least one-fifth of the time should be spent on fun (at this time children can play freely, with minor participation of the teacher);
2) At least one-fifth of the time (in the case of younger children – a quarter of the time), children should spend in the kindergarten garden, the playground, park, etc. (there should be organized various kinds of games including those involving physical activity, sports, nature observation, household chores, cleaning tasks and gardening);
3) At most one-fifth of the time should be spent on different types of didactic classes, realized according to the chosen program of pre-school education;
4) The remaining time – two-fifths of the time – the teacher can spend on activities selected by him/her (but these two-fifths also include care activities, self-care tasks, organizational tasks and others).

Primary education

In a primary school there is a division into two didactic cycles – integrated education (grades 1–3) and block education (grades 4–6).

| Integrated education (no distinct subject areas) | Grades 1–3 | Age 6–9 |
| Block education (subject based) | Grades 4–6 | Age 10–13 |

In grades 1–3 there are not separate subjects such as Polish, mathematics, etc. and the teacher conducts lessons according to their own schedule, adjusting the time of classes and breaks to suit students' activities. The only guideline is organizing didactic-upbringing processes in such a way that every day there are sport activities with a total weekly time of at least three hours.[4] From grade 1, students are obliged to attend religion or ethics classes which are conducted at schools for an hour a week.[5]

Educational objectives at this stage aim at facilitating holistic and harmonious students' development, in particular of:

- Skills necessary for acquiring knowledge (reading, writing and calculating);
- Abilities to initiate and maintain proper contacts with other children, adults, the disabled, representatives of other nationalities, etc.;
- A sense of belonging to school, local, regional and national community;
- Abilities to act in various situations at school and outside school;
- Creating the need of contact with nature.[6]

Education organization changes in grades 4–6. In the school schedule, the following subjects appear: Polish, history and society, foreign language, mathematics, nature, music, arts, technology, computer studies, sports and in some regions the language of a national minority or ethnic group.

As well as those subjects, from grade 6 there also appear educational-upbringing paths: reading and media education, health education and education for social life. The task of the teacher is to include the content of a selected path in their subjects. School can also organize additional hours of classes devoted to the paths.

ICT and literacy

The ability to use modern information and communication technologies in line with the assumptions of the Core Education Curriculum for Comprehensive Education at Primary Schools are among the most important skills acquired by pupils in the course of comprehensive education at a primary school.

Pupils develop this ability at computer classes. It is assumed that pupils completing the first class will: use the computer within the basic range of its operation (start a program using the mouse and keyboard) and know how to use a computer in such a way so as not to endanger their health. Then, after completing the third class, their knowledge will be enriched and they will know the names of the computer's components, as well as the dangers of anonymous contacts and making their address available to other people. In addition to this, the pupils will have better skills as for: (1) the use of selected programs and educational games; (2) the use of options in the programs; (3) searching for and using information (surfing through the websites selected by the teacher, e.g. the website of their school, and playing animations and multimedia presentations); (4) creating texts and drawings (the pupils should be able to type (using the keyboard) letters, numbers and other characters, words and sentences, as well as make drawings using selected graphics editor).

Mathematics

Within the program assumptions (in the Core Education Curriculum for Pre-School Education and Comprehensive Education for Primary Schools valid since the school year 2009/10) in the field of mathematics, the emphasis was put on computational efficiency, memorizing things such as the products, naming and recognizing geometric figures, using binomial expressions in practical situations, knowing the decimal system as well as efficient counting and writing numbers. The Core Education Curriculum does not include mathematical studies of children's concepts, experimentation as a way to develop mathematical thinking, noticing relationships and dependencies between the numbers in mathematical tasks or didactic games. These elements of the teaching program concerning mathematics – which are associated with individual strategies to solve problems in everyday life – have not received proper recognition yet.

The importance of languages

The graduate of the first stage of education should be able to: respond verbally and non-verbally to simple teacher's commands in a foreign language, understand sentences from listening, read the words and simple sentences with understanding, ask questions and answer questions in the scope of the acquainted expressions and use reference books as well as multimedia tools.

The basic goal of a language education on the second stage of education (IV–VI class) is effective communication in a foreign language in speaking and writing. Even though the language correctness plays a pivotal role, it's not a supreme teaching result. The second stage refers to the six reference levels defined by the Council of Europe in the Common European Framework of Reference for Languages: Learning, Teaching and Assessment as to a standard for grading an individual's language proficiency.

The voice of the child

TOMEK: Mom selected the school with a language focus. She takes me to private math classes, not because I have problems but because my parents think that together with English this is the most important subject at school.

KASIA: I have problems at school mainly with English classes. No-one at home can help me with homework.

Approaches to assessment and achievement

Pre-school assessment

An important element of pre-school education is assessment. A kindergarten, being responsible for the quality of the preparation of its pupils to school, at the beginning of the year preceding the moment when a child is going to start learning in the first class of a primary school, must make an assessment concerning the level of a child's readiness for school education (pre-school assessment). The task of the kindergarten teacher is to observe the children in order to get to know the abilities and developmental needs of the children under their care and to document these observations. The purpose of such analysis is to gather information that may help:

- The parents,
- The kindergarten teacher,
- The employees of the psychological-pedagogical counseling office for Special Educational Needs.

In Poland, the assessment system for children aged 6–9 (attending grades I–3 in a primary school) does not use marks. It's a descriptive report of students' strengths and deficits as well as recommendations for further work. From grade 4, students are assessed in the scale 1–6 (1 is the lowest and 6 is the highest).

Since 2002, after primary school a grade 6 test has been introduced. It is an obligatory test of the skills required in the Core Education Curriculum and it does not perform any selecting functions.

A lower secondary school finishes with compulsory exams in humanistic subjects, science and a foreign language, whose results decide about admission to a secondary school. During the exam, the following skills are checked:

- Reading
- Writing
- Reasoning
- Applying information
- Applying knowledge in practice.

The voice of the child

TOMEK: Mom is worried when I don't do well at school. She would like me to study at a good university in Europe, but in order to get there you need not only good marks, but also fluent foreign languages.

Whose childhood in the context of the educational system do we talk about?

Two 11-year-old students, living in different social settings of Łódź, were asked to talk about their schooling.

Examples from childhood

Case study 1

Kasia is ten years old and attends the 3rd grade of the public primary school situated in one of impoverished neighbourhoods in Łódź. Despite it being the city centre, the majority of people are tenants of the flats in beautiful but dilapidated nineteenth century terraced houses.

FIGURES 11.2, 11.3 Exhibition 'We and our neighbourhood', in the International Museum of Artists, Łódź, 19–30 November 2004. Authors: Rafał Krzeszewski, Kuba Kulesza, Łukasz Lamecki, Rafał Nockowski, Przemek Nowakowski, Curators: Anita Gulczyńska, Jerzy Grzegorski.

She spends her leisure time in a courtyard, a concrete rectangular surrounded by four walls of low-rise brick houses. Kasia's courtyard lacks functional spatial division which would take into account a younger generation's needs. It's where dwellers of different ages spend their leisure time. This situation has its advantages and disadvantages. Deprivation facilitates children's imagination and creative attempts to transform the neighbourhood. They build tents out of blankets and plunks, play circus in the courtyard, play hide-and-seek, paint the houses' walls, organize their own exhibitions, etc.

FIGURES 11.4, 11.5 Exhibition 'We and our neighbourhood'

Some of those forms, however, annoy grown-up neighbours or administrators, etc. Kasia's grandma pops them up into the courtyard and gives them a hard time, because 'it is the kids who matter'.

The world beyond the neighbourhood is accessible through a way leading through two dark gateways – places occupied by local youth groups. They are a border separating the neighbourhoods from a busy street.

FIGURES 11.6, 11.7 Exhibition 'We and our neighbourhood'

Kasia's uncle often stands at one of the gateways and the 'grandma is angry' because 'it is not a good company and only problems later come out of it'. Her uncle, when being asked who he is, replies 'I'm from (here he quotes the street name)'. She already knows 'all deserving respect' and that 'one cannot show weaknesses'. She is being acquainted with this local theory by her significant others from the family and neighbourhood.

Since she was eight, Kasia has been bravely walking to school on her own. Passing the busy anonymous street which belongs to the world beyond the neighbourhood, she starts to get to know it on her own. She loves her family very much, particularly her mother who works hard as a seamstress and who takes her to school daily every other week as she works shifts and her grandma takes care of her and her sister. She sees her dad rarely because he works outside Łódź.

Case study 2

Tomek is 11 and lives in a newly built house outside the city. His closest friends are not related to his local community. Tomek attends a private primary school which is the only one in the city which has a bilingual curriculum, i.e. from the first year of education (age seven) all lessons are conducted both in Polish and English. Every day his mom drives him to school which takes an hour one way.

FIGURES 11.8, 11.9, 11.10, 11.11 Tomek's school (private collection of the authors)

He spends most of his time outside school with his friends from a horse riding club. He shares with them a love of horses and of sport and competition. He competes and achieves first serious successes. Tomek is closely attached to his parents, particularly to his mom who since his birth has been devoted to him. As his parents run a company together, his mom adjusts her schedule to suit her son's. She takes him to and back from school, goes to extracurricular activities, is in constant touch with the teachers and always supports him in homework. His dad works till late, so he has a poorer contact with his son, but it allows him 'to provide a better future for his son'. He tries to make it up at weekends. Then they go to the cinema, go bowling or play 'laser games' in a local entertainment centre. Grandparents are eagerly involved in the care of their grandson too.

Individual biographies reflect the society and their experiences.

Examples of the Polish education system

The voice of the child

KASIA: I went to school when I was seven. I was not afraid because I knew many children as they live nearby. In my class there have been friends from my courtyard since grade one. In the beginning my mom took me to school. She even showed me her teachers as they still teach there…

TOMEK: Mom looked for a school for a long time. I had to take an exam to get into school. I was very afraid but we had been preparing for a long time and everything went well. I did not know anyone and was afraid, but should not have been. Then, when a new school was created at a very good secondary school, they moved me there. Half of my class went there as everything is in English. We all passed the exam. We drive with my mom to school for almost an hour.

Selection of a primary school reveals differences of opportunities for educational success. In the case of Kasia, a selection of the school is determined by its closeness, both physical and symbolical. Kasia attends a local public school situated just across 'her street', the school which became a part of her mom's and uncle's experience. The world of Kasia's communication shows a strong connection with the neighbourhood. Her schoolmates recruit mainly from there as well.

Tomek's education from its beginnings is separate from his local community. The criterion for the school selection seems to be a presumably high quality of education. It is a private school whose students are the group unified by their parents' expectations of the standard of educational services.

The organization of a school day

Organization of a school day in a primary school is determined individually for each of them. A general rule is dividing students into grades, which work in a lesson-subject system and consist of students born in the same year (with the exception when a student repeats the same grade or when faster developing children start their school career earlier). In big schools education takes place in two shifts; in smaller ones lessons start in the morning.

An integrated education schedule example

Lessons are separated by breaks – the time which formally is meant for rest – however it has a locally constructed meaning:

The voice of the child

KASIA: During the breaks we run a little, when the teachers do not watch us. It is fun when it is warm because they open a playground.

TOMEK: Fortunately there are breaks at school. Short ones, but a lunch break lasts 20 minutes. We have a wi-fi internet so we often play. In the library we can use computers and play online. We monkey around in the class. Recently we have been throwing a cassette to each other, the cassette was thrown on the pavement where two ladies were walking. They complained to the headmistress. There was a big fuss about it. Since then we cannot stay in the classroom during breaks.

TABLE 11.1 An example of a grade 2 schedule in Poland

No	Hor	Monday	Tuesday	Wednesday	Thursday	Friday
1	8:00–8:45	—	—	Early school education	English	—
2	8:55–9:40	—	English	Early school education	Religion	—
3	9:50–10:35	—	Sports	Musical education	Social education	—
4	10:45–11:30	Sports	Early school education	Computers	Early school education	—
5	11:50–12:35	Early school education	Early school education	Religion	Early school education	Early school education
6	12:45–13:30	Early school education	Early school education	—	—	Early school education
7	13:40–14:25	Arts	—	—	—	Early school education
8	14:35–15:20	—	—	—	—	Sports

Source: http://sp12otwock.edu.pl/plan/

School lunch – the voice of the child

KASIA: I do not eat lunches at school; I have better ones at home. My grandma gives me sandwiches for school.

TOMEK: In my school there is no kitchen only catering. Mom every day asks me if I liked my lunch and if I am hungry she buys me something on our way or if we have more time she takes me somewhere for a quick lunch.

Most Polish schools give homework which, depending on the education stage, takes up to several hours every day. In the majority of public schools there are day-rooms whose caring and educational role is expressed in homework support and leisure time activities.

Homework – the voice of the child

KASIA: I do homework in a dayroom at school or at home. I prefer the dayroom because grandma quickly gets annoyed with me because I do not understand or because I do not write legibly.

TOMEK: After school I always go to some extra sport activities or private lessons. When I have them I do my homework there.

Reflective questions

Consider the role of a family's social status and its influence on school selection.

Consider the role of a poor neighbourhood and its influence on education.

What are the benefits and limitations of organizing children's leisure time?

Summary

To conclude, education in Poland is influenced most significantly by student's family socio-economic status as well as by the values and life-styles of their local community. Education always takes place *somewhere* and the children are influenced both socially and educationally by that locality (Mendel: 2006: 26).

Further reading

Bernstein B. (1975) Sources of Consensus and Disaffection in Education. *Class, Codes and Control*. London: Routledge and Kegan Paul.

Cumming D. and Cumming D. (1968) The Everyday Life of Delinquent Boys, in D. Irvin and E. Thomson (eds) *Among the People: Encounters with the Poor*. New York and London: Basic Books, Inc., Publishers.

Lavoie R. (2005) *It's So Much Work to Be Your Friend: Helping the Child with Learning Disabilities Find Social Success*. New York: Touchstone.

Petrie P. (2003) Social Pedagogy: An Historical Account of Care and Education as Social Control in Rethinking Children's Care, in J. Brannen and P. Moss (eds) *Rethinking Children's Care*. Buckingham: Open University Press.

Wilson T.P. (1973) Normative and Interpretative Paradigms in Sociology, in J.D. Douglas (ed.) *Understanding Everyday Life: Toward the Reconstruction of Sociological Knowledge*. London: Routledge and Kegan Paul.

Notes

1　A superintendent authority in Poland is a governmental administrative unit dealing with educational supervision and implementing educational state policy in a given region.
2　That seemed to be a solution to uneven educational opportunities which are traced back to the exclusion of representatives of some communities – mainly children from rural areas or from families of lower socio-economic status – from pre-school education (Pilch, 2010).
3　The European agreement in the area of education and training has set the objective of 95 per cent of four-year-olds and older children who have not yet reached the school age to be included in the education system (**The Report on the State of Education 2010**).
4　The Core Education Curriculum.
5　Only Catholicism is taught as this is the predominant religion in Poland.
6　The Core Education Curriculum.
7　That was the final of the Project sponsored by the Municipality of Łódź. The authors constitute a group of teenagers from the same neighborhood as one of our study actors – Kasia – whose uncle was one of the photo's authors.

References

Blumer H. (1954) 'What is Wrong with Social Theory', *American Sociological Review*, 18, pp. 3–10.
Berger P.L. and Luckmann T. (1966) *The Social Construction of Reality: A Treatise in the Sociology of Knowledge*. Garden City, NY: Anchor Books.
Dz.U. Nr 137 z 2003 roku, poz. 1304, Ustawa z dnia 27 czerwca 2003 r. o zmianie ustawy o systemie oświaty oraz o zmianie niektórych innych ustaw, art.14, ust.3.
Klus-Stańska D. (2009) „Problemy Wczesnej Edukacji", Numer specjalny: *Sześciolatki do szkół a€fakty, polemiki, emocje*, Polskie Towarzystwo Pedagogiczne.
Konarzewski K. (ed) (2000) *Szkoły podstawowe i gimnazja w pierwszym roku reformy systemu oświaty: fakty i opinie*. Raport cząstkowy w ramach programu „Monitorowanie reformy systemu oświaty" przygotowany na zlecenie i we współpracy z Zespołem ds. Monitorowania Reformy Systemu Edukacji przy Prezesie Rady Ministrów, Warszawa grudzień: Instytut Spraw Publicznych.
Konarzewski K. (2004) Reforma oświaty. Podstawa programowa i warunki kształcenia, Warszawa: Instytut Spraw Publicznych.
Mendel M. (2006) *Pedagogika miejsca i animacja na miejsce wrażliwa* in M. Mendel (ed.) *Pedagogika miejsca*, Wrocław: Wydawnictwo Naukowe Dolnośląskiej Szkoły Wyższej Edukacji TWP.
Pilch T. (2010) "Społeczeństwo wobec szkoły-szkoła wobec przyszłości. Rozważania o polskiej polityce oświatowej", in S. Janusz and M. Kulesza (eds) *Ciągłość i zmiana w edukacji szkolnej—społeczne i wychowawcze obszary napięć*, Wydawnictwo Uniwersytetu Łódzkiego, pp. 21–33.
Podstawa programowa wychowania przedszkolnego oraz kształcenia ogólnego w poszczególnych typach szkół obowiązująca od roku szkolnego 2009/10 [The Core Education Curriculum 2009/10], Warszawa 2009.
Raport o stanie edukacji [The Report on the State of Education] (2010) *Społeczeństwo w drodze do wiedzy* [Society on the Path to Knowledge]. Warszawa: Instytut Badań Edukacyjnych [Institute of Education Research].
Regulation of the Minister of National Education and Sport of 26 February 2002, annex no 2 (2002) (Rozporządzenie Ministra Edukacji Narodowej i sportu z dna 26 lutego 2002 r., dz. cyt., załącznik nr).
Śliwerski B. (2004a) Reformowanie oświaty w Polsce, in Z. Kwieciński and B. Śliwerski (eds) *Pedagogika: podręcznik akademicki*. Warszawa: Wydawnictwo Naukowe PWN.
Śliwerski B. (2004b) Polski system oświatowy, in J. Prucha (ed.) *Pedagogika porównawcza: podręcznik akademicki*. Warszawa: Wydawnictwo Naukowe PWN.

Wołoszyn S. (1994) *Dzieje wychowania i myśli pedagogicznej w zarysie.* Warszawa: Wydawnictwo Naukowe PWN.

Wołoszyn S. (2003) *Oświata i wychowanie w XX wieku*, in Z. Kwieciński and B. Śliwerski (eds) *Pedagogika.* Warszawa: Wydawnictwo Naukowe PWN, pp. 155–170.

12

Education in rural South Africa

Chris Bryan

Acknowledgements

I would like to thank Anthony M. Nderitu, a South African teacher, whose comments have provided insight and perception.

My gratitude also goes to the staff and pupils of the senior-primary school in Limpopo Province at which this research took place; their enthusiasm and resilience provides the inspiration for this chapter.

Introduction

This chapter examines how socio-economic background and curriculum reform impacts upon the development and achievement of children in a rural senior-primary school in Limpopo Province, South Africa. It will focus on early childhood through to 13 years, with particular reference to the 10–13 year old age range. Using data collected in September 2011, pupil diaries and non-participant observation provide insight into the reality of life for children in Limpopo Province.

The chapter will first outline the demographic, historical and socio-economic context of South Africa. An overview of the structure of the educational system since independence in 1994 is described, together with the key features of curriculum reform. Finally, challenges to teaching and learning in rural South Africa are identified and discussed, leading to the question 'What lessons can we learn from the South African educational reform experience?'

South Africa in context

Demographic context

Covering an area of approximately 1,220,813 square kilometres, South Africa has an estimated population of 50.6 million of which 40.2 million are black Africans, 4.6 million are coloured, 4.6 million are white and 1.2 million are Indian or Asian in origin (SSA, 2011). With a rich traditional culture and 11 official languages, English being the most commonly used and understood, the country is divided into nine provinces each having its own legislature, premier and executive council. The South African constitution also recognises the institution and status of traditional leaders who play an important role within rural communities.

Limpopo Province is situated in the far north of South Africa, covering an area of approximately 125,755 square kilometres and bordering Mozambique, Botswana and Zimbabwe. It has a low population density of an estimated five million, 98 per cent of which are black African (SSA, 2011) and is a fertile, predominantly agricultural region with valuable mineral deposits. Despite government investment in the area, the infrastructure is poor with many houses lacking electricity, running water and sanitation.

Historical context

South Africa is a parliamentary democratic republic with a President who is elected by the National Assembly, the dominant national party being the African National Congress. Nelson Mandela, who in 1994 was the first democratically elected President, named South Africa's diverse ethnic population the 'rainbow nation' with constitutional values based on human dignity, human rights and equality.

Since independence in 1994, South Africa has undergone a period of rapid political and social change; however, in the 1940s the societal context was very different. Apartheid, a word meaning 'separate development', racially segregated the population as white, Indian, coloured (mixed race) or black. Blacks were not allowed into white areas, marriage between whites and blacks was illegal and children attended different schools according to their racial group. A system of Bantu education for the black population operated with inadequate funding, overcrowded classrooms, insufficiently qualified educators and few resources. Moreover, the Bantu curriculum was designed to address the perceived needs and abilities of the black population, supporting their subsistence living and low-level service occupations. The resultant poor literacy limited the chances of learners entering advanced education; this situation was compounded in 1953 with the passing of the Bantu Education Act 1953, which restricted the access of blacks to progress into higher education. South Africa is now a democratic republic underpinned by an ideology of social justice and egalitarianism, however, as Barbarin and Richter (2001) suggest, the legacy of apartheid had a devastating effect upon the consciousness of the country, the accumulated effects of which will take many years to resolve.

Recommended further reading

In their book 'Mandela's Children: Growing Up in Post-Apartheid South Africa', Barbarin and Richter (2001) present an excellent in-depth consideration of child development from birth to ten years in South Africa, following Nelson Mandela's release from prison in 1990.

The socio-economic context

Unemployment in Limpopo Province is high, particularly among the black population, resulting in chronic poverty with 56 per cent of young learners living within the poorest areas (CREATE, 2009). For children growing up in these deprived socio-economic conditions, life can be very hard. Poverty leads to hunger and malnutrition, lower classroom concentration and poor school attendance. It also affects home circumstances such as inadequate lighting to read after sunset, no facilities to do homework and lack of books and toys. Moreover, poverty can cause stressful home conditions with an increase in the familial use of alcohol and subsequent violence. The following quote from a child's school diary reveals one of the consequences of this situation: 'My stepfather drinks and then he comes home and beats my mom and sometimes us too. He drinks when he gets paid at the end of the week. We hide when he comes home' (A child from the school, aged ten).

HIV/AIDS, which is endemic in South Africa, has further exacerbated the challenges caused by poverty. In 2009, UNAIDS estimated that 5.6 million of the population were infected with HIV, of which 17.8 per cent were aged 15–49. This has resulted in approximately 1.9 million AIDS orphans being raised by aunts and grandparents, many of whom have poor levels of education and high levels of illiteracy and are therefore unable to support the learning of the child. Moreover, the responsibility of childcare has increasingly been left to older siblings who themselves miss out on education. The devastating effects of HIV/AIDS together with the mass migration of males seeking work in urban areas have resulted in women playing a progressively important role as principal wage earner often in low paid, menial work.

Nyriba and Bachri's story...

Nyriba (not her real name) is 12 years old. She lives in a small brick house in the village with her young sister and aunt; both their parents have died of AIDS. Although the paint is peeling off the walls and red African dust covers every surface, Nyriba knows she is fortunate to live in her aunt's house which has its own water and electricity supply.

At 5.30am she gets ready for school. She boils some water, washes her face and puts on her school uniform. Having had breakfast of bread and tea, she packs her school bag and at 6.30am begins the 30-minute walk to her senior-primary school. On her way she meets Bachri, also 12 years old but small for his age, who lives in a house with a roof that leaks and a shared water standpipe that at times does not work. His home has no toilet and food is cooked outside over an open wood fire.

Neither Nyriba nor Bachri have books or toys at home and with few playing areas and no clubs for them to join, most evenings are spent watching television, if the electricity supply is working. Nyriba is afraid to go out after dark as there are people around who may attack her and she is usually in bed by 8.30pm having completed her homework. Her aunt sees education as an important part of Nyriba's development; being very poor and with little support at home, Bachri struggles to complete his homework and his motivation to learn is low.

Education in South Africa

The ideological principles

> Education is the great engine of personal development.
>
> (Mandela, 1995:194)

For Nelson Mandela, education in post-apartheid South Africa was central to social transformation and economic success. Education reform that followed independence sought to

- Redress past injustices in educational provision
- Provide an education of progressively high quality for all learners to develop their talents and capabilities
- Advance the democratic transformation of society, combat racism, sexism and all other forms of unfair discrimination and intolerance
- Contribute to the eradication of poverty and economic well-being of society, protect and advance diverse culture and languages
- Uphold the rights of all learners, educators and parents and promote acceptance of their responsibility for the organisation, governance and funding of schools in partnership with the State.

(South African Schools Act, 1996)

As part of this vision, all restrictions of racial mixing were abolished and school attendance became compulsory for children aged seven years (Grade 1) to 15 years or the completion of Grade 9, whichever came first. The South African government now provides a national educational framework which is administered by each of the nine provinces, with elected members of the community having a legal right to representation on the school governing body; traditional leaders continue to have considerable influence on schools in local towns and villages.

Further reading

An authoritative reference overview of South African government departments and policies, *The South Africa Yearbook*, is published annually and can be accessed at www.gcis.gov.za/content/resourcecentre/sa-info/yearbook.

The structure of the South African education system

There is provision for two types of school in South Africa:

1. Government-funded public schools
2. Independent schools, which are mostly privately funded.

Both types of school are expected to follow the same basic national curriculum. Government funding for public schools covers teacher salaries, textbooks and stationery, with most schools charging school fees to cover non-teaching personnel and the upkeep of buildings. The level of payment is based on a national poverty score (quintile), using local income, unemployment rates and level of education within the community; the quintile score is then used to gauge the level of poverty experienced by the school. The school that Nyriba and Bachri attend is designated a 'no fee school' as it has a high poverty rating.

Education in South Africa is divided into three bands: **General Education and Training**, **Further Education and Training** and **Higher Education and Training** as shown in Table 12.1.

The Department of Basic Education is responsible for General Education and Training, providing compulsory basic education for Grade 1 to Grade 9, and comprises **Foundation** (Grades R–3), **Intermediate** (Grades 4–6) and **Senior** (Grades 7–9). Promotion to the next grade is by age unless a child is assessed to be academically unable to perform at the next level, at which point additional support should be given. For rural schools with limited resources this is often challenging, leaving children with Special Educational Needs profoundly disadvantaged.

Early Childhood Development

During apartheid, pre-school and early childhood education for black children was mostly disregarded, the void being filled predominantly by non-governmental organisations. With the recognition that quality early years provision enhanced the life chances of young children through the acquisition of the basic cognitive skills, the South African government

TABLE 12.1 The structure of education in South Africa

Band	Grade	Age (years)	Qualification
Higher Education and Training		18+	**Tertiary education at graduate and post-graduate level.** A Matriculation Endorsement of the National Senior Certificate is the minimum legal requirement for entry to university.
Further Education and Training Non-compulsory high school education	12	18	**National Senior Certificate** Matriculation
	11	17	
	10	16	
General Education and Training Compulsory education			
Senior phase	9	15	Compulsory education ends
"	8	14	
"	7	13	
Intermediate phase	6	12	
"	5	11	
"	4	10	
Foundation phase	3	9	
"	2	8	
"	1	7	Compulsory education begins

TABLE 12.2 The structure of Early Childhood Development in South Africa

Band	Grade	Age (years)	Qualification
Early Childhood Development	R	5–6	Not all primary schools have a reception class
"		0–4	Early Childhood Development Centres

has invested significantly in a policy of Early Childhood Development (ECD). The Department of Basic Education oversees ECD across the country for pre-school children (0–4 years) and Grade R children (5–6 years). A child may enter Grade R aged five, however parents can choose not to send their child to school at this age if they feel the child is not ready; many schools carry out an assessment of children to determine if a later admission would be in the best interests of the child.

Government funding for ECD comes from two sources:

(i) the Department of Education for the expansion of Grade R, principally in public schools
(ii) the Department of Social Development for pre-school children in community based ECD facilities.

A survey was carried out by the Department of Basic Education, Department of Social Development and UNICEF (2011) assessing the public expenditure and service quality of ECD in South Africa. The results indicated that Grade R provision in public schools appeared to be relatively well organised, however the situation for privately run ECD community based centres was variable. Where the site owners had developed an infrastructure, facilities were good; other locally run community ECD centres suffered from large classes, inadequate toilet facilities, poor safe water supply, lack of electricity and insufficient classrooms. The report also noted that despite government subsidies, many families from poorer rural regions did not have access to quality ECD centres due to an inability to pay school fees.

Curriculum reform

Central to the vision of equality, democracy and social justice was the introduction of 'Curriculum 2005'. Based on models from the USA and New Zealand and somewhat rapidly introduced in 1998, it was seen as South Africa's version of a learner-centred, outcomes-based curriculum, with problem solving and creativity underpinning a relevant knowledge base. However, following criticism that it lacked content specificity and had poor assessment procedures, 'Curriculum 2005' was revised in 2002 to become the 'Revised National Curriculum Statement for Grades R–9'. In 2009 a further review of the curriculum suggested that teachers were experiencing 'curriculum overload'. This resulted in the development and implementation of the Curriculum and Assessment Policy Statements, which rationalised the curriculum and assessment process from Grade R (age five years) to Grade 12 (age 18 years) and were implemented in 2012.

TABLE 12.3 Summary of curriculum reform in South Africa 1994–2012

Year	Development	Comment
1994	All references to racist and sexist elements were removed from the curriculum.	Beginning of post-apartheid curriculum reform.
1998	Introduction of Outcomes-based Education – 'Curriculum 2005', reflecting the new values and principles of the country.	The curriculum had eight new Learning Areas. Education was child-centred with the teacher as the facilitator.
2002	'Curriculum 2005' revised to become 'Revised National Curriculum Statement for Grades R–9'.	This resulted in the streamlining of the design and simplifying of terminology. National Curriculum Statements implemented by structured learning programmes.
2009	Review of the National Curriculum Statement Grades R–12. A movement away from outcomes-based education towards essential subject knowledge.	Reduction in the number of Learning Areas from eight to six for Grades 4–6 (Intermediate phase). Regular external assessment in Mathematics, Home Language and First Additional Language for Grades 3, 6 and 9.
2012	National Curriculum Statement Grades R–12 (January 2012).	Rationalisation of the curriculum and assessment process. The planned date for completion is 2014.

Curriculum content

'Curriculum 2005' identified eight Learning Area Statements (later called 'subjects') for Grades R–9; these were Languages (a home language and a first additional language), Mathematics, Natural Sciences, Social Sciences, Arts and Culture, Life Orientation, Economics and Management and Technology. For the majority of schools in South Africa, English is the recognised additional language and is the language of learning and teaching. The national curriculum also included the key skills of communication, critical thinking, activity and information management, group and community work and evaluation skills. Following a review in 2009, the Intermediate phase curriculum, which includes Grade 4 (age ten years) to Grade 6 (age 12 years), was reduced from eight to six subjects (Department of Basic Education, 2011a).

TABLE 12.4 Subjects and time allocation per week for the Intermediate phase

Subject	Time allocation per week (hours)
Home Language	6
First Additional Language	5
Mathematics	6
Natural Science and Technology	3.5
Social Skills	3
Life Skills – including Physical Education, Creative Arts, Personal and Social Well-being	4
TOTAL	27.5

Source: Department of Basic Education (2011c)

TABLE 12.5 Subjects and time allocation per week for the Foundation phase

Subject	Grade R (hours)	Grade 1–2 (hours)	Grade 3 (hours)
Home Language	10	7–8	6–7
First Additional Language		3–2	5–4
Mathematics	7	7	7
Life Skills	6	6	7
TOTAL	23	23	25

Source: Department of Basic Education (2011c)

Significantly, whilst western based knowledge remains in the South African national curriculum, the government recognises the value of indigenous traditional and local knowledge, particularly in rural areas; thus the principle of Indigenous Knowledge Systems (IKS) underpins the national curriculum.

Reflective activity

Curriculum review often occurs following claims of 'curriculum overload'. To what extent does the curriculum with which you are familiar experience this problem? You may wish to read a report by Oates (2010) – 'Could Do better: Using International Comparisons to Refine the National Curriculum in England' – to consider wider international contexts. This can be accessed at: www.cambridgeassessment.org.uk/ca/digitalAssets/188853_Could_do_better_FINAL_inc_foreword.pdf.

A typical day at a senior-primary school

At the time of the research (2011), the school that Nyriba and Bachri attended had 219 girls and boys, aged between 10–13 years, a Principal, seven teachers and approximately 30 pupils in each class. All the teachers at the school had been educated during the apartheid period in a local teacher education college and possessed a Primary Teaching Certificate, targeted towards black teachers; one teacher had gained a BEd. Significantly, during the 1990s many teacher education colleges were incorporated into universities as they were deemed to be of poor quality, producing under-qualified teachers. The closing of the colleges has led to a shortage of teachers, particularly in rural areas, thus in 2012 the Department of Higher Education and Training announced the re-opening of three teacher training colleges across the country, with an emphasis on Foundation phase teachers, especially African language speakers.

Lottery-funded football, tennis and netball facilities were very popular at the school, with teachers organising some after-school team games. The school also had a computer room, however, lack of finance and poor telephone infrastructure prevented internet access. Outside facilities included eight pit latrines, a standpipe supplying fresh drinking water and a wooden hut that operated as a wood store and lunchtime kitchen.

The school day

School assembly

Nyriba has been asked to read a passage from the Bible at the school assembly which begins at 7.15am and is held in the open air. Although Nyriba's home language is Tshvenda, she will read in her first additional language which is English. Bachri's teachers tell him he is clever, however, he does not want to read aloud because his reading is poor and there is no-one at home to help him.

Lessons 1 and 2

Lessons begin at 7.30am and last for approximately an hour. Nyriba and Bachri walk into the classroom, which has tables and chairs for each learner, and a blackboard. They open their new government-issued Maths workbook and listen as the teacher explains multiplication using their home language. The class repeats together the words written in English on the blackboard and complete some Maths problems.

When the hand bell rings, the children move to another classroom. Each subject is taught by a different teacher and Nyriba listens intently as she learns about her traditional culture. She hears how in the dry season grandmothers can be seen sprinkling crushed herbs and chanting for rain, a traditional custom. She is also taught about the importance of ancestors to the Venda culture and how in the past men had more than one wife, each wife living in their own mud hut within a compound. The lesson finishes with Venda songs, which the children love to sing.

Lunchtime

At approximately 10.00am, Nyriba and Bachri line up with the rest of the school for lunch which today is 'pap', a traditional South African food made of smooth maize meal, cabbage and a bean stew. The lunch, which for many children is the only meal of the day, is served in plastic containers brought from home. It is cooked outside in huge pots hung over wood fires. The children sit on the dusty ground to eat their lunch using spoons or their fingers. The teachers also have a school lunch which is eaten in the staffroom or under the shade of a tree. After about 40 minutes the children go to their next lesson.

Lessons 3–5

With a short break at 12 noon, lessons 3–5, which are English, Tshvenda and Natural Science follow a similar pattern involving movement from classroom to classroom and teacher-led instruction. Nyriba and Bachri listen to each teacher, put their hand up to answer questions and copy notes from the blackboard.

The school day ends

At 2pm the school day ends. Nyriba starts to wash the dusty floors of the classrooms with her friends. Sometimes she stays at school and plays netball or performs traditional dances accompanied by drums and singing, but usually she walks home to help her aunt with household chores. Bachri enjoys a game of football after school and then walks home. His parents are trying to find work in Johannesburg so he lives with his older sister and a family friend who has an alcohol problem.

Challenges to teaching and learning

'Curriculum 2005' was fundamentally at variance to that experienced by most black South Africans and placed unprecedented demands on schools, particularly in poor rural areas. With equal importance placed on subject knowledge and outcomes-based learning, it assumed that teachers were effective practitioners and had a secure subject knowledge. However, with limited support and few resources, the role of the teacher changed from the traditional, authoritarian, didactic approach of the apartheid period towards a facilitator of child-centred learning. These changes, which ignored the significance of school and classroom context, led Jansen (1999) to suggest that the introduction of 'Curriculum 2005' was 'context blind'. Research carried out in 2006 by Bryan (2011) confirmed this assertion, with teachers in Limpopo Province stating that lack of resources, poor subject knowledge and inadequate professional development had been, and continued to be, key factors limiting the quality of teaching and learning. Furthermore, the requirement to teach in English, the language of learning and teaching, placed additional demands on teachers whose own expertise of the language was limited. This lack of vocabulary resulted in a return to traditional approaches to whole class learning, far removed from the child-centred, outcomes-based style originally intended for 'Curriculum 2005'.

Reflective question

Child-centred learning, based on the work of educational researchers such as Vygotsky and Piaget, sees the child taking an active role in their learning. In what way does the role of the teacher change when moving from a traditional, didactic style of teaching to a facilitator of learning?

The introduction of an outcomes-based curriculum also resulted in an excessive and complicated system of criterion referenced, outcomes-based assessment. The assessment of each subject was designed to put less emphasis on written tests and provide 'indications of learner achievement in the most effective and efficient manner' (Department of Education, 2002:18). However, an outcomes-based curriculum required a process of continual assessment using learner portfolios and project work, about which the educators had little knowledge and for which they were ill-prepared. What is more, those children living in poverty had few resources to satisfactorily complete their project work. Support for schools to raise attainment came from district officials, who have a responsibility to ensure that centralised government education policies are managed and administered effectively. However, with limited understanding of outcomes-based assessment and at times dysfunctional school organisation, many schools did not conform to the national curriculum assessment requirements. In response, district officials deployed an approach described by Plowright (2011) as excessively bureaucratic and somewhat mechanistic, with little impact on improvement of teaching and learning in the classroom and subsequent raising of attainment.

Lessons from the South African education reform experience

This chapter has explored the challenges facing learners and teachers in a poor, semi-rural school in Limpopo Province, South Africa. It has identified three contextual inter-relationships challenging the vision of quality education for all:

The context of the learner

Children arrive at school with a range of experiences, values and beliefs, which will affect their ability and motivation to learn. Limpopo Province continues to be one of the poorest provinces in South Africa, with high illiteracy rates, chronic poverty, debilitating unemployment and endemic HIV/AIDS. Such disadvantaged, often fractured life experiences have led Van der Berg (2008:9) to conclude that home background was the 'single most significant factor influencing educational outcomes in most developed and developing countries'. These challenges have resulted in a number of provincial, national and international initiatives targeting the welfare of primary school children in the province. Exemption from payment of school fees for children for families in the poorest areas, together with the National Schools Nutrition Programme providing a cooked school lunch five days a week, have had a considerable impact upon the health and well-being of learners. Significantly, this service is not open to children attending Early Childhood Development community centres, consequently these children are more vulnerable to malnutrition. With children from disadvantaged families often having poor classroom performance, high absenteeism and a high drop-out rate, Early Childhood Development has a significant role to play for learners within this context.

The context of the school

The South African experience demonstrates the need for education reform to acknowledge the context within which schools operate. A westernised child-centred curriculum may be appropriate within a westernised context and culture, however, there is evidence to suggest that a new, hastily introduced curriculum, with insufficient support and resources for teachers to develop innovative pedagogic skills, can jeopardise the quality of teaching. Similarly, assessment that is ambiguous, inappropriate and incorrectly deployed can be de-motivating and lead to excessive bureaucratic procedures. Effective learning requires effective teaching. Effective teaching requires well qualified teachers who experience on-going and appropriate professional development.

With these limitations it is perhaps not surprising to note a disappointing examination profile for Limpopo Province schools in the Annual National Assessments (ANA) taken in February 2011. Involving six million learners in public primary schools across South Africa, the ANA focused on Grade 3 (literacy and numeracy) and Grade 6 (Maths and Languages); marking was carried out by educators within the school, reviewed by district officials and the marks were collated on a national data base. The results indicated that primary schools in the Limpopo Province underachieved for Mathematics and Languages compared with other schools in the country (Department of Basic Education, 2011b).

The South African education experience also highlights the significance of relevant knowledge. The introduction of IKS challenges the extent to which westernised knowledge provides an appropriate curriculum for the indigenous population. For some, IKS celebrates the distinctiveness of local knowledge, context and culture, providing a structure that more directly meets the developmental needs of the community. For others, IKS appears to reflect the education of apartheid, where black children were given appropriate knowledge for their basic needs, with little international focus. Interestingly, the requirement to provide a contextually relevant curricula, which addresses political ideology whilst meeting the employment needs of society, is one which faces many countries throughout the world.

Reflective question

Areas of social deprivation can be found in the UK; the number of children claiming free school meals is an indicator of such regions (Department of Education (2012) www.education. gov.uk/aboutdfe/foi/disclosuresaboutchildrenyoungpeoplefamilies/a00271/free-school-meals can provide you with regional data). To what extent do you think lack of resources or limited income can impact upon the quality of learning, with a consequent lowering of attainment?

The context of society

South Africa is a signatory to the United Nations Millennium Development Goals, which include national targets to combat hunger, poverty and illiteracy and there is evidence to suggest that improvement, if somewhat relative, is being made. The South African Millennium Development Goals Country Report (Republic of South Africa, 2010) for example, indicated a decline in absolute poverty and an improvement in literacy rates. However, the report continues by suggesting that it is unlikely that all goals relating to decreasing unemployment and eradicating poverty and hunger would be met by the target date of 2015. Moreover, research carried out by Kyei and Gyekye (2011) in Limpopo Province suggests that poor literacy, an indicator of underdeveloped societies, remained the key predictor of unemployment in the area. When placed within a globalised context, the problems become increasingly grave. Whilst the alleviation of poverty and hunger is seen by the South African government to be a fiscal priority, UNESCO suggests that global financial insecurity threatens to diminish past gains. It continues by warning that 'the financial crisis and steep food prices have created "perfect storm" conditions for a major setback' (UNESCO, 2010:19).

Post-apartheid South Africa has undergone considerable change since independence. Huge investment has gone into low-cost housing, improved sanitation and electrification, together with the provision of a welfare grant system. However, problems of administration and bureaucracy still exist. In 2012, textbooks from the government failed to arrive in the province until well into the school term, and in 2011 the national government took control of Limpopo Province finances as it became clear that the province was effectively bankrupt. Despite these challenges, South Africa continues to work towards a just and equal society, however there is an urgency to ensure that the gap between the rich and poor does not increase with the pace of globalisation.

Last words...

An understanding of child development requires recognition of the complex contextual inter-relationship between the child, the school and society. It is important, however, not to give context determinist powers; despite considerable disadvantages, learners can and do exhibit resilience. The very poorest schools in Eastern Cape, for example, showed considerably better attainment for Mathematics in the Annual National Assessments 2011 than equivalent schools in Limpopo Province, suggesting that poverty alone was not a predictor of underachievement. Similarly, the 2011 report by the Organisation for Economic Co-operation and Development (OECD, 2011) indicated that despite disadvantaged socio-economic backgrounds, the population of Korea has one of the highest reading performances of OECD countries, alongside Canada, Finland and Shanghai-China.

Nyriba's story supports this finding. Despite coming from a disadvantaged home background, she is succeeding at school, values education and has high aspirations. Like many 12-year-old girls across the world she styles her hair fashionably, cares about her appearance and studies hard. The socio-economic context in which she lives and the school context within which she learns present many challenges. Despite these difficulties Nyriba sees education as a way forward. It is to Nyriba, with thanks, we leave the last words of hope for the future.

Everyone must have a dream. My dream is to become a pilot. Without education you are nothing. I promise you I will never give up my learning because education is the key to success. That's why I love school and education.

(Nyriba, aged 12, 2011)

References

Barbarin, O. and Richter, L. (2001) *Mandela's Children: Growing Up in Post-Apartheid South Africa*. New York: Routledge.

Bryan, C. (2011) Professional Development During a Period of Change: A Small-Scale Case Study Exploring the Effect of Context on Practice in a South African Rural School. *Professional Development in Education* 37(1): 131–141.

Consortium for Research on Education, Access, Transitions, and Equity (CREATE) (2009) 'No fee' schools in South Africa. Policy Brief Number 7. [Online]. Available from: www.create-rpc.org/pdf_documents/Policy_Brief_7.pdf (Accessed: 8 January 2012).

Department of Basic Education (2011a) Curriculum News. [Online]. Available from: www.education.gov.za/Curriculum/CurriculumNews/tabid/348/Default.aspx (Accessed: 6 January 2012).

Department of Basic Education (2011b) *Report on the Annual National Assessments of 2011*. Pretoria: Department of Basic Education.

Department of Basic Education (2011c) Curriculum News. [Online]. Available from: www.education.gov.za/Curriculum/CurriculumNews/tabid/348/Default.aspx (Accessed: 24 June 2012).

Department of Basic Education, Department of Social Development and UNICEF (2011) *Tracking Public Expenditure and Assessing Service Quality in Early Childhood Development in South Africa*. Department of Basic Education, Department of Social Development and UNICEF.

Department of Education (2002) *Revised National Curriculum Statement Grades R–9 (Schools)*. Pretoria: Department of Education.

Department for Education (2012) Free School Meals. Available from: www.education.gov.uk/ aboutdfe/foi/disclosuresaboutchildrenyoungpeoplefamilies/a00271/free-school-meals (Accessed: 23 November 2012).

Government of South Africa (2011) The South Africa Yearbook [Online]. Available from: www.gcis. gov.za/content/resourcecentre/sa-info/yearbook (Accessed: 29 December 2011).

Jansen, J. (1999) The School Curriculum Since Apartheid: Intersections of Politics and Policy in the South African Transition. *Journal of Curriculum Studies* 31(1): 57–67.

Kyei, K. and Gyekye, K. (2011) Determinants of Unemployment in Limpopo Province in South Africa: Exploratory Studies. *Journal of Emerging Trends in Economics and Management Science* 2(1): 54–61.

Mandela, N. (1995) *Long Walk to Freedom*. London: Abacus.

Oates (2010) 'Could Do Better: Using International Comparisons to Refine the National Curriculum in England'. [Online]. Available from: www.cambridgeassessment.org.uk/ca/ digitalAssets/188853_Could_do_better_FINAL_inc_foreword.pdf (Accessed: 2 January 2012).

OECD (2011) Education at a Glance 2011: OECD Indicators, OECD Publishing. [Online]. Available from: http://dx.doi.org/10.1787/eag-2011-en (Accessed: 10 January 2012).

Plowright, D. (2011) *School Improvement and the Role of District Education Officials in South Africa*. Paper presented to the BERA Annual Conference 2011, 6–8 September, Institute of Education, London, UK.

Republic of South Africa (2009) *Report of the Task Team for the Review of the Implementation of the National Curriculum Statement* Final Report, October 2009. Pretoria: Government Printer.

Republic of South Africa (1996) *South African Schools (Act No 84 of 1996)*. Pretoria: Government Printer.

Republic of South Africa (2010) *Millennium Development Goals Country Report 2010*. Government Printer.

Revised National Curriculum Statement Grades R–9 (2002). [Online]. Available from: www.info. gov.za/view/DownloadFileAction?id=70257 (Accessed: 6 January 2012).

Statistics South Africa (SSA) (2011) *South African Statistics 2011*. Pretoria: Statistics South Africa.

UNAIDS (2009) South Africa HIV and AIDS Estimates (2009) [Online]. Available from: www. unaids.org/en/regionscountries/countries/southafrica (Accessed: 1 January 2012).

UNESCO (2010) 'Education for All' Global Monitoring Report 2010, *Reaching the Marginalised*. Oxford University Press/UNESCO.

Van der Berg, S. (2008) *'Poverty and Education'*. Education Policy Series 10. UNESCO and International Academy of Education.

13

Education in the United States of America

Michelle Appleby

Acknowledgements

I would like to acknowledge the other contributors of this chapter and my former students, Lilia Bouzit, Madeline Erba, Melanie Bussell and Victoria Westhead, who have lent me their voices to help exemplify topics I have discussed. Their insight and experience adds depth and a personal element to a discussion of education on a very broad and generalised scale. I would also like to acknowledge my family for their unending support and encouragement.

Introduction

The United States of America is a country in the Western Hemisphere consisting of 48 contiguous states, in addition to Alaska and Hawaii. The country shares borders with Mexico to the south; Canada to the north; is bordered on the west by the Pacific Ocean and on the east by the Atlantic Ocean. The total area of the United States is comparable to that of China, making it the world's third largest country; technically smaller than Russia and Canada, but bigger than China (CIA, 2012). The topography varies across the country from mountains to flatlands, sub-tropical mangrove wetlands to rolling hills and temperate forests to arid deserts. As equally diverse are the cultures contained within the United States; characterised by its unique dialect, music, arts and cuisine. This wide range of diversity is a direct result of the large-scale immigration from many different countries throughout history. As of July 2011, the population of the United States was estimated around 311 million people with around 292,000 students currently enrolled in education ages three and above (United States Census Bureau, 2010). In 2009, in an evaluation of 65 countries, the Programme for International Student Assessment (PISA) ranked the US 17th in reading, 31st in math and 23rd in science (OECD, 2011).

Although difficult to discuss a topic as broad as education in the United States due to the vastness and diversity of the country itself, an attempt will be made to look at the structure and organisation of primary education, underlying philosophies, governmental policies, achievement and assessment. Every attempt will be made to avoid over-generalisation but it is certain that exceptions to ideas discussed will occur.

Structure and organisation in the United States

In order to understand education in the United States it is important to note that the American education system is rooted in a democratic, republic political system whereby the people choose representatives to make political decisions on their behalf and constituents can decide on policy matters by voting on ballot initiatives and referendums. Education is a highly politicised arena and is often hotly debated in every election at all levels. Education policy is governed in large part by the political party in power. Similar to other Westernised countries, the American government operates on three levels: national, state and local (city or countywide) level. Funding for public education in the United States is mainly provided by the tax collection of the government from these three levels. At a national or federal level, the government is mainly responsible for setting national achievement and financial standards for all schools across the country. However, the largest proportion of funding for education comes from the collection of local property taxes. This means schools in fairly affluent areas will receive more funding at a district level because they are based on the value of the local property. This situation creates a discrepancy in resources available for students in the more affluent areas versus students in poorer areas. Examples of decisions also made at a district level are numbers of student to teacher ratios, curriculum adoption and school catchment areas. All school districts establish their own starting and finishing times and transportation requirements based upon guidelines set by the state. These decisions are made by a school board which is elected in local elections. The school board appoints an official, called a superintendent, to manage the schools in the district. The superintendent receives directives from the state legislation who, in turn, must meet national requirements.

Funding

Schools which receive funding from the government to support their financial needs are called public schools, a contrasting demarcation from public schools in the United Kingdom. In theory, most students have a choice to attend free, tax-subsidized schools or fee paying private schools. However, location and cost of education are always considerations for families.

Public schools

In American public schools, students can attend school for free and are not usually required to wear a uniform. The schools are generally within the local community; however, in rural areas some pupils may travel many miles every day to attend school. Attendance to public schools is based on residence and school board determined catchment areas. Transportation to school is generally free, especially for younger children, and paid for by the local school district. Transporting students to and from school is a major financial concern for most school districts. Most of this transportation occurs on the typical yellow school bus which is commonly associated with schools in the United States. School start times are decided by the school district to coordinate bussing for the three levels of school. Typically there will be three starting times in a district: one for elementary, one for middle and one for high school. Based on the ideas of democracy, and inherent in that is the right to education for all (Dewey, 1916), most state constitutions have written within them a legal right for students within the catchment area to attend which makes it therefore difficult to have students removed, expelled or excluded from these schools – even in extreme circumstances. This has major implications for behaviour management in public schools.

Private schools

Private schools in the United States are similar to what are called public schools in the United Kingdom. Also included in this category are faith schools which are aligned with a certain religion; here students receive lessons based on the religion and the beliefs upon which the school was founded. Students and their families are required to pay fees to attend the school and generally wear a strict uniform. The fees cover various rates depending on reputation, location, expenses and tuition. For families which cannot afford the fees, scholarships or bursaries are available but most pupils' parents pay the full amount. Unlike the government funded counterpart, private schools are under no obligation to accept students that do not meet their entry criteria which can be based on achievement, parental support and involvement and behaviour requirements. Students attending private schools generally benefit from lower class size, more rigorous curriculum and the schools they attend generally have better national and international reputations (Evans, 2004).

Phases of education

In most American public and private schools, education is divided into four phases: preschool, elementary school, middle school (sometimes called junior high school) and high school where students will graduate with a qualification called a diploma. Among the four census regions (Northeast, Midwest, South and West) in 2003, the proportion of people who had completed high school ranged from 88 per cent in the Midwest to 82 per cent in the South (United States Census Bureau, 2003). After graduation from high school, students can go on to college for up to two years and/or university to achieve graduate and postgraduate diplomas. Placement into year groups is determined by age. The first stage of formal schooling in the United States is kindergarten which is the youngest grade in elementary school going through to grade 12 in high school. Most children begin kindergarten at the age of five or six in August or September after a summer vacation which lasts around ten weeks after each school year. For the purposes of this chapter, more attention will be paid to the beginning of the student's learning journey in elementary school in the United States.

TABLE 13.1 Early learning in the United States

Ages	Level of schooling	Grades
3–4	Nursery school/pre-kindergarten	n/a
4–5	"	n/a
5–6	Kindergarten	n/a
6–7	Elementary school	1
7–8	"	2
8–9	"	3
9–10	"	4
10–11	"	5
11–12	"	6

Source: Adapted from the Institution of Education Sciences

Preschool and the Head Start Program

Preschool is not a mandatory educational level. However there has been national recognition of the importance of the early years (Bertram and Pascal, 2002) and this was demonstrated by the government funding preschool, health and social care programmes for low income families with young children called Head Start. Families that do not meet the criteria to qualify for the Head Start Program must fund preschool or childcare for this age range themselves (Vinovskis, 2005).

The Head Start Program was initiated by the United States Department of Health and Human Services and provides education, health and parenting services to children and their families in need. It began in 1964 (Currie and Thomas, 1995) and was initially a summer programme to help children who were struggling and lacked access to resources and services, because they were from low income families, to catch up with their peers. The programme was meant to help children to prepare for kindergarten with a stress on pre-reading and writing skills and basic number sense ideas (Gonzalez-Mena, 2009).

Elementary education

Attendance in school is mandatory for all children in the United States, but the age range for starting and leaving school varies from state to state (United States Department of Education, 2004). On average, children begin compulsory schooling in elementary school at age five or age six in kindergarten. Elementary school structures can vary as well. Most elementary schools finish at the end of 5th grade when children are ten or 11. However, because local districts and private alternatives can dictate regulations to schools, some elementary schools can go to 4th, 6th or even 8th grade.

The main focus in elementary school in terms of curriculum is mastery of basic subjects such as reading, writing and mathematics. Students often remain with their classroom teacher all day except to receive tuition in specialist subjects such as physical education (often called gym), music, art and library. These specialist subjects are taught by a specialist teacher who only teaches these subjects during a school day allowing classroom teachers time to organise and plan the day and to focus on the more commonly considered academic subjects.

Student voice: 'In my elementary school, I think I got a lot of valuable and unique teaching experiences as well as learning experiences that I probably wouldn't have gotten anywhere' – Victoria Westhead.

Pedagogic practices

The role of the elementary school teacher

The main role of the elementary school teacher in the United States is to prepare younger students for future schooling by teaching basic subjects such as literacy and math. Teachers of this age group tend to engage in lesson planning of subjects with a focus on subjects such as reading and maths, and teach life skills such as how to study and learn independently and how to work with others as a team. Elementary school teachers spend a great deal of time assessing students to evaluate their abilities, strengths and weaknesses and tend to teach in a large group or in small groups the lessons which they have planned. American teachers communicate with parents about children's progress in the forms of newsletters, emails, conferences and report cards where children are graded on their achievement approximately three times a year.

Teachers of this age range also typically work toward preparing students for achievement on standardised tests required by the state in which they live. They develop and enforce classroom rules to teach children proper behaviour, often using incentives for positive reinforcement such as adding marbles to a jar which when filled can result in a reward such as a class party or a treat (United States Department of Labor (USDL), 2012).

Teachers in primary school are required to supervise their class outside the classroom during playtimes up to three times a day. Many teachers use a hands-on approach, including props, to help students understand abstract concepts, solve problems and develop critical thinking skills. For example, they may show students how to do a science experiment and then have the students do the experiment. They may have students work together to learn how to collaborate to solve problems. (USDL, 2012).

In some schools with older students, teachers work in teams. These teachers often specialise in teaching one of two pairs of specialties, either English and social studies or math and science. Generally, students spend half their time with one teacher and half their time with the other. Some kindergarten and elementary school teachers teach special classes, such as art, music and physical education.

Some schools employ teachers of English as a second language (ESL) or English for speakers of other languages (ESOL). Both of these types of teachers work exclusively with students who are learning English, often referred to as English language learners (ELLs). The teachers work closely with students individually or in groups to help them improve their English skills and to help them with assignments received in other classes.

Students with learning disabilities or emotional or behavioural disorders are often taught in traditional classes. Teachers work with special education teachers to adapt lessons to these students' needs and monitor the students' progress. In some cases, kindergarten and elementary school teachers may co-teach lessons with special education teachers (USDL, 2012).

Curriculum

Emergent literacy

Most American early years teachers embrace the term 'emergent literacy' which relates to the process of acquiring literacy skills in early childhood. The term is used to denote the idea that the acquisition of literacy is best thought of as a developmental continuum as opposed to a skill-set which develops when children start school (Whitehurst and Lonigan, 1998). There is a strong movement to assume that reading, writing and speaking develop simultaneously and in association with each other from the moment a child is born. This development is reliant upon interactions in the social environment of those around them and even in the absence of formal instruction.

It is believed that the skills necessary for emergent literacy and those which are stressed in early years settings in the United States are: semantic and syntactic knowledge; conventions of print; encouragement of 'pretend reading and writing' behaviours; knowledge of graphemes; and phonological awareness (Whitehurst and Lonigan, 1998). The development of these elements can be found in most early years settings in the United States. Equally important is the environment where literacy takes place which supports or impedes development. There is a strong connection between home literacy environments and emergent literacy, so a strong connection between reading, writing, school and home is nurtured and prioritised in most early years settings.

There is no national curriculum in the United States. School districts choose and adopt curriculum which addresses the state's learning standards and benchmarks for each grade level. The times these topics are taught and how they are taught is completely up to the school districts to decide. Each state must meet these learning standards or goals to meet the national standard of Adequate Yearly Progress (AYP) mandated by the national initiative No Child Left Behind discussed later in the chapter.

Public elementary school teachers typically instruct classrooms of 20 to 30 students. Because inclusion is mandated by law in the United States, children in a classroom may require a number of teaching modifications in order to address varying abilities and special needs. These individuals could range from being identified as having special educational needs to students who are academically and artistically gifted. Teachers in schools and wider school districts typically collaborate to develop materials that supplement and support the diverse range of learners in their classrooms. It is considered good practice to post most curriculum and materials on school websites for parents to access in an effort to allow parents to help their children more effectively at home. Most student books and materials for students are provided by the school in state-funded education.

> Student voice: 'I feel that my attitude towards different races, religions, and cultures in general, was very strongly influenced by my early exposure to such a varied group of classmates in elementary school' – Melanie Bussell.
>
> Elementary school teachers are trained with an emphasis on human cognitive and psychological development and the principles of curriculum development and instruction. Teachers typically earn either a Bachelor's degree in Early Childhood and/ or Elementary Education. Qualification standards for most teachers are determined by the individual states with state universities determining the programmes necessary for

future teachers. Some states require future teachers to not only achieve a Bachelor's degree but also take content areas tests and instructional skills tests before certification. Teachers qualified in one state may not necessarily be able to teach in other states without having to take university classes and/or take these tests first.

Other topics studied in elementary school by students are social studies (American history, geography and economics), science (biology, chemistry, physics, ecology and physiology). Because AYP, as dictated by No Child Left Behind, is highly determined on literacy and mathematics scores, it is possible that children may receive less instruction in these other academic areas.

TABLE 13.2 A typical week in an American elementary school

	Monday	Tuesday	Wednesday	Thursday	Friday
8:30–8:45	School commences, attendance taken and whole class circle time				
8:45–9:45	Mathematics	Mathematics	Mathematics	Mathematics	Mathematics
9:45–10:15	Physical education	Music	Art	Library	Physical education
10:15–10:30	Recess and Snack time				
10:30–11:30	Writing	Writing	Writing	Writing	Writing
11:30–12:15	Lunch and recess				
12:15–1:15	Reading	Reading	Reading	Reading	Reading
1:15–2:15	Science	Social studies	Spelling/ handwriting	Science	Social studies
2:15–3:15	Spelling/ handwriting	Science	Social studies	Spelling/ handwriting	Science or social studies
3:15–3:30	Story read aloud or recess				
3:30	Dismissal				

Student voice:

I liked working on projects both in and out of class in elementary school because I could see my accomplishments, whereas it was harder for the 10 year old version me to "see" what I learned in a normal day of school. I truly believe that starting to work on projects like those at a young age helped my work ethic now – Lilia Bouzit.

Extracurricular activities

A characteristic of American schools which is often depicted in the media is the high number of extracurricular activities on offer to students including sports, clubs and volunteering activities which benefit the local community. Extracurricular activities are educational activities not falling within the scope of the regular curriculum but managed and mostly funded by the school. Parents of children in activities may have to pay a fee for materials or uniforms. Teachers get paid a supplement to their salary to organise and manage after school activities which is a motivating factor to put in extra hours and comprehensive activities often raise the profile of the school in a competitive educational marketplace where parents can often choose where to send their children for schooling.

These activities can extend to large amounts of time outside the normal school day; home-schooled students, however, are not normally allowed to participate and students in lower socioeconomic areas do not often have access to the wide range of activities which are available to more affluent students. Students who participate in these activities are found to have a higher social and academic self-concept, higher educational aspirations, more successfully academic coursework submissions, a higher rate of homework submission, less absenteeism, higher academic achievement and a higher rate of post-secondary qualifications (Marsh, 1992; Mahoney and Cairns, 1997).

Reflective task

Think for a minute about the discrepancy mentioned so far in the chapter with regard to students from more affluent families and students coming from lower socioeconomic backgrounds. In what ways are poor students disadvantaged? Keep note of these areas as you continue to read.

National policies and law

This chapter has already discussed the government's role in education and the highly politicised nature of education in the United States. The Federal Department of Education plays a role in setting standards for education and is also responsible for funding it. Children are required by law to attend school in most states until the age of 16 but that can vary to up to 18 years old depending on the state laws (United States Department of Education, 2004). Students can also be schooled at home which will be discussed later on in the chapter. Compulsory education requirements can generally be satisfied by educating children in public schools, state-certified private schools or an approved home-school programme.

In the United States, the federal law which states that all governmental educational services must meet the individual needs of students, including those with special educational needs is called Individuals with Disabilities Education Act (IDEA). IDEA says that all students with special needs are entitled to a free and appropriate public education (FAPE). It is the schools responsibility to meet with the parents or guardians to develop an Individualized Education Program (IEP) that determines best placement for the child. IDEA also states that students must be placed in the least restrictive environment (LRE) that is appropriate for the student's needs. Government-run schools that fail to provide an appropriate placement for students with special needs can be taken to due process wherein parents may formally submit their grievances and demand appropriate services for the child. Schools may be eligible for state and federal funding for the (sometimes large) costs of providing the necessary facilities and services.

Approaches to assessment and achievement

Standardised testing and No Child Left Behind

Near the end of a student's high school experience, students may opt to take one or more standardised test depending on if they decide to go on to university or not. The main rationale for administering these tests is to measure the overall level of achievement of the students. The Scholastic Aptitude Test (SAT) and the American College Testing (ACT) exams are two examples of nation-wide exams which provide the main basis for university admissions in the United States.

No Child Left Behind

Under the No Child Left Behind Act (NCLBA), all American states must test students in public schools state-wide to ensure that they are achieving the desired level of minimum education. This Act was presented by President George W. Bush on 23 January 23 2001 and was subsequently passed by both the House of Representatives and the Senate later that same year. The Act became a law one year later in January 2002. It requires all schools which receive government funding to administer a state-wide standardised test annually to all students. The students' scores on the test, which may take up to two weeks to complete, determine how well the teachers have taught the students. Educational standards and standardised testing decisions are usually made by state governments. States will develop their own method of assessment such as the Michigan Educational Assessment Program (MEAP) or the Florida Comprehensive Assessment Test (FCAT). Students who are educated at home or in private schools are not included in these assessments. The NCLBA requires that students and schools show growth which has been deemed as AYP. This means that schools must show student achievement every grade, every year. If the school's results are repeatedly poor, then steps are taken to improve the school (Borman and Cotner cited in Ballantine and Spade, 2008).

> Student voice:
> I don't remember much about the MEAP, only that it was pretty stressful. It wasn't until I was told by my parents that the test was more to evaluate the teachers than the individual students that I stopped worrying about it quite so much. Looking back, I think the early exposure to standardized testing was a good thing. Taking more important standardized tests in later years was, at least, nothing I hadn't experienced before' – Melanie Bussell.

Schools that do not achieve AYP for two years in a row are publically labelled as 'In need of improvement' and are required to write a two-year plan detailing how the school will address failing subject areas. Students at this point are given a choice as to whether they want to transfer to a different school in the same school district if that choice exists. If the school misses AYP for a third year in a row the school is bound by law to offer free tutoring and other supplemental supports for struggling students at the cost of the school. Missing AYP for a fourth year means that the school is labelled as needing 'corrective action' which can involve replacement of staff members, introduction of a new curriculum or extending the hours in a school day. A fifth unsuccessful year results in a complete restructure of the school which will be implemented after the sixth time of failure. Some of these plans go as far as to close the school completely, change the school into a Charter School or asking the State Department of Education to run the school itself.

The NCLBA requires that all teachers are 'highly qualified'. Each state defines what this means in terms of teacher training and continued professional development for its teachers. Curriculum standards are set by the state which applies to all schools within that state. All states must meet a 100 per cent student proficiency level by 2014 (Borman and Cotner cited in Ballantine and Spade, 2008).

Supporters of the NCLBA are quick to point out increased accountability that is required of the school and its leaders. The yearly standardised tests are the mark to which everything is judged with an end result of withdrawal of state funding if targets are not met. The link between students' outcomes and state academic standards is made very clear. The law sets a standard that all children's progress is being measured and monitored and teaching is adapted to meet the requirements of students' needs. Parents are kept informed of the school's progress with yearly school report cards of how the school is faring on the whole. As per NCLBA, parents are notified when their child is being taught by a professional who does not meet the 'highly qualified' requirements as explained earlier.

Student voice:

I wish I could say that the MEAP tests were useless, but I think that taking standardized tests at a young age eventually helped me with the ACT/SAT. I still think it would be best if standardized tests were removed from education, because they are taking time out of the year and teachers are forced to teach to the test – Lilia Bouzit.

Criticisms of NCLB

Opponents of the law argue that this punitive system is unsupportive in helping schools address high failure rates of students where there are wider sociological issues such as poverty and students learning to speak English as a second language. Linn et al. (2002) state that the NCLBA of 2001 substantially increases the testing requirements for states and sets demanding accountability standards for schools, districts and states with measurable AYP objectives for all students and subgroups of students defined by socioeconomic background such as race and ethnicity, English language proficiency and disability. It is interesting to note that states' curriculum standards, the depth of their testing instruments, the levels at which they decide a teacher's 'highly qualified status' vary greatly across the United States. As a result, the percentage of students who score at a proficient level vary greatly from state to state and the likelihood of all schools scoring 100 per cent proficiency rating in 12 years is unlikely (Linn et al., 2002). While states were being forced to make budget cuts, including in the area of education, they had to incur additional expenses to comply with the requirements of the NCLBA. The funding they received from the federal government in support of the NCLBA was not enough to cover the added expense necessary to adhere to the new law (Sunderman et al., 2005).

Student voice:

> I found standardized testing preparation to be a waste of time. For about two
> months of the school year, our elementary school was so concerned about the
> teachers and school getting a good score they would try to inflate their scores by
> pumping the students with stuff expected to be on the exam. School shouldn't be
> about preparing for test scores, it should be to teach students what they need to
> know about in the real world. In 5 years no one cares about their test scores –
> Madeline Erba.

As always with standardised testing, the practice of giving all students the same test, under
the same conditions, has been accused of inherent cultural bias because different cultures
may value different skills. In addition, the NCLBA can be critiqued in that some schools are
deemed as failing if all students are not labelled as what has been deemed as proficient, even
if students have made great progress within one year. It has been shown that some students
may take more time to achieve targets than others and that standardised tests with high
stakes outcomes do not accommodate for this (Reville, 2007).

Reflective task

The NCLBA is promoted as requiring 100 per cent of students (including disadvantaged and
special education students) within a school to reach the same state standards in reading and
mathematics by 2014.

What are your thoughts on this? Why do you think this way? Give examples.

More recently, in September 2011, President Barack Obama announced that his
administration would provide relief from the NCLBA for schools who were having trouble
meeting the 100 per cent attainment rate by 2014 as outlined by the Act. Because so much
emphasis was put on schools to achieve a pass on the tests, other important skills were not
being taught and this target was seen to be prohibiting states from achieving other educational
reforms which were needed to help students gain important employability skills. The
flexibility granted by the Obama Administration will help states move forward with
education reforms that are based on rigorous college- and career-ready standards, state-
developed accountability systems that reward progress and address achievement gaps, and
meaningful educator evaluation systems that support increased student achievement. This
flexibility will still ensure that every single child is getting an excellent education, but the
rationale is that a more skills-based approach will be considered so all students can feel they
have the skills necessary to be competitive in a global economy (The White House, 2012).

Current challenges and issues

Including the current challenges of achievement gaps between the different socioeconomic
classes, United States' education faces many other challenges and issues such as teachers leaving

the profession, parental involvement and student reading ability; all of which may hinder progress in education (Boyer and Wolf-Hamil, 2008). It is no surprise that teaching is a very demanding profession full of responsibility and a new level of accountability for American teachers. Many American teachers find the high stress levels too difficult to cope with for any length of time. Jalongo and Heider (2006 cited in Boyer and Wolf-Hamil, 2008: 2) state that, 'forty-six percent of new teachers in this country quit teaching after five years or less, with that percentage growing to fifty percent in urban areas.' On a related note, lack of parental involvement could be leading teachers to feel so overburdened. Although parents of children in elementary are still quite involved, middle and high school parents tend to be less accessible and supportive of their children's education. Padgett (2006 cited in Boyer and Wolf-Hamil, 2008) cites reasons such as hectic work schedules, school distance, language and cultural barriers as reasons many parents are hesitant to get involved with their child's school. Another challenge is that of the lack of reading skills of students in American education. A large majority of the nation's students are not reading at their expected level for their age which greatly impacts American students' education. Boling and Evans (2008 cited in Boyer and Wolf-Hamil, 2008) say that more than eight million American students cannot read or comprehend what they read even at a basic level. This challenge impacts dropout rates of students who feel demotivated and disengaged from school and choose not to complete their programme of study to attain their degree.

Conclusion

This chapter has discussed the educational system in a vast country and has made every attempt to avoid over-generalisations. The structure and organisation of American education was discussed with a focus on the early experiences of American students in elementary school. Although there is no national curriculum in the United States, the No Child Left Behind policy has had lasting and noticeable effects on schools nationally but some signs are evident that it is beginning to change. Some of these effects are the increased inclusion of standardised testing into the curriculum with greater and sometimes serious implications for schools. American teachers continue to face challenges with teacher motivation, parental support and reading achievement especially in lower social classes.

Further reading

Bowles, S. and Gintis, H. (1977). *Schooling in Capitalist America: Educational Reform and the Contradictions of Economic Life*. London: Routledge and Kegan Paul.

Ekstrom, R., Rock, D. and Goertz, M. (1988). *Education and American Youth: The Impact of the High School Experience*. London: Falmer.

Murray, C. (2009). *Real Education: Four Simple Truths for Bringing America's Schools Back to Reality*. New York: Crown Publishing.

Riele, K. (2009). *Making Schools Different: Alternative Approaches to Educating Young People*. London: Sage.

Ryerson, E. (2008). *A Special Report on the Systems and State of Popular Education on the Continent of Europe, in the British Isles, and the United States of America: With Practical Suggestions for the Improvement of Public Instruction in the Province of Ontario*. Ontario: Dept. of Education.

References

Ballantine, J. and Spade, J. (2008). *The Sociology of Education*. (6th ed). Englewood Cliffs: Prentice-Hall.

Bertram, T. and Pascal, C. (2002). *Early Years Education: An International Perspective*. Birmingham: Centre for Research in Early Childhood.

Boyer, A. and Wolf-Hamil, B. (2008). *Problems Facing American Education*. Available from: www.nationalforum.com/Electronic%20Journal%20Volumes/Boyer,%20Ashley%20Problems%20Facing%20American%20Education.pdf date accessed: 29 January 2012.

Central Intelligence Agency, CIA. (2012). The World Factbook. Available from: https://www.cia.gov/library/publications/the-world-factbook/rankorder/2147rank.html date accessed: 12 April 2012.

Currie, J. and Thomas, D. (1995). Does Head Start make a Difference? Available from: www.econ.ucla.edu/people/papers/Currie/Currie14.pdf date accessed: 13 April 2012.

Dewey, J. (1916). *Democracy and Education: An Introduction to the Philosophy of Education*. New York: Free Press.

Evans, G. (2004). The Environment of Childhood Poverty. *American Psychologist*, 59(2): 77–92.

Gonzalez-Mena, J. (2009). *Child, Family, and Community: Family-Centred Early Care and Education*. London: Pearson.

Linn, R., Baker, E. and Betebenner, D. (2002). Accountability Systems: Implications of Requirements of the No Child Left Behind Act of 2001. *Educational Researcher*, 31: 3–16.

Mahoney, J. and Cairns, R. (1997). Do Extracurricular Activities Protect Against Early School Dropout? *Developmental Psychology*, 33(2): 241–253.

Marsh, H. (1992). Extracurricular Activities: Beneficial Extension of the Traditional Curriculum or Subversion of Academic Goals? *Journal of Educational Psychology*, 84(4): 553–562.

OECD (2011). Lessons from PISA for the United States, Strong Performers and Successful Reformers in Education. Available from: http://dx.doi.org/10.1787/9789264096660-en date accessed: 12 April 2012.

Reville, S. P. (2007). Stop the Narrowing of the Curriculum by 'Right-Sizing' School Time. *Education Week*, 27(9): 30–36.

Sunderman, G., Kim, J. and Orfield, G. (2005). NCLB Meets School Realities: Lessons From the Field. London: Sage.

The White House (2012). Education. Available from: www.whitehouse.gov/issues/education date accessed: 13 April 2012.

United States Census Bureau (2003). Educational Attainment in the United States: 2003 Population Characteristics. Available from: www.census.gov/prod/2004pubs/p20-550.pdf date accessed: 12 April 2012.

United States Census Bureau (2010). Current Population Survey. Available from: www.census.gov/hhes/school/data/cps/2010/tables.html date accessed: 12 April 2012.

United States Department of Education (2004). Digest of Education Statistics. Washington D.C.: National Center for Educational Statistics.

United States Department of Education, Office of Special Education and Rehabilitative Services. (n/d) History: Twenty-Five Years of Progress in Educating Children with Disabilities through IDEA.

United States Department of Labor (USDL) (2012). Occupational Outlook Handbook: Kindergarten and Elementary School Teachers. Available from: www.bls.gov/ooh/Education-Training-and-Library/Kindergarten-and-elementary-school-teachers.htm date accessed: 13 April 2012.

Vinovskis, M. (2005). *The Birth of Head Start*. Chicago: University of Chicago Press.

Whitehurst, G. and Lonigan, C. (1998). Child Development and Emergent Literacy. *Child Development*, 69(3): 848–872. Available from:
http://rachaelrobinsonedsi.wiki.westga.edu/file/view/child+development+and+emergent+literacy.pdf date accessed: 27 January 2012.

Conclusion

Mabel Ann Brown and Jon White

In conclusion, this book, *Exploring Childhood in a Comparative Context* has offered the reader an opportunity to reflect. Should educationalists be repeating the same practice or should they be considering ways to improve? As Albert Einstein is reported to have said, it is 'Insanity: doing the same thing over and over again and expecting different results' (Einstein).

'Society has moved far from considering the child as a blank slate, only as white paper, or wax, to be moulded as one pleases (Locke 1693) or imbued with innate innocence or purity' (Rousseau (1762) as cited in Paige-Smith and Craft 2008:179).

The children have rights and a voice and practice is changing. It should be clear from reading this book that the contested philosophies driving the care and education of young children find themselves at a critical point in their development. As this is written in 2013, there are news reports from many countries of a rise of anti-immigrant sentiments, created in part by stringent economic pressures. Political parties appear to fear the increased influence of extremist voices, apparently intent on closing borders and repatriating migrant workers. Additionally, there are significant environmental concerns, as population growth and the drive for more material goods puts pressure on manufacturing and industry. This in turn has led to a widening of the gap between the rich and poor communities, both within and between nation-states.

Similar evolving structures are to be seen in other countries outside of Europe. The identity of citizens and the gradual change in the underpinning strength of economies (in particular the move from industrial to post-industrial) has resulted in new and challenging pressures on the adults who are responsible for the preparation of children for life in an uncertain future. Throughout these chapters, it has been clear that the writers have returned to this theme: how can we be confident in how we are preparing children for life when the world in which we are living now is likely to evolve and so become a very different place in the future? This is at the heart of the dilemma of how we are preparing children to see the world of which they are a part. Will the world be seen as a threatening place, full of problems and insecurities, where there are people ready to exploit you and you need to exercise caution and prudence to avoid disaster? Or is the world becoming a global village, consisting of people like us, where the principles of honour, integrity and fairness are the basis for daily dealings. Is the separation of people through language, custom and culture to be seen as a threat or the opportunity for enrichment?

External agencies responsible for Quality Assurance exist in all the countries included in this review. However, it appears that the concept of Quality is actually a socially constructed phenomenon, so may not transfer reliably from one context to the next. And yet, as we develop a more global view of childhood and children find themselves to be part of families who are mobile, there is an increasing need for us to understand that children are being subjected to a wide range of competing influences, all of which claim to be High Quality. The OECD PISA collates information from 34 OECD countries and 41 partner countries and economies but as the sign in Einstein's office in Princeton said 'Not everything that counts can be counted, and not everything that can be counted counts.' Thus much good practice frequently goes unrecorded.

Security concerns are also a fundamental issue within the many national states. The strength of modern models of tolerance and freedom are being tested as disruption from legitimate mass protest and fear of terrorist incidents may increase the tendency of security forces to act in the 'national interest' to limit the traditional freedoms of citizens.

Continued enlargement over recent years has clearly enriched the concept of what it means to be both a European citizen and a citizen of the world. Going beyond the early general charters, the European model may be characterised as providing a sense of 'belonging', as suggested by Osler and Starkey (2005) leading to a status, a feeling and a practice. These themes reinforce the sense that to be truly a world citizen is to participate in a culture that is developing and evolving. For example, the concept of the European nation-state as an active ideological framework in which to live has a complex and contested nature and it is felt that it is through the education of its children and young people that the social justice across the European community and beyond can be achieved.

In comparison, there is a contrast with the world citizenship model implicit in a Capitalist framework, which has evolved into a value system advocating the acquisition of wealth and promotion of individual development. These values are instilled at an early age through a system of education and socialisation that embody an 'American' ideal in a federally co-ordinated way which is almost unimaginable were it to be transposed to a European context.

So while the development of citizenship and the role of early years practitioners and teachers of young children may be at a political crossroads, there are several defining features which emerge from reading the commentaries in this book. Firstly, there appears to be a trend towards listening to children and affording them status by engaging with them in the decisions that affect their lives. This is a pre-cursor to being active citizens as adults. To feel as if you are a stakeholder in the social world of which you are a part is likely to instil a sense of social responsibility and a willingness to contribute to supporting those less able to support themselves. A strong sense of empathy emerges as adults try to anticipate the demands that a turbulent world will place on the young people of the future.

Linked to this is the second theme of resilience, defined by Fongay et al. (1994) as 'normal development under difficult conditions'. This recognises that in their transition between the multiple contexts of childhood, they will need to re-acquire understandings of the rules and assumptions made for them by the adults who construct their world. It is clear that many of the national systems embody the *promotion* of resilience as an underpinning driver, over and above the content of the curriculum. This is exemplified by how the adults treat the children in their care and that it is 'OK not to know'. The feeling that they are accepted as 'emerging' citizens with rights and responsibilities appears fundamental to the educational provision across the world.

The third and final aspect again draws on the sense of belonging identified earlier. In practice, there is recognition of the importance of social partnerships and that the networks within the lives of children serve to enrich and deepen their sense of individual identity and ability to participate in meaningful activities. Involvement of parents and wider family networks, together with access to a complex diversity of social and cultural activities allow children to demonstrate their interests and competence.

These beliefs appear to be fundamental to the creation of a sense of belonging that children across the world are being encouraged to develop and demonstrate the criticality of embedding social and community values through the provision of high-quality education and care. It is the mechanism by which this can be achieved that we can now turn. The austerity which now pervades our institutions is nothing new. Successive governments have forever seen the costs of providing early years education and care as a burden on the state which has, at best, a long term outcome of producing citizens capable of contributing to the wealth of the nation. Using phrases such as 'wealth' and 'contributor' is setting a tone that is challenged in many countries, as this implies that the early childhood institution is a 'factory' producing a 'product' – the child ready to enter the next phase of their education, ready to reproduce cultural norms and values on their journey.

Children's childhoods are determined by the society they grow up in but our greater awareness of the the more global approaches may enable providers to consider their practice in the light of their new knowledge. Aitken and Powell (2005:186) consider that some systems such as Te Whariki could be 'transferable models of excellence' but in reality what they offer is a 'shared understanding' but this can never be a complete understanding as each country has different systems and different politics and people.

Children need to develop social and emotional skills as recognised in Finland or Japan but perhaps ultimately we are aiming for a world Te Whariki or woven mat as there will always be differences, but with imagination these differences can enhance the world and can be woven together to enable the world to move forward. Our children are our global future and the voices expressed in this book are a glimpse into other practices. It is an opportunity to reflect and hopefully create a global future that works for everyone.

References

Aitken, E. and Powell, J. (2005) 'International Perspectives' in Jones, L., Holmes, R. and Powell, J. (eds) *Early Childhood Studies: A Multiprofessional Perspective*. Berkshire: Open University Press.

Einstein, A. Online. Available from: www.alberteinsteinsite.com/quotes/einsteinquotes.html (Accessed on 20 March 2013).

Fongay P., Steel M., Steele H., Higgit A. and Target M. (1994) The Theory of Practice of Resilience. *Journal of Child Psychology and Psychiatry*, 33(2): 231–257.

Osler A. and Starkey H. (2005) *Changing Citizenship: Democracy and Inclusion in Education*. Berkshire: Open University Press.

Paige-Smith A., and Craft A. (2008) *Developing Reflective Practice in the Early Years*. Maidenhead: Open University Press.

Index